PRIVATE LEARNING, PUBLIC NEEDS

TEACHING

⮞CONTEMPORARY⮜

SCHOLARS

Shirley R. Steinberg & Joe L. Kincheloe
General Editor

Vol. 3

PETER LANG
New York • Washington, D.C./Baltimore • Bern
Frankfurt am Main • Berlin • Brussels • Vienna • Oxford

Eric J. Weiner

PRIVATE LEARNING, PUBLIC NEEDS

THE NEOLIBERAL ASSAULT ON DEMOCRATIC EDUCATION

PETER LANG
New York • Washington, D.C./Baltimore • Bern
Frankfurt am Main • Berlin • Brussels • Vienna • Oxford

Library of Congress Cataloging-in-Publication Data

Weiner, Eric J.
Private learning, public needs: the neoliberal assault
on democratic education / Eric J. Weiner.
p. cm. — (Teaching contemporary scholars; v. 3)
Includes bibliographical references and index.
1. Critical pedagogy—United States. 2. Education—Economic
aspects—United States. 3. Literacy—United States.
4. Conservatism—United States. I. Title. II. Series.
LC196.5.U6W45   370.11'5—dc22   2003025891
ISBN 0-8204-6200-4
ISSN 1533-4082

Bibliographic information published by **Die Deutsche Bibliothek**.
Die Deutsche Bibliothek lists this publication in the "Deutsche
Nationalbibliografie"; detailed bibliographic data is available
on the Internet at http://dnb.ddb.de/.

Cover design by Joni Holst

The paper in this book meets the guidelines for permanence and durability
of the Committee on Production Guidelines for Book Longevity
of the Council of Library Resources.

To my mom, who never gave up on me

Contents

Part 1. Neoliberal Globalization and the Question of Adult Literacy Education

Part 2. The Work of Critical Theory in a Neoliberal Age

◉ Part 3. Critical Pedagogies and Literacies for a Neoliberal Age

Acknowledgments

There are several people who have made this book possible. But it is a difficult task to decide where to begin historically in acknowledging their influence and support. If I go way back, I would have to thank Lynn Dorfman, my fourth-grade teacher, whose spirit and compassion, more than twenty-five years after the fact, still informs my sense of what a great elementary school teacher should be.

Elizabeth (Libby) Fay challenged me as an undergraduate and then again as a graduate student to "read" literature and the world critically and with passion.

Donaldo Macedo, whom I met because of Libby, I owe a great debt. He literally took me in, mentored me, and supported me when I was struggling to find my way. He saw in me things I did not see myself, and for that I am eternally grateful.

It is extremely difficult to find the right words to thank my mentor Henry A. Giroux. When you work with someone closely for three years, a unique relationship gets formed. He challenged me as no other person ever had and I worked hard under his tutelage, trying to make him proud of the work I was doing. His commitment to the work and passion for intellectual projects in my experience is unmatched. I can only hope that some of it rubbed off on me.

I would also like to thank Patrick Shannon, who has always been extremely generous with his time, knowledge, and support. His guidance in literacy has been invaluable as well as his ability to laugh with me at the absurdities that too often characterize the academy.

Dierdre Glenn-Paul has been an enormous help in assisting me mediate academic life as an assistant professor.

Joe Kincheloe and Shirley Steinberg encouraged me to write this book and were kind enough to put it in their series. Together they do more than any other academics I know to encourage and directly help young scholars get published. Their generosity is to be admired and emulated.

Last, I must thank Catherine, whose love and support inspires me every day.

Thanks to the following publishers for allowing reprints of the following articles:

University of Calgary for:
"Paths from Erich Fromm: Thinking Authority Pedagogically." Journal of Education Thought (JET), Vol. 37:1, pp. 59–76

Taylor and Francis
"Secretariat Paulo Freire and the Democratization of Power: Toward a Theory of Transformative Leadership." Educational Philosophy and Theory, Vol. 35:1, pp.88–104

IRA
"Beyond Remediation: Toward Ideological Literacies of Learning." Journal of Adolescent and Adult Literacy, 46:2, pp. 150–168

Introduction

Neoliberal Globalization and the Manufacturing of Common Sense

For me, writing this book was an exercise in hope and possibility, ire and frustration. As a dreadful student who was kicked out of school before eleventh grade began, passed the GED, washed dishes for inadequate pay, and was a cheesesteak hack for many years, school was a place of ridicule, intimidation, hostility, and embarrassment. Teachers represented themselves as authoritarian overseers who had the power (and were not afraid to use it) to discipline and punish whenever my friends and I would veer from the established rules of the institution. I was unable to understand how the knowledge that the teachers and the school had determined was important for me to learn had any bearing on my life. As such, I remember almost nothing in terms of "official knowledge" from high school, though I did learn many things.

As the "problem" kid, I was often called into the principal's office and interrogated about other students' actions. I would never rat out my friends, but I learned how not to be intimidated by authority, thereby questioning its validity and integrity whenever it made itself visible. I also learned not to trust teachers, schooling, and the educational apparatus. The mistrust of these things, in the end, has made all the difference. To make a longer story shorter, after a few years I ended up going back to community college as a part-time student, transferred to a university in Boston, and then transferred again to the University of Massachusetts Boston.

UMass Boston is an extraordinary place because of its responsiveness to diversity, quality of professors, and small class size. At the time, the average age of undergraduates was twenty-eight, which was perfect for me because I did not want to be the oldest student in my freshman seminars. The diversity at UMass was not simply the multicultural diversity that is celebrated in current educational discourse; it was more. Age, sexual orientation, class, ideology, race, ethnicity, and life experience (Vietnam veterans programs, single-mother programs, etc.) made the practice of diversity tangible because it was coupled, for the most part, with a critical curriculum and pedagogy: I had, for the first time in my life, found a school and teachers who seemed truly interested in taking the experiences of the student body and channeling them into courses and pedagogical approaches to knowledge that pushed us to think critically about local and global situations. For example, a class on media, war, and social consequences almost spun out of control (this is a positive description!) when four of the students, Vietnam veterans, took issue not only with the representation of that war in films like *Platoon*, but with other students who believed that Hollywood's representations were realistic. In almost all of the classes I attended at UMass Boston, we debated, argued, fought, and struggled over meanings and history, knowledge and power. As students, our stories mattered, just as our literacies and knowledges were respected.

I came back to UMass Boston a few years after graduating to begin a master's program in literature, mainly because the world of business seemed a strange and empty place. Unfortunately, the graduate program in literature was not as dynamic an experience as the undergraduate experience for reasons beyond the scope of this brief autobiographical introduction. Suffice it to say, the diversity that drove the undergraduate world was almost entirely absent in the graduate world. In spite of this, Professor Elizabeth (Libby) Fay, who was also a significant influence for me as an undergraduate, not only introduced me formally to my first brush with critical thought through her noncanonical reading of Romanticism's canon, but provided a supportive environment as I worked to develop a more critical vocabulary. Seeing where my intellectual curiosity was heading, Libby introduced me to Professor Donaldo Macedo, stating directly that once I began to study with him, I would leave the discipline of English, never to return.

Donaldo introduced me to texts that helped give voice to the experiences I had as a high school student and, in a somewhat different form, continued to have as a young adult. It was an amazing moment for me, a validation of something that I felt, but could not yet give words to. Working with Donaldo, I began to further develop a language by which I could begin to articulate my educational experiences of marginalization, humiliation, and rebellion. I continued my graduate studies at Penn State with Professor Henry A. Giroux, who opened up to me the complex world of critical theory, postmodernist thought, feminism, critical race theory, the "field" of critical pedagogy, postcolonial theory, and other insurgent perspectives on life, language, work, and schooling.

I offer this account as an introduction to *Private Learning, Public Needs: The Neoliberal Assault on Democratic Education* because I want the reader to understand that I am not the typical (if there is such a thing) educational thinker; that is, I did not get into the educational debate or the position of teacher-educator because I had such a great experience in school and wanted to share it with others. As I've said, my experience was quite the opposite. The reality is that bad teachers, bad schooling, and bad political policies—not necessarily bad intentions—threaten our students every day. More often than not, the kids get blamed for their failures, even though it is the educational system that is failing the poor, the working class, and students of color by brutally ignoring their literacies, knowledges, histories, and dreams. More pernicious is the fact that this institutional failure is often interpreted and internalized by those whom it has failed as their own personal problem.

In short, I work in the educational sphere because I want to help transform the conditions of schooling and the larger contexts that shape it (and that it shapes). Poor and working-class students, nonwhites, and other students marginalized or oppressed because of their ideas, attitudes, languages, and literacies should be able to develop the skills, dispositions, attitudes, and intellect to think and act as socially connected individuals, responsible for each other, just as they learn to work with each other toward democratic ends. In relation to my privileged students, I am motivated by the same "utopian" project, but in their case it is not necessarily a question of learning as much a question of unlearning: unlearning normalcy for privilege, making visible the power that hides behind appeals to science, technology, gender neutrality, color blindness, and classlessness. Not to be misunderstood, both groups—the privileged and the oppressed—struggle under different forms of "false consciousness." False consciousness, in this context, is confusing a political part for ideological wholes, not, as it is sometimes defined, being unconsciously ignorant even of the parts. The different forms of false consciousness—the different parts to the sociopolitical puzzle that are known and how they are understood—have different pedagogical implications, but all must be addressed as ethical considerations against the backdrop of social and political values.

The irony that I am a teacher-educator does not escape me, and the reader should not ignore it. Being certified as a teacher is different from knowing how to teach or knowing how to think critically about the contexts in which learning takes place, and too many teachers and the systems that employ and educate them are helping to destroy the hopes and dreams of all our students, from the very young to adults who struggle to learn to read, by ignoring what it means to educate for a public democracy. "Public democracy," as David Sehr explains, "sees people's participation in public life as the essential ingredient in democratic government. Public participation arises out of an ethic of care and responsibility, not only from oneself as an isolated individual, but for one's fellow citizens as co-builders and co-beneficiaries of the public good."[1] No longer an acknowledged priority of many teacher education programs and elementary and secondary schools, democratic values and "skills" have been sacrificed at the altar of neoliberalism. Neoliberalism supports "a [privatized] conception of democracy [that] minimizes the role of ordinary citizens as political actors who can shape their collective destiny through participation with others in public life."[2] As Sehr reminds us, the lifeblood of "private democracy" runs deep in the history of "Western" democratic theory. *The Federalist Papers*, authored by Madison, Hamilton, and Jay, make it clear that the "masses" were to be controlled and contained; they were not to be trusted with the responsibility of self-government.

Four years into the new millennium, the antidemocratic ideological force of neoliberal capitalism dominates the sphere of cultural reproduction, including formal school systems, informal "educational" industries, such as film, television, and print media, and political/economic policy on a local and global scale. Neoliberalism both exaggerates and reframes "privatized" democracy by hollowing out the state apparatus as a democratic force, just as it uses state power as a weapon against democratic actions of insurgency, like the ongoing revolts against the World Trade Organization, the World Bank, and global trade initiatives. Neoliberalism, according to Jean Comaroff and John L. Comaroff, "aspires, in its ideology and practice, to intensify the abstractions inherent in capitalism itself: to separate labor power from its human context, to replace society with the market, to build a universe out of aggravated transactions."[3] This is the force of reproduction in the early twenty-first century, and it has altered the way we must think about the processes of schooling and education, literacy and language, curriculum and pedagogy, and theory and resistance. The abstractions of neoliberal capitalism pose particular problems for progressive and critical educators because the language of democratic agency and social responsibility is erased under the prerogative of private values and concerns. As Comaroff and Comaroff write

> Once-legible processes—the workings of power, the distribution of wealth, the meaning of politics and national belonging—have become opaque, even spectral. The contours of "society" blur, its organic solidarity disperses. Out of its shadows emerges a more radically individuated sense of personhood, of a subject built up of traits set against a universal backdrop of likeness and difference. In its place arise collectivities erected on a form of mechanical solidarity in which me is generalized into we.

> In this vocabulary, it is not just the personal is political. The personal is the only politics there is, the only politics with a tangible referent or emotional valence. By extension, interpersonal relations come to stand, metonymically, for the inchoate forces that threaten the world as we know it. It is in these privatized terms that action is organized, that the experience of inequity and antagonism takes meaningful shape.[4]

Neoliberal globalization, Fernando Coronil argues, "has led to a contradictory combination of new patterns of global integration and heightened social polarization within and among nations."[5] As Coronil reports, using information from both the United Nations Conference on Trade and Development and a document written by Subcomandante Marcos of the Zapatista movement in Mexico, this reality is spurred on by the economic slowdown, the widening gap between developed and developing nations, the gains in wealth by the world's elite classes, the growth of employment and income insecurity, and the growing gap between skilled and unskilled labor on a global scale.[6] Undergirding these disturbing trends is neoliberalism's pernicious imperative to treat people as capital, or more accurately, to evaluate human worth against the value of humans as a "source of wealth," like natural resources.[7] As Coronil correctly observes

> [T]he value of people can only be compared to the value of things only because both are reduced to capital. The definition of people as capital means that they are to be treated as capital—taken into account insofar as they contribute to the expansion of wealth, and marginalized if they do not.[8]

This perspective informs not simply a culture of consumption—people consuming "things" as well as each other as part of their deep psychology as consumers—but more importantly, neoliberal discourse includes, at a base level, the commodification of everyday life. From sitting idly in front of the television to attending school, our world is constructed, in large part, through a *political* process that turns almost all actions and thoughts into things that can be bought and sold. If, by chance, we do something or go somewhere that has escaped the commodifying grasp of neoliberal logic, then its value—social, material, or otherwise—will assuredly be questioned.

Beyond the productive capacities of neoliberalism to manufacture an atomized consumer citizen, the absences in neoliberal discourse are profound and include, but are not limited to, democratic needs, such as the establishment of institutions that encourage political equity; cultural pluralism; public institutions that function outside the logic of markets; and the production of knowledges that can claim legitimacy beyond the narrow strictures of positivistic measurement. Within this broad sphere of sociological and political life, *Private Learning, Public Needs: The Neoliberal Assault on Democratic Education* examines neoliberalism's power to position teaching, education, schooling, and literacy as overly functional endeavors that not only work in the service of neoliberal interests directly, but help to reproduce the institutional structures that leave unmet the needs that neoliberalism helps to create.

🐚 Critical Pedagogy in the Age of Neoliberalism

Over the last thirty years, critical studies in education, schooling, pedagogy, and curriculum have brought attention to the reproductive nature of dominant modes of learning. It has been/is argued that schooling reproduces social and political/economic inequity due to any number of variables, including racism, sexism, and class bias; tracking; the "hidden" curriculum; the division between high and low culture; and disciplinary pedagogical models that encourage docility and automated student responses. What is being reproduced specifically, critical educationalists argue, is primarily an antidemocratic capitalistic system that denies the basic right of collective political agency to individuals due to the perpetuation of economic and cultural inequities.

The reproductive model of schooling took aim at a form of capitalism in its economic and cultural manifestations. Framed initially within a neo-Marxist framework, the critiques of schooling became increasingly complex as they moved from a primarily class-oriented, modernist perspective to a more inclusive postmodernist perspective that took into account racism, sexism, nationalism, and (post)colonialism. Nevertheless, monopoly capitalism was the primary force of reproduction, churning out workers and elites beneath the veil of a "neutral" public education system.

Of course, the reproductive thesis has gone through numerous transformations, responding to the changes that history initiates. Most notable for my discussion throughout this book is Giroux's contribution to the theory of reproduction: resistance.[9] No longer automatons following the social order, students have been, in fact, resisting the reproductive process in specific and important ways. Often these behaviors of resistance are labeled by dominant society as criminal or pathological, but they nevertheless demonstrate, to an important degree, that people are not simply dupes of a system that is impenetrable and beyond change. The notion of resistance is vital to critical studies of schooling and learning if democratic education is to be at all relevant.

Recognizing the dialectic between resistance and reproduction makes the notion of hope concrete, and without hope for a future characterized by caring as opposed to violence, learning as opposed to indoctrination, struggle as opposed to oppression, and freedom as opposed to constraint, there is no need for democratic education. Democratic education describes a process indebted to the belief that individual agency must be the catalyst for the collective organization of the public sphere. The individual, in this context, is understood as one who is in relation to others. As such, individuals experience themselves negatively, within a matrix of different power relations. We are, in many significant ways, that which we are not. Therefore, individual power is only as forceful as the social conditions it to be (i.e., a strong democracy would translate into strong individuals). Individualism, by contrast, is the process by which ideology produces the individual positively, that is, outside of his or her relations to others. This formulation of the individual leaves the individual, by consequence, as weak-kneed and atomized in the face of powerful social forces.

Ironically, individualism threatens the democratic project by disempowering the individual to act collectively to resist elite interests that, more often than not, differ from interests of working and poor people throughout the world.

Within the dialectic between reproduction and resistance is an explicit repositioning of pedagogy as more than the "the practice of knowledge and skills transmission."[10] The continued reduction of pedagogy to this narrow stricture of "real" practice does more than simply reproduce the false dichotomy between theory and practice; it ignores the rich body of social theory that has theorized pedagogy "as a form of political and cultural production deeply implicated in the construction of knowledge, subjectivities, and social relations."[11] This is not to say that methodological "practice" is not a relevant subject for research and theory, but rather that the concept of pedagogy must be understood

> as a discursive practice, an unfinished language, replete with possibilities, that grows out of particular engagements and dialogues. It offers up new categories, examples and insights for teachers and others to engage and rethink everything from the purpose and meaning of schooling to the role that educators might play as cultural workers. Its specificity and value lie in its success in providing a language that ruptures the business-as-usual relationship between theory and practice, pedagogy and teaching, and schools and critical public cultures. It means comprehending pedagogy as a configuration of textual, verbal, and visual practices that seek to engage the processes through which people understand themselves and the ways in which they engage others and their environment.[12]

Conceptualized in this way, critical pedagogy must not only stay responsive to the changing social realities of the day, but it must also be a force for breaking into the common sense that neoliberalism, over the course of many years, has manufactured. As such, democratic education in the age of neoliberalism necessitates more than teaching students the skills and dispositions demanded by democratic life, private or public. In short, it means teaching teachers, students, and other political workers both how to reimagine "democracy" and how to transform the ideological and material structures of neoliberalism that delimit public participation in local and global affairs.

Through a "pedagogical" process, neoliberal ideology manufactures common sense at an incredibly efficient rate. The type of common sense that is manufactured is primarily sociological in nature, causing a form of what I call "imaginative inertia." This imaginative inertia is characterized by an inability to think beyond the parameters of dominant sociological structures. If we cannot imagine radically, then we cannot act radically. The reality of imaginative inertia on a mass scale does not mean, however, that people are automatons, blindly thinking and acting, dupes of powerful sociological structures. More accurately, imaginative inertia reflects a state of *limited* and *limiting* activity; that is, it points to the power of sociological borders as they manifest themselves at the level of the psychological and affective

registers to define both dominant and insurgent discourses. The state of imaginative inertia, for example, is seen explicitly, as I will discuss in chapter one, in how a
society manufactures needs and their satisfactions.

🍵 Literacy in a Neoliberal Age

Literacy education, in its dominant manifestations, suffers from imaginative inertia under neoliberal rule by being reduced to no more than a set of basic skills, sanctioned by the federal government, state agencies, and many academics, and assessed
by positivistic forms of measurement. Literacy has been effectively reduced to
"reading" or, more directly, decoding and the "proper" pronunciation of texts by influential committees like the National Reading Panel.[13] The notion of meaning plays
a small role in the overall conception of literacy and is categorized under the heading "comprehension." Comprehension relates to a process by which the reader dis-
covers the meaning in the text as though the meanings "found" are unrelated to the
contexts in which the text itself is being read. This is more than an oversight and
articulates with neoliberalism's fetish with technological rationality, as well as with
its more insidious mythology of language learning as a means toward capitalistic
gain. In this formulation, literacy and language are severed from power and knowledge, making the latter invisible and the former a subject for cognitive science, positivistic studies, and drill and skill initiatives.

In contrast and outside neoliberal logic, literacy has not only been pluralized,
but understood as an important, however insufficient, means toward realizing freedom in oppressive conditions.[14] In this form, language is understood as an ideological tool, making its power formidable in the construction of false realities and false
consciousnesses. Becoming literate, from this perspective, means, in short, critically engaging language, revealing its power to frame reality in a way that privileges,
in our current context, business interests, the interests of the white minority (speaking globally), and men. In this discourse, literacy education is directly tied to
liberation.

Literacy has also been thought of specifically in light of its relationship to language and learning. Linguist James Gee convincingly argues, in his development of
a theory of literacy, that "literacy is control of secondary uses of language (i.e., uses
of language in secondary discourses)."[15] A discourse, in Gee's scholarship, is a
"socially accepted association among ways of using language, of thinking, and of acting that can be used to identify oneself as a member of a socially meaningful group
or 'social network.'"[16] Recognizing the intrarelationship between literacy, language,
and learning, Gee argues for a notion of literacy that includes an analysis of how
language is used; the cultural capital a person is granted through his or her fluen-

cy in specific kinds of discourses; and the powerful social and political connections that are nurtured among members of discourse communities. Anyone who has ever been berated by a teacher, for example, for not speaking "proper" English will appreciate the insight of Gee's conceptualization of literacy. "Proper" English is not anymore proper than any other way of speaking or writing the language. It is only "proper" because of its location within a more general context of behaviors and beliefs. In other words, power shapes our notions of what is proper and what is not. This is not a new argument, I know, but for those readers who have been trained to reduce literacy to a skill-based decoding of decontextualized words and letters that is, at the same time, apolitical, and nonevaluative, this position on literacy needs to be made clear.

The pedagogical implications of Gee's conception of what it means to be literate, combined with the concepts and practices of "critical literacy," are significant. Neither "whole language" nor "phonics" can adequately address the demands of these two positions, separately or together, although "whole language"—with its focus on contexts, meaning construction, and phonemic fluency—comes close. Missing from whole language studies generally, and there are exceptions of course, is a direct confrontation with power and ideology. Both of these infiltrate language learning at a fundamental level, making the process of teaching a student how to read words a lesson in the world that those words help to create. Gee's understanding that there are dominant discourses that legitimate certain meanings and pronunciations over others is important methodologically because it means that reading teachers must be responsive to the exclusive nature of discourses, their ideological parameters, and what other discourses they are defining themselves against. Of concern, in this context, is not simply the "how" of reading instruction, which is too limiting and ignores the relationship between language and power. Rather, the "why" and "what" of language instruction must be developed in a way that addresses the intimacy between language and power as an *ethical* concern. This means that literacy teachers have decisions to make in the face of concrete situations that have been interpreted in specific ways due to the relationship between language and power. In the neoliberal age, the literacy level of the literacy teacher needs to be developed so that he or she can respond ethically to the demands of language learners, demands that arise out of the contradiction between neoliberal interests on one hand and democratic needs on the other.

🎵 Conclusion

These four concepts—critical pedagogy, public democracy, neoliberalism, and literacy—are interrogated and used for interrogation throughout the book. These

terms and ideas are highly contested, but nevertheless they are fundamental referents in our current context for mapping the relationship between power, education,
learning, and democratic possibilities. This is not to say that these are the only referents that could be used, and in this way, the book you are about to read, either in
parts or as a whole, is speculative and not without its absences. In spite of this, I
believe these referents draw attention to many of the social, political, ideological,
pedagogical, and cultural ramifications of power and privilege in the local and
global spheres. For example, these referents provoke and address certain questions
throughout the book: What roles will the "neoliberal" state play in directing public school curriculum, pedagogy, and assessment? How has corporate culture's "public pedagogy" effectively crossed into our educational institutions, and what is the
effect on our students' learning? On our teaching? How have "postmodern" theories of globalization challenged modern theories of resistance and change? What
kinds of literacies are needed in our neoliberal age to enhance individual and collective agency? Have we, as some have argued, exchanged power for comfort? Has
the cultural sphere—primarily made up of media, the "popular" and consumerism—
superseded the formal educational sphere in its influence over what, how, and why
we learn what we do? How do state standards at the elementary and secondary levels affect teacher-education curriculum? How does an overly functionalized curriculum and pedagogy create a "deskilled" workforce? How does this deskilling affect
teachers' political agency, both within and beyond the classroom? What would a
teacher-education program look like that educates teachers as both practitioners and
intellectuals? What knowledges would support such an undertaking? What practices—pedagogical, political, curricular—would make this conception of teacher
agency operational in the service of academic freedom and cultural responsibility?
At stake in understanding and trying to answer these questions in this book, I
believe, is our individual power to think and act collectively in the service of our
common concerns, even as they arise out of our individual differences. These questions are directly and indirectly addressed in the following chapters.

Part I, "Neoliberal Globalization and the Question of Adult Literacy
Education," is broken into two chapters. Chapter one is a study of neoliberalism and
its relationship to globalization. Specifically, the changing role of the state is examined in terms that bring attention to globalization's capacity to ignore nation-state
borders, especially in the context of finance and culture. Through a discourse of
needs and satisfactions, neoliberal globalization is rationalized as the only viable
means by which to realize modernity's goals of progress and rationality. The role of
the state is then discussed in light of its influence on local agencies and on local institutions. Of issue is the interiorization of neoliberal globalization at the material levels of educational life, namely curriculum standards and development. Through the
imposition of certain kinds of standards, teacher education programs must make

some hard decisions about whether they will, on the one hand, satisfy the needs manufactured by neoliberal interests as they manifest themselves in curricular and pedagogic mandates, or, on the other, will use their authority to challenge and confront that which they know is detrimental to democratic principles and good teaching practices.

Chapter two examines how neoliberal interests have impeded the goals of adult literacy education. By ignoring the violence of poverty, racism, and sexism as constituently linked to the project of literacy, adults have been left behind in the fight not only for a literate global population, but also in the eradication of oppressive ideologies and their material effects. These two issues, I will argue, must be seen as correspondences, the latter driving the former. Finally, the question, Why read? is addressed in the context of democratic, economic, and cultural concerns, troubling three of the major justifications of literacy development in the United States and abroad.

Part II, "The Work of Critical Theory in a Neoliberal Age," takes up the work of two prominent critical theorists in and beyond education: Erich Fromm and Paulo Freire. These two theorists make practical interventions into the discourse of neoliberalism, which is necessary before any reconceptualization of neoliberal ideology can take place. Chapter three discusses Fromm's important alternative to top-down discourses of power and authority. His work suggests fascism as a viable outcome of an unchecked authority like neoliberalism, with its penchant for atomization and rampant individualism. In chapter four, Freire's work in São Paulo as Secretary of Education is studied for what it can teach us about the importance and possibility of structural transformations. More than an ideological project, Freire's work represents a radical reconstruction of an entrenched educational system, beginning with the democratization of power within the structure itself.

Part III, "Critical Pedagogies and Literacies for a Neoliberal Age," is broken up into two chapters. Chapter five is a practical disruption of standard remedial literacy practices. Neoliberalism demands a particular functionality, and remedial literacy programs are notorious for fulfilling this ideologically driven mandate. Moving beyond this mandate, I examine what it would mean to teach literacies of ideology within a remedial reading course. Chapter six is also a practical disruption, developing pedagogical strategies that encourage cultural studies of critical pedagogy. In this chapter the primary considerations of cultural studies and critical pedagogy are conceptualized in practical terms. By engaging these concepts at the strategic level, the critical act is on its way to becoming transformative.

I encourage the reader to read these chapters critically. These ideas are meant to inform as well as provoke; they are, in the best sense, part of an ongoing dialogue. As such, they are directed discussions in the service of understanding complex social and political forces. The reader must disrupt, challenge, investigate, question, inquire, and struggle to both understand and critique my contributions to the larger critical discourse on schooling, literacy, pedagogy, and learning. In the spirit of dialectical thinking, these studies must be positioned as a continuation of the critical process, a process indebted to the notion that, through our ability to imagine a world beyond the parameters of neoliberal ideology, we can transform our "public" institutions of private learning so that they become responsive to our democratic needs.

Neoliberal Globalization and the Question of Adult Literacy Education

Neoliberal Ideology, State Curriculum Standards, and the Manufacturing of Educational Needs

Notes on the Transformation of State Power, Ideological State Apparatuses, and Teacher Education in the Age of Globalization

What is at stake are the needs themselves. At this stage, the question is no longer: how can the individual satisfy his needs without hurting others, but rather: how can he satisfy his needs without hurting himself, without reproducing, through his aspirations and satisfactions, his dependence on an exploitative apparatus which, in satisfying his needs, perpetuates his servitude?[1]

Neoliberalism is the defining political economic paradigm of our time—it refers to the policies and processes whereby a relative handful of private interests are permitted to control as much as possible of social life in order to maximize their personal profit. Associated initially with Reagan and Thatcher, for the past two decades neoliberalism has been the dominant global political economic trend adopted by political parties of the center and much of the traditional left as well as the right. These parties and the policies they enact represent the immediate interests of extremely wealthy investors and less than one thousand large corporations.[2]

Introduction

These two epigraphs, although written during different times, speak to what I will describe as one of the most disturbing trends in contemporary social-economic-political-educational culture. Taken together, the words of Herbert Marcuse and Robert McChesney point out the relationship between individual needs and satisfactions on one hand and their constitutive relationship to corporate power and private interests on the other. In the context of education and schooling in New Jersey, the local state government has either sanctioned neoliberalism as the guiding ideology for curriculum and pedagogical policy, or it has forfeited ideological control of its schools through "privately" administered whole-school reform (WSR) initiatives, which in turn, work to legitimate and strengthen the relationship between neoliberal globalization and the "new" role of the nation-state. New Jersey's position raises the following important questions about the future of public education, the role of both local state and nation-state power, and the hegemonic effects of ideological state apparatuses (ISAs) in an age of neoliberal globalization: What are some of the implications—democratic, cultural, curricular, pedagogical, economic— of this forfeiture or sanctioning? What might the effects of running our public educational system in the service of private interests be on our sense of the "public"? What responsibility do local states have to satisfy public needs publicly? How has globalization affected local state agencies' power to control the form and function of their public schools? What are some of the implications of neoliberal globalization on teacher education?

In what follows, I address these questions primarily through a theoretical discussion about neoliberal ideology by addressing the implications its philosophical principles and ideological practices have on the role of the nation-state. Neoliberalism represents a "nonsystemic" system, that is, an ideological system of language, thought, and behavior that detests and, as P. Bourdieu argues, wants to destroy "collective structures which may impede the pure market."[3] As a global economic, political, and cultural force, neoliberalism challenges us to rethink the role of the "modern" nation-state. Notions like "state sovereignty"—as it translates into the economic, political, ideological, and cultural power a nation-state has to control what occurs inside and condition what occurs outside of its national borders— must be revised in the face of globalization's penchant to ignore national borders and interrelate the economies and cultural practices of nation-states.

Further, I discuss how neoliberal globalization manufactures particular needs in the service of specific interests at the local and regional level. From this perspective, neoliberalism's strength lies not in its ability to reproduce itself per se, but rather in its ability to adjust to the "underdetermined" evolution of its own policies and practices, in large part by producing in cooperation with ISAs, a "discourse of needs." Through this discourse of needs, ISAs and the nation-state create a causeway by which neoliberal globalization travels down, affecting the democratic control local and regional agencies have over what needs are met and by what means. Bob Jessop describes this process as "interiorization."[4] In the educational context of New Jersey, interiorization, I will argue, is the effect of WSR models articulating with the neoliberal interests of the nation-state, which in turn articulates with the goals and objectives of global financial markets. The strong relationship between WSR and the larger global context disempowers local and state governments from determining which goals and objectives are appropriate for their communities. The authority of WSR models, like *Success for All*, to negate local state mandates suggests a subtle transformation in the form and function of ISAs in the age of neoliberal globalization.

I ground these discussions in a critical analysis of New Jersey's Core Curriculum Standards. Curriculum standards are a valuable measure of both ideological perspective, local government influence, and, in our present conjunction, state power. Looking at two of New Jersey's Core Curriculum Standards, one of which illustrates local government's investment in neoliberal ideals and one that directly contradicts them, I critically analyze how these standards, in the first instance, perpetuate a neoliberal discourse of needs and, in the second instance, challenge this discourse. In the second instance, I discuss how the challenge is rendered benign through WSR control of the schools.

Lastly, I consider some of the challenges the state's neoliberal agenda presents to "progressive" teacher-education programs, using the College of Education at Montclair State University in New Jersey as an example. One question that frames my analysis of teacher education in a neoliberal age is, Do teacher educators and progressive teacher-education programs, by pragmatically satisfying educational needs that are manufactured in the service of neoliberal interests, help perpetuate the ideological thinking and apparatuses that went into the creation and normalization of those needs in the first place? This is no small matter if higher education generally, and teacher education specifically, are to play a leadership role in disrupting the hegemony of neoliberalism on one hand and establishing a radically democratic project on the other. By working in the service of a democratic project, teacher education can become more than the preparation of classroom managers and technicians; it can become the training of teachers to respond to the changing needs of a radically diverse and democratic society, where issues of equity and individual power find a common project in collective actions of dissent and freedom.

🕮 Welcome to the Jungle: Barbarism in a Neoliberal Age

Neoliberalism is an economic, political, and cultural system that requires a certain level of political docility, social cynicism, and economic fatalism on behalf of its constituencies to maintain its hegemony. "It is precisely in its oppression of non-market forces that we see how neoliberalism operates not only as an economic system," writes Robert McChesney, "but as a political and cultural system as well."[5] These three parts together give neoliberalism its force as well as its coherence. But for analytical purposes, it is fruitful to separate out its interrelated parts. By doing so, its "totality"—its hegemony—is better understood and more forcefully challenged.

Economics

The neoliberal age is defined by five major economic principles: (1) an uncritical acceptance of the market's determining both private and public needs, (2) a concentration of wealth and power, (3) "deregulation" and corporate welfare policies, (4) privatization, and (5) an emphasis on individual accountability at the expense of social responsibility (i.e., individualism). These principles have come to define local, national, and global practices throughout the world. The International Monetary Fund (IMF) and the World Bank are often referenced as primary tools of neoliberal ideology, leveraging countries through the dissemination of financial loans and other development initiatives. As David Hursh points out, "The U.S. dominated World Bank and International Monetary Fund has required national governments to develop economic policies that emphasize economic growth and property rights over social welfare and personal rights."[6] Once these loans have been granted, the World Bank and IMF then have the "right" to tell the leaders of these countries how to run their economies. Neoliberal principles always guide the "recommendations" that are made, generally under the name "country assistance strategies."

Greg Palast, investigative reporter for news organizations like the BBC and *The Guardian*, speaking to Joseph Stiglitz, ex–chief economist of the World Bank and 2001 Nobel Prize winner in economics, uncovers what is essentially a four-step program toward neoliberal rule.[7] Stiglitz contends that step one, as mentioned above, is privatization. In real-world terms, this means that countries are required to sell off public assets like water and electricity to private interests. In exchange, leaders of these countries receive "commissions paid to Swiss bank accounts for simply shaving a few billion off the sale price of national assets."[8] Stiglitz claims that the U.S.-backed privatization program in Russia, for example, "cut national output nearly in half, causing economic depression and starvation," while it "paid" President Yeltsin through campaign kickbacks.[9] Knowing that this type of information sounds conspiratorial, Palast reminds his readers that Stiglitz was a "member of Bill Clinton's cabinet as chairman of the president's Council of Economic Advisors." In other words, he was there helping to make these decisions.

The next step in the manufacturing of neoliberal rule is called "Capital Market Liberalization." Palast explains that this "means repealing any nation's law that slows down or taxes money jumping over borders." In neoliberal utopia this kind of deregulatory policy encourages the flow of capital both in and out of countries.

But the reality for countries like Indonesia and Brazil is "the money simply flowed out and out."[10] Palast reports that Stiglitz called this the "hot money cycle," and it has the effect of depleting a nation's reserves very quickly. In response to this capital flight, and in an effort to attract investors back to the suffering nation, "the IMF demands these nations raise interest rates to 30 percent, 50 percent and 80 percent,"[11] with the result, Stiglitz says, that "higher interest rates demolished property values, savaged industrial production and drained national treasuries."[12]

The next step in the plan, according to Palast's discussion with Stiglitz is called "Market-Based Pricing," meaning simply that nations are required "to raise the price on food, water, and domestic gas." Stiglitz states that when a nation is struggling under the burden of the first two policies, "the IMF takes advantage and squeezes the last pound of blood out of them. They turn up the heat until finally, the whole cauldron blows up."[13] Backing up this claim, Palast points to the case of Indonesia in 1998 when riots overtook the nation in response to the IMF's cutting off water and food subsidies for the poor. In addition he points to the riots in Bolivia in 2000 and in Ecuador in 2001. Especially important about Palast's treatment of this particular step in the "Assistance Strategy" is his willingness to report that the upheavals are "written into the plan." He points to the "Interim Country Assistance Strategy" for Ecuador in which the World Bank stated "that they expected their plans to spark 'social unrest.'"[14]

The fourth step is ironically called the "Poverty Reduction Strategy," better known as "free trade." As in the deregulatory plan, there is a utopian ideal at work here. The free trade, too, is marred by the unequal operation of force and power. Stiglitz compares the World Trade Organization's (WTO) conception of the free market to the Opium Wars, in that the barriers to capital are only being knocked down in the service of U.S. and European interests. Inversely, U.S. and European markets are heavily fortified against foreign competition by the imposition of "impossible tariffs" upon developing nations.[15]

This economic framework, argues Pierre Bourdieu, is "founded on a formidable abstraction. For, in the name of a narrow and strict conception of rationality as individual rationality, it brackets the economic and social conditions of rational orientations and the economic and social structures that are the condition of their application."[16] This bracketing, according to Bourdieu, is a fatal theoretical flaw (and therefore a practical flaw as well) because the dichotomy between "a properly economic logic, based on competition and efficiency, and social logic, which is subject to the rule of fairness" is false.[17] In other words, there is no economic theory separate from the social practices that it informs and in which it is informed. For to think about competition and efficiency outside the ethical demands of fairness would lead, almost by historical design, to brutal delineations of power, coupled with the violent and oppressive tactics of an unchecked authority. Neoliberalism, as is evident in its effects, privileges its advocates while denunciating its critics, just as it leaves developing nations and their workers struggling under economic inequities that only continue to grow.[18] Its gesture to "pure theory"[19] is no more than the "displace(ment) [of] political sovereignty with the sovereignty of 'the market,' as if the latter had a mind and morality of its own."[20]

The four steps to neoliberal rule as sanctioned by the World Bank and IMF have numerous ethical implications, especially and specifically in regard to the "rules of fairness" that social logic demands. Notions of equity are absent in the neoliberal age, and conversely, inequity is the only means by which modern society can live freely. This Orwellian logic is, in fact, the logic of neoliberalism. Inequality will set you free, while fairness or equity will imprison the individual in a matrix of regulation, restriction, and constraint. By perpetuating the myth of pure theory, neoliberalism severs power from privilege, just as it sutures freedom to the economic market. The equation provides justification for social irresponsibility, as well as a rationalization for the corporate-government complex.

Politics

These four economic steps ostensibly frame, according to Bourdieu, the "utopia of neoliberalism—thus converted into a *political problem*."[21] He positions neoliberalism as a "strong discourse" because it has the ability to make the world that, in turn, makes it what it is.[22] Beyond the economic, neoliberalism, Bourdieu argues, is a "political project" underway. The goals of the project are simply to devise and undertake a "programme of the methodological destruction of collectives."[23] The destruction of collectives suggests an ethical position, one that obviously devalues collective organizations of power. One might wonder what kind of citizen this value system produces and celebrates. Henry Giroux argues, "As society is defined through the culture and values of neoliberalism, the relationship between a critical education, public morality, and civic responsibility as conditions for creating thoughtful and engaged citizens are sacrificed all too willingly to the interest of financial capital and the logic of profit-making."[24] The subject produced by the sacrifice of these ideas can be described as possessing a combination of political impotency and economic competitiveness. The combination is disturbing in that subjectivities are manufactured that primarily possesses freedom in terms of individual and economic competition. This makes systems of thought and behavior invisible to the indoctrinated "eye," just as it positions people as rivals and enemies fighting for inadequate resources in the "free" marketplace.

This sacrifice can be read as a violent intervention into political and democratic life because it effectively destroys personal and collective agency and replaces them with nothing comparable. As Giroux writes, "It assaults all things public, mystifies the basic contradiction between democratic values and market fundamental-ism, and weakens any viable notion of political agency by offering no language capable of connecting private considerations to public issues."[25] When it becomes impossibly difficult to make these kinds of connections, what, as civically engaged people, can we do that can rightfully be called politics? Politics in its ideal form depends, at the least, on the creation and development "of social institutions that depend on explicit collective activity."[26] Moreover, politics demands support for *collective* struggle over power and meaning vis-à-vis our individual experiences as they unfold in, and as an effect of, the *public* and *social* spaces that we occupy. As a consequence, "There is a strong argument to be made that neoliberal capitalism in its millennial moment portends the death of politics by hiding its own ideological underpinnings in the dictates of economic efficiency."[27] In pragmatic terms, the death of politics is initiated, according to McChesney, by an attack on democratic connections, manifested in the decimation of noncommercial organizations and institutions, like "community groups, libraries, public schools, neighborhood organizations, cooperatives, public meeting places, voluntary associations, and trade unions."[28]

Appealing to the logic of economic efficiency continues to be an effective strategy for defending neoliberal rationality. In this context, efficiency correlates directly with economic (goods and services) production, distribution, and consumption. The cheaper the better, as the saying goes, the one caveat being that "quality" is not to be sacrificed. There are a few obvious problems and contradictions with this idea of efficiency. First, "cheaper" in a neoliberal context refers not to the profits shareholders are to enjoy, but rather the salaries and benefits of the workers who produce the goods and services. The neoliberal argument is that if shareholders and corporations continue to enjoy profits, while the workers get paid nominally, then capital investments can be made at the higher levels of power, while consumer spending at the lower levels will still actively stimulate the economy. This places workers in the eyes of shareholders as profit liabilities. So, in this way, neoliberal efficiency refers to the least amount possible that can be spent on workers measured against the most money shareholders can put into their pockets. This strategy, against reason, takes money *out* of the public sphere (out of the pockets of the mass of consumers) and gives it voluntarily to a small minority of people to "reinvest" at their will. As the privileged and wealthy have historically shown a great penchant for collectively hording their capital, as evidenced by the legacies of wealth and power in this country and throughout the world, this strategy exacerbates social and economic inequality while justifying it as the most rational means by which society should be economically and politically organized.

Second, the notion of economic efficiency dismisses, by contrast, notions of political, democratic, educational, and social efficiency. These notions of efficiency balance economic values against social and political values. Efficiency in these contexts means that resources are distributed in a way that encourages mass-based participation in democratic, social, educational, and political life. Measuring efficiency in these separate, but related, contexts rests on our ability as citizens to shape collectively our own worlds. No longer dictated to by the irrational rationality of neoliberal efficiency, the efficiency of politics is measured against people's "opportunities" (i.e., the resources they possess) to critically reflect, collectively organize, act against institutions that abuse power and authority, and to create institutions that signify competing ideas. As Zygmunt Bauman argues, "Critical reflection is the essence of all genuine *politics* (as distinct from the merely 'political'—that is, related to the experience of power). Politics is an effective and practical effort to subject institutions that boast *de facto* validity to the test of *du jour* validity."[29] The critical act is often economically inefficient, but democratically efficient. The opposition of these ideas has signaled an ideological war, with two of the serious casualties being a viable notion of the "public" and our ability to maintain an "engaged critique."[30] Giroux explains that by positioning the "market as final arbiter of social destiny . . . neoliberalism empties the public treasury, hollows out public services, and limits the vocabulary and imagery available to recognize non-commercialized public space, antidemocratic forms of power, and narrow models of individual agency."[31]

Ideologically, neoliberalism's hostility to the public is only matched by totalitarianism's hostility to the private. In their hostilities, they are profoundly united to make the thoughts of individuals, alone or in social groups, "impotent, irrelevant and of no consequence for the success or failure of power."[32] Public displays of collective agency, as we saw in Seattle and, more globally, leading up to the U.S. war on Iraq, are discounted as inconsequential, or they are positioned as a threat of some kind needing to be disciplined or punished. By positioning social and collective dissent as a threat to freedom, neoliberal ideology effectively transforms the political into the criminal. This transformation directly threatens the democratic project. By demonizing at best, and criminalizing at worst, what constitutes public and collective political action, neoliberalism leaves only individual expressions of dissent as acceptable "political" responses to institutional and systemic initiatives. As Giroux argues,

> As democratic values give way to commercial values, intellectual ambitions are often reduced to an instrument of the entrepreneurial self and social visions are dismissed as hopelessly out of date. Public space is portrayed exclusively as an investment opportunity, and the public good increasingly becomes a metaphor for public disorder. That is, any notion of the public—for example, public schools, public transportation, or public parks—becomes synonymous with disrepair, danger, and risk.[33]

In this respect, neoliberalism is a conservative ideology, hostile to democratic control of power, privilege, and authority. Its conservatism finds meaning in its attack on publicly oriented projects, like public education. In the end, from an ideological perspective, it is impossible to tease apart the conservative agenda against publicly oriented projects on one hand and neoliberalism's dogmatic support of privatization on the other. Together they manufacture, at the level of common sense, a culture of positivism, self-help, and corporate rationality, all undergirded by the belief in the individual as separate (i.e., located inequitably within the free market structure) but equal. As such, neoliberalism is also a cultural phenomenon that transgresses the borders of the political and economic to create a cultural logic that celebrates "the absence of questioning; its surrender to what is seen as the implacable and irreversible logic of social reality."[34]

Culture

Neoliberalism's grip on the political and economic realities of people naturally affects how and what we think about each other, social reality, and the future. The affect of neoliberalism is felt at the level of (un)consciousness; it is experienced in greater degrees as a matter of common sense. This is evident in the reactions of its advocates when they confront its critics. As Giroux writes, "Within this discourse, anyone who does not believe that rapacious capitalism is the only road to freedom and the good life is dismissed as a crank."[35] These dismissals, more than a matter of economic and political import, suggest that neoliberalism operates as a cultural *practice*. As a cultural practice, neoliberalism is lived out and reproduced within corporate culture:

> [C]orporate culture . . . refer[s] to an ensemble of ideological and institutional forces that functions politically and pedagogically both to govern organizational life through senior managerial control and to fashion compliant workers, depoliticized consumers, and passive citizens. Within the language and images of corporate culture, citizenship is portrayed as an utterly privatized affair whose aim is to produce competitive self-interested individuals vying for their own material and ideological gain. Reformulating social issues as strictly private concerns, corporate culture functions largely to either cancel out or devalue social, class-specific, and racial injustices of the existing social order by absorbing the democratic impulses and practices of civil society within narrow economic relations. Corporate culture becomes an all-encompassing horizon for producing market identities, values, and practices.[36]

The articulation between neoliberalism and corporate culture creates a seamless flow of knowledge and power, made hermetic by one rationalizing the other. For example, corporate culture demands not only an adherence to market-based principles, but rewards those who embody the identities manufactured and legitimated by neoliberalism. Neoliberal identities are characterized by a number of different cultural practices. Like all identities, these are not stagnant, nor are they without internal contradictions. Moreover, people embody multiple identities simultaneously. Nevertheless, it's helpful to create a working typology to help describe a few major neoliberal identities and the cultural practices that inform them:

(1) *The Marketeer* practices an unquestioning acceptance of the market as the final arbiter of all things social. The people who embody this aspect of neoliberal identity position all private and public actions within the context of market rationality. In this context, the market is omniprescient and brutally indiscriminate. If an action fails or succeeds, the Marketeer chalks it up to the logic of the market. The successful Marketeer establishes him- or herself as a beneficiary or victim of the market, adding to the market's mythological status as an indiscriminate player in the mysterious world of free market capitalism.

(2) *The Rugged Corporatist* practices a form of Wild West individualism. He or she is often represented in popular culture as the successful (i.e., wealthy) or future successful business guru in the corner office, who dismisses the "social" and "public" as the place and space of "welfare," choosing instead to go it alone. Ignoring the highly evolved cultural network that assists the Rugged Corporatist in climbing the corporate latter, this neoliberal subject embodies the "bootstrap" spirit of capitalistic lore.

(3) *The "Cultured" Corporatist* invests heavily in the high-low culture dichotomy, taking pride in his or her fluency in bourgeois life. Most notable for his or her humanist impulses, this neoliberal identity celebrates "high" culture as the pinnacle of human achievement. These achievements are argued to be made possible by unrestrained capitalism, competition fueling creativity or, in corporate-speak, research and design. Public intervention into private life is understood as a threat to both the perpetuation and production of high culture. In this context, the influence of the "masses" is seen as a threat to the "good life," constraining the "natural" evolution of cultural inventiveness and sophistication.

(4) *The Materialist* dogmatically pursues the acquisition of material goods, making little to no distinction between who he or she is and what he or she owns. Giroux writes, "The good life, in this discourse, 'is construed in terms of our identities as consumers—we are what we buy.' The good life now means living inside the world of corporate brands."[37] The Materialist invests in corporate culture's promise of wealth and prestige, the fulfillment of the promise being the reward for the ideological investment. This identity is the most publicly visible and therefore has an implicit pedagogical dimension. That is, it "teaches" the lessons of neoliberalism through a display of its potential rewards. MTV's popular show *Cribs*, which takes viewers on tours of wealthy musicians' houses, can be read as an advertisement for neoliberalism.[38] Absent in this advertisement is the fact that most musi-

cians struggle simply to make ends meet and, without corporate sponsorship, are almost destined to go unrecognized by the public eye.

(5) *The Fatalist* practices a form of cultural and historical homicide through his or her embodiment of neoliberal destiny. For Fatalists, neoliberal destiny has already arrived. Present-day Fatalists are not without predecessors, like those in the "Roaring Twenties [who] confidently assumed that labor had been crushed for good and the utopia of the masters achieved. . . . But again the celebration was premature. Within a few years . . . the business run society par excellence, was forced by popular struggle to grant rights" to poor people, workers, women, and others oppressed by the business class.[39] In spite of history, the Fatalist plays the role of "Chicken Little," yelling that history is over, our destinies are determined, and that resistance is futile. The right-wing talk shows that litter television and radio are effective public relations tools for the Fatalist perspective. The sheer repetition of the message, matched by the power of the medium, gives the message an authority difficult to combat. Moreover, this level of cultural saturation "normalizes" the message, just as it makes dissention (i.e., hope and possibility) sound strange.

This brief typology is just a beginning, and, as all typologies are, it is oversimplified. Identities are complex social, political, and psychological phenomena that are interrelated and dynamic. Nevertheless, by analytically identifying and critiquing some of the major neoliberal identities being manufactured and reproduced through corporate culture, we can begin to draw connections between the knowledge these identities create and legitimate and the power and authority that they represent. More to the point, corporate culture creates these identities, while successful corporate workers, to a greater or lesser degree, embody them.

The embodiment of corporate culture, at the level of identity, is important because it draws attention to the affective and psychological dimensions of neoliberalism. In other words, corporate culture seeps into the folds of civil society, transforming the way we all "see" the world and each other. It is not just workers on Wall Street who are affected by the power of corporate culture or rewarded for their docility. It's also the schoolteacher who thinks of his students as "clients" or "consumers." It's the artist who sells her talent to corporate advertising. It's the athlete who plays for endorsements instead of the challenge. It's the parents who enter into contractual agreements with their children. Corporate culture's ideological power lies is in its ability to shape our identities and perceptions—to condition our social conscience—beyond the walls of traditional corporate formations.

The movement from the boardroom to the classroom, the art studio, the recording studio, the family, and the playing field signals the rise of an ideological state apparatus, or ISA, transformed by state power under the influence of neoliberal globalization. Before discussing the subtle transformation of the ISA into what I will call the ideological corporate apparatus (ICA), it is necessary to review

Louis Althusser's understanding of the state and how neoliberalism and globalization challenges us to think differently about state power and its function.

🕮 The State in Neoliberal Times

Althusser worked out his theory of ISAs on the back of what he referred to as a Marxist theory of the state. Summarizing the theory, he writes that

1. The state is the repressive state apparatus.
2. State power and state apparatus must be distinguished.
3. The objective of the class struggle concerns state power and, in consequence, the use of state apparatus by the classes holding state power as a function of their class objectives.
4. The proletariat must seize state power in order to destroy the existing bourgeois state apparatus and, in a first phase, to replace it with a quite different, proletarian, state apparatus, then in later phases to set in motion a radical process—the destruction of the state (the end of state power, the end of every state apparatus).

Althusser complicates this theory of the state by arguing that the state apparatus "contains two bodies: the body of institutions which represent the Repressive State Apparatus on the one hand, and the body of institutions which represent the body of Ideological State Apparatuses on the other."[40] These two bodies of institutions work in concert with the state apparatus securing through repression "the political conditions for the action of the Ideological State Apparatus."[41] Describing the relationship even more specifically, Althusser argues that the state apparatus works as a "shield" so that the body of ISAs—especially education—can "secure the reproduction specifically of the relations of production."[42] Althusser, building on Antonio Gramsci's politicization of education, is "very aware that, unlike previous modes of production capitalism with its segmented spaces and the separation of workers from the means of production relies on the institutions of the state in the broad sense in order to secure the expanded reproduction of society."[43]

Given the neoliberal reality of globalization, I will argue that this theory of the state must be amended so that it reflects the new mediations of power that are occurring across the globe. This is not at all intended to imply that the state has become a useless category to analyze political, economic, and ideological practices and effects. On the contrary, the state might, in fact, be the glue that holds the globalizing effects of neoliberal ideology together.

Globalization, Bauman writes, is not about, in the first instance (although it is often used in this way), a description of global "effects, notoriously unintended and unanticipated. . . . [Rather] the idea of 'globalization' explicitly refers to von Wright's 'anonymous forces,' operating in the vast—foggy and slushy, passable and untamable—'no man's land,' stretching beyond the reach of the design-and-action capacity of anybody's in particular."[44] David Held writes that "globalization [from a transformalist perspective] is portrayed . . . as a force that erodes . . . the capacity of nation-states to act independently in the articulation and pursuit of domestic and international policy objectives."[45]

From this perspective, neoliberal globalization has transformed the modern role of the state by disabling its "military, economic and cultural self-sufficiency, indeed self-sustainability."[46] Bauman clarifies this observation by arguing that the territorial distinction between "inside" and "outside" the state no longer accurately describes the relationship between the state and the larger global context in which it is a part. For Bauman, this reality is implied by global forums like the World Economic Forum sponsored by G8 countries (nation-states) to convene on issues of global significance, issues like trade, immigration, human rights, terrorism, security, and world courts. In the context of these global issues, the modern state's sovereignty is transformed, creating a quasisovereignty, that is, a sovereignty that is experienced and balanced against the interdependencies imposed by globalization. This "transformalist" perspective, as Held points out, sees the modern state as "increasingly trapped within webs of global interconnectedness permeated by quasi-supranational, intergovernmental and transnational forces, and unable to determine its own fate."[47] These interdependencies, from a transformalist perspective, suggest that the nation-state is experiencing a change in how its political, economic, and ideological power gets exercised in the global arena.

Economically, the transformalists argue, the state cannot control nor "resist for more than a few days the speculative pressures of the 'markets.'"[48] The state is now subjected to a kind of market-based disciplinary control in which world finances enjoy the freedom and mobility (i.e., the sovereignty) once enjoyed by states. State power is compromised due to a lack of economic freedom as it exists against the power and freedom that world financial markets have to cross borders, infiltrate localities, and manipulate state bureaucracies. As Bauman points out, "It is not difficult to see therefore that the replacement of territorial 'weak states' by some sort of global legislative and policing powers would be detrimental to the interests of 'world markets.'"[49]

Bauman's point is important theoretically because it acknowledges that territoriality is indeed not only a property of the state, but a *productive* effect of world "markets." For example, world financial markets move *through* the territorial borders of nation-states, giving evidence at one and the same time of the state apparatus and state power (or lack thereof). This need to "move through" territorial nation-state borders is direct evidence not only that the inside and outside are intact, but that power, within the context of globalization, is *directed* and *situated*. If it is to move through borders, it must begin from somewhere. Its mobility is made manifest through the economic, ideological, and political structure of the nation-state, even as the nation-state's modern structure is transformed by neoliberal globalization.

Politically, dominant Western nation-states function as a "subservient" power bloc, deriving influence and authority not from their individual state sovereignty (i.e., the sovereignty that the ruling classes assume they have by right of their position), a thoroughly modern conception of state power and rights, but from "giving" it up. This is not to say that the G8 countries, for example, do not exert an enormous amount of *ideological* pressure on the World Bank and IMF agencies, but they do so *without sovereignty*. As Held points out, "states have had to increase the level of their political integration with other states . . . and/or increase multilateral negotiations, arrangements and institutions to control the destabilizing effects that accompany interconnectedness."[50] In this instance, "political fragmentation" and "economic globalization" are constitutive processes.[51]

It is important to highlight the inequities of power that inform political integration in this new global interconnectedness. Political power is located directly within the borders of nation-states. The United States, for example, has an enormous amount of control to centralize its own interests within the global sphere. So, although we might have a more integrated formulation of sovereignty within globalization, the circumstances of nation-states—economically, politically, and ideologically—are still conditioned by the operation and maintenance of the state apparatus if not state power.

Ideologically, nation-states struggle to secure their borders, and immigration arises, for many advanced Western nations like Germany and the United States, as the biggest stated threat to "cultural" sovereignty. They are losing this struggle because it is very difficult, if not impossible, to let goods and services through borders while keeping people out. It is almost inconceivable to think of a "nonporous" state border established by a state that is not, at the same time, a police state. Technology also has affected states' ability to filter out undesirable cultural messages. Whether it is China struggling with the Western democratic and economic ideas that filter through the Internet and other global media; Iran whose cultural sovereignty is upset by secular radio messages that come from exiled Iranians in the United States; or the United States' struggle to "colonize" an increasingly "resistant" immigrant population through the imposition of English-only mandates[52]; states fight to resist "foreign" incursions into their cultural spheres. Held writes,

> In these circumstances, the traditional link between "physical setting" and "social situation" is broken; the new communication systems create new experiences, new commonalities

and new frames of meaning independently of direct contact between people. As such they serve to detach, or disembed, identities from particular times, places, traditions, and can have a "pluralizing impact" on identity formation, producing a variety of options which are "less fixed or unified." Moreover, these systems operate in large measure independently of state control and are, accordingly, not easily amenable to direct political regulation.[53]

One might conclude, given the weakening of the nation-state to exert sovereign power over its dominion that the nation-state as a geopolitical reality would be faltering. This is not the case, and since the fall of the Soviet Union, we have seen a renewed effort to reterritorialize borders once erased under the totalitarian pressures of Soviet-style communism.[54]

As neoliberal globalization distributes power and resources throughout the world the nation-state continues to function as a "geocapitalistic" marker, suggesting that, according to S. Aronowitz and P. Bratsis, the property of territoriality is *specific* to the capitalist state, and therefore "tied to capitalist exploitation and its organization/reproduction by the state."[55] According to Aronowitz and Bratsis, the notion of territoriality makes problematic theories of globalization that negate an "apparatus" because the notion of territoriality necessarily draws a line between inside and outside. As such, if an alternative power is to exist beyond the apparatus of the state, we must identify a space that can appropriately generate and become the locus for that power.[56]

Metaphysical spaces notwithstanding, political, economic, and ideological power must have a location—a geography—if they are to exercise that power effectively. In this context, neoliberal globalization creates a geopolitical "dystopian" network of nation-states in which "people do not change their position, they simply move around."[57] This post-Marxian conception of the state is important because it inverts liberal and post-structural paradigms of globalization. In other words, rather than understand the state in terms dictated by the high priests of globalization and neoliberalism, a rethinking of the state in radical terms means changing the terms of the debate. When we view the state from the context of globalization, it appears weak and fragile against the invisible network of ubiquitous forces that conceptually inform the discourse of globalization. By contrast, when globalization is understood in the context of the state, (1) it appears less overdetermined; (2) its structure now appears as a spatial reality—it has a geography that can be mapped and transformed; and (3) state power can be captured, through revolution or politics, globally affecting the economic, ideological, and political realities of people within the borders of allied nation-states.

Explaining the phenomenon of consistency between the territorial principle and globalization, Bauman writes,

> For their liberty of movement and for their unconstrained freedom to pursue their ends, global finance, trade and the information industry depend in the political fragmentation . . . of

the world scene. They have all, one may say, developed vested interests in "weak states"—that is in such states as are *weak* but nevertheless *remain states*. Deliberately or subconsciously, such inter-state, supra-local institutions as have been brought into being and are allowed to act with the consent of global capital, exert coordinated pressures on all member or independent states to destroy systemically everything which could stem or slow down the free movement of capital and limit market liberty. . . . Weak, quasi-states can be easily reduced to the (useful) role of local police precincts, securing a modicum of order required for the conduct of business, but need not be feared as effective brakes on the global companies' freedom.[58]

This relationship between globalization and territorialization, Bauman argues, suggests a global ordering that separates the political from the economic, but does not, at the same time, decouple power from the operation of capital. Rather, capital commutes through an "anonymous" ideological authority, while politics function as the means by which states manage that ideology and the inequities of power that it reproduces. Named "glocalization" by Roland Roberts, this "mutually complementary process benefits the wealthy, while leaving destitute the majority of the world's population."[59] Bauman writes in 1999 that the UN's latest *Human Development Report* states that

> [T]he total wealth of the top 358 "global billionaires" equals the combined incomes of the 2.3 billion poorest people (45 percent of the world's population) . . . only 22 percent of the global *wealth* belongs to the so-called "developing countries," which account for about 80 percent of the world population. . . . [Moreover] in 1991, 85 percent of the world's population received only 15 percent of its income. . . . No wonder that the abysmally meager 2.3 percent of global wealth owned by 20 percent of the poorest countries thirty years ago has fallen by now still further, to 1.4 percent.[60]

These realities of neoliberal globalization pronounce not the death of the nation-state, but its transformation.[61]

In contrast to Althusser and Marx, Bauman's "post-Marxist" theory of the state rests on a geography of power that is informed by the "contradiction" of territoriality on one hand and globalization on the other.[62] It can be summarized as follows:

1. The state is a globally interdependent territory
2. The state apparatus is economically impotent, while state power is exercised primarily in the service of security and policing at the local level.
3. The primary role of state is to maintain security in defense of market mobility, while defending its citizens from the "more sinister consequences of market anarchy."
4. Without economic, military, and cultural "sovereignty," states lose their ability to stop the neoliberal trends (which together they helped to start) of "deregulation, liberalization, flexibility, increasing fluidity, facilitating the

transactions on the financial and real estate and labour markets, easing the tax burden, etc."

5. State power, regardless of who takes it, has little or no possibility of "re-forging social issues into effective collective action."

6. As such, the reproduction of the conditions of production *inside* the state is driven by global markets and ideological forces *outside* the state, although this process is regulated by both state power and more localized institutional forces. These localized forces take shape in the form of what I referred to above as ideological corporate apparatuses, or ICAs.

An ICA corresponds to Louis Althusser's famous discussion of the ISA in significant ways. Most directly, ICAs, like ISAs, function to "reproduce the conditions of reproduction" through pedagogical strategies, hegemonic in their effort to make "reality" a matter of common sense. "To put this more scientifically," writes Althusser,

> I shall say that the reproduction of labour power requires not only the production of its skills, but also, at the same time, a reproduction of its submission to the rules of the established order, i.e., a reproduction of submission to the ruling ideology for the workers and a repro-duction of the ability to manipulate the ruling ideology correctly for the agents of exploita-tion and repression, so that they, too, will provide for the domination of the ruling class "in words."[63]

Moreover, ICAs like ISAs are "multiple, distinct, [and] 'relatively autonomous' . . . [and] *function 'by ideology.'"* This is not to say that repression is not used by ICAs and ISAs alike. Rather, repression, argues Althusser, functions as a secondary strat-egy of control, "attenuated and concealed, even symbolic." ICAs and ISAs also cor-respond in significant ways in formation: education, family, church, temple, media, and health care. These diverse ideological apparatuses are unified by the means in which they function, namely and "predominately by ideology . . . insofar as the ide-ology by which they function is always in fact unified, despite its diversity and con-tradictions, *beneath the ruling ideology,* which is the ideology of 'the ruling class.'" The unification of these formations is significant for Althusser because the (repressive) state apparatus's ruling ideology must be understood in concert with the ruling ide-ology of the ISAs, that of the ruling class. As he writes, "To my knowledge, *no class can hold State power over a long period without at the same time exercising its hegemo-ny over and in the State Ideological Apparatuses."* This is apparently still true in our neoliberal age.

However, ICAs, unlike ISAs, function not only in concert with the interests of the ruling class within the state, but now they function as extensions of global for-mations, most directly financial markets and media oligopolies. Within states, but in response to and as an effect of global realities, ICAs condition "glocalities" in a way that manufactures, as a matter of common sense, the fatalism of neoliberal globalization, as well as positions it as a priority of local development. In this sense ICAs are primarily responsible for ensuring political fragmentation, economic globalization, and the further deterioration of local governing agencies' democratic autonomy *through privatizing initiatives*, while legitimating the reproduction of the conditions of production as they transpire globally.

The major ICAs within the United States, in name, are not so different from Althusser's ISAs, with a few additions:

1. The educational ICA (adult, secondary, primary, and early childhood [private and public])
2. The family ICA ("traditional" and untraditional unit)
3. The legal ICA (made more significant by the establishment of the International Criminal Court)
4. The political ICA (ostensibly an ideologically one-dimensional business party, dominated by corporate money)
5. The cultural ICA (film, literature, music; what might be accurately called the "Supraculture Industrial Complex")
6. The energy ICA (composed of oil and nuclear industries)
7. The transportation ICA
8. The health care ICA
9. The pharmaceutical ICA

When Althusser identified the institutions that functioned as ISAs, he needed to address the fact that many of them were not public formations, but private. His response came out of Gramsci's work, which accurately pointed out that the difference between private and public, in this context, was missing the point because the "distinction [was] internal to bourgeois law, and valid in the (subordinate) domains in which bourgeois law exercises its 'authority.' . . . [T]he State, which is the State *of* the ruling class, is neither private nor public; on the contrary, it is the precondition for any distinction between public and private."[64]

In the context of neoliberal globalization, the private nature of ICAs (even in the case of "public education," which gasps for breath as more and more local agencies privatize public education) does not call for such a response. In other words, neoliberal globalization is the precondition for justifying the *erasure of any distinction between the public and private*, with private interests decimating not only the public sphere, but all things public. Here, privatization becomes a defining objective of state power, to the extent that it benefits the mobility of global capital markets, markets of the ruling elite. Ironically, the effect this erasing of the "public" has on state power is, in large part, the deterioration of the authority a state has to control its public resources, while one major ideological effect is the political deflation of public troubles into private concerns. The erasure of all things public positions the state as a repressive *client-state*, its "employers" being global financial markets and corporate oligopolies:

> With its material basis destroyed, its sovereignty and independence annulled, its political class effaced, the nation-state becomes a simple security service for the mega-companies. . . . The new masters of the world have no need to govern directly. National governments are charged with the task of administering affairs on their behalf.[65]

Within this context, the educational ICA and the cultural ICA, above and beyond all other ICAs, function to help reproduce the relations of neoliberal production. The educational ICA does this, as Althusser and others have argued, through a process of intense indoctrination. Noam Chomsky explains:

> Because they don't teach the truth about the world, schools have to rely on beating students over the head with propaganda. . . . [T]his is well known by those who make policy . . . The Trilateral Commission referred to schools as "institutions" responsible for the indoctrination of the young. The indoctrination is necessary because schools are, by and large, designed to support the interests of the dominant segment of society, those people who have wealth and power. . . . And schools succeed by operating within a propaganda framework that has the effect of distorting or suppressing unwanted ideas and information.[66]

Moreover, as Paul Willis's famous study of the lads attests, not only do schools function to reproduce through suppression, they also provoke a kind of resistance in students that, in the end, works to reproduce exploitative class relationships.[67] Althusser pointed out that education's indoctrination of the young into an exploitative system was as successful as it was because the

> mechanisms which produce this vital result for the capitalist regime are naturally covered up and concealed by a universally reigning ideology of the School, universally reigning because it is one of the essential forms of the ruling bourgeois ideology: an ideology which represents the school as a neutral environment purged of ideology.[68]

In the neoliberal age, the ideological appeal to neutrality has been replaced by an overt appeal to the logic of neoliberal interests. No longer do schools need to defend themselves as institutions beyond ideology. Rather, as educational ICAs they enthusiastically embrace the knowledge of neoliberalism, appealing to common sense as the final marker of reason. The success of the educational ISA provides the groundwork for the educational ICA. Successfully indoctrinated into the relations of capitalist production, citizen-consumers of the state are easily transformed into global citizen-consumers. The knowledge that legitimates the relationship between global citizen-consumers and neoliberal glocalization moves out of the shadows of neutrality and into the domain of "correct" thinking, which means that the ideology of neoliberalism as it gets rehearsed in the educational ICA is no longer "hidden" in the neo-Marxist sense of the word. Through standardization and testing mandates—pedagogical and curricular—the state functions as a sanctioning agency of glocalization. In other words, educational ICAs are "glocal" formations, turning the neoliberal commitment of the state into a material reality at the local level. Importantly, this frees local state agencies to produce standards of education that can appear to contradict the ideological demands of the state. The political power that the contradiction might hold is made impotent by the introduction of WSR models, as I will discuss in the next section, that articulate with the needs manufactured by the power of the neoliberal state.

Cultural ICAs, like educational ICAs, function pedagogically as "teaching machines" and, in our current context, have enormous power to condition not only the way people think, but what they think about as well.[69] From Hollywood and television conglomerates to radio dynasties (e.g., Clear Channel) and the music industry, cultural ICAs "teach" as well as they do because, unlike schooling, their pedagogy is, at the same time, entertainment. Giroux argues that the cultural industry's products "function as public pedagogies by articulating knowledge to effects, purposely attempting to influence how and what knowledge and identities can be produced within a limited range of social relations."[70] Similarly, Michael Parenti argues that media and its content are "more akin to education than to industry" and should be evaluated accordingly.[71] Raymond Williams writes, "For who can doubt, looking at television or newspapers, or reading the women's magazines, that here, centrally, is *teaching*, and teaching financed and distributed in a much larger way than is formal education."[72] These theorists position this kind of public pedagogy "both in its affective and ideological capacities as the copula of indeterminacy between popular culture and its consumption." By taking up the cultural in pedagogical terms, we get outside the text itself:

> Because teaching is never divorced from the context in which it occurs, a focus on a film's teaching strategies and capacities and the lessons it promotes leads to an engagement with the socio-political context of the film. As such, a film's pedagogy takes on relevance outside the limited scope of the film itself.[73]

Unlike educational ICAs, which struggle to legitimate themselves beyond appeals to neutrality, cultural ICAs still make appeals to neutrality by situating their products as "entertainment." As entertainment, they escape the accusation of being pedagogical, that is, of having any significant influence on how people think and what they think about. This appeal to entertainment is ideological; it hides the fact that we "learn" more aptly when we are enjoying what we are doing at the time at which we learn. It also ignores the semiotic reality of cultural production; that is, cultural ICAs rhetorically distance themselves from their constructivist power to produce knowledge and the material history that corresponds to that knowledge. This is no small matter. When truth becomes no more than the byproduct of ideology, and knowledge the direct effect of dominant power, an individual's social agency becomes a strange fruit indeed.

Cultural ICAs produce what Giroux calls "public pedagogies because they play a powerful role in mobilizing meaning, pleasures, and identifications."[74] As formations of public pedagogies, cultural ICAs must be held accountable, just like schools, to the histories that they create and the futures that they imply. Their power to shape glocal discourses should not be discounted as the innocent effect of entertainment, people "choosing" to participate in and live out the corporatist knowledge that is produced through cultural ICAs. Choice is only a substantive referent if we have the resources to make good choices. With the concentration of corporate power in the media, the choices people have regarding the "entertainment" they consume are significantly limited.[75] In this context, the public pedagogies that cultural ICAs produce "legitimize some meanings, invite particular desires, and exclude others."[76] Given the concentration of power that cultural ICAs represent, this "discriminatory" process is antidemocratic; that is, the meanings that are legitimated and excluded and the desires that are invited are thought to be beyond the pale of democratic influence. I say these formations are antidemocratic and not simply nondemocratic because they work *productively* to close down "open discussion and deliberation among alternative political viewpoints and platforms."[77] They do this through an appeal to the neoliberal logic that argues that the "free" and "unregulated" market will provide the conditions of freedom, even though neoliberalism, as it is made operational by the World Bank and IMF in the international sphere and the ICAs on the glocal level, is a highly regulated and monitored political and ideological practice.

This contradiction reveals the primary role of the ICAs and the state apparatus in the neoliberal age. That is, through an ideological and political appeal to corporate freedom, the state reinforces its power and ideological formations against the intrusion of democratic needs. In our neoliberal age, those who embody state power—the ruling elite—use the state apparatus to help privatize public formations, instrumentalize knowledge, and dismantle collective structures that threaten powerful states' domination of global and local systems of finance, culture, politics, and ideology. Contrary to the "postmodern" version of globalization, this does not mean that the state loses its power; it means that its power is transformed to meet the new needs that have been manufactured through, and as an effect of, the dominating discourse of neoliberal globalization. Both state power and the (repressive) state apparatus are transformed to respond to the privileging of corporate power and culture on one hand and the dismantling of individual democratic agency on the other.

In the United States, one major consequence of this transformation is that ICAs hold significant ideological power over local government formations, aligned instead with the centralized and privatizing power of the state and larger global formations. In the neoliberal age, it is the interrelationship between ICAs and the state in a global context that threatens "decentralization in the control of economic and political institutions, and pluralism in the institutions of everyday life."[78] The production of a neoliberal discourse of needs is one mechanism by which this threat is manifested.

🐚 Manufacturing and Rationalizing Needs in a Neoliberal Age

As I have been discussing, cultural ICAs and educational ICAs are both powerful pedagogical/political formations in their interrelationship with state power. Their influence to shape a person's consciousness can be witnessed by examining the human condition at its most basic level, the level of needs and satisfactions. But even at this level, we find a discourse, a "discourse of needs." James Gee describes a discourse as "a socially accepted association among ways of using language, of thinking, and of acting that can be used to identify oneself as a member of a socially meaningful group or 'social network.'"[79] Additionally, discourses are either dominant or secondary, the dominant being the one that creates the conditions upon which other distinctions are made. The dominant discourse of needs corresponds to neoliberal ideology in significant ways, bringing attention to the process by which the discourse of neoliberalism helps manufacture and rationalizes specific needs, just as it positions other requisites—social, political, pedagogical—as unimportant or irrelevant. One of the primary effects of the interrelationship between cultural and educational ICAs and the state is to manufacture needs and their satisfaction through the utilization and reproduction of a neoliberal discourse. In other words, ICAs rationalize their practices through a discourse of needs, a discourse that positions needs as "natural" byproducts of the only viable economic, cultural, and political system, namely neoliberalism. In "scientific" terms, needs are positioned as neutral signifiers of the human condition. The key to understanding the significance of needs and structures is not the fact that ideological systems prioritize, produce, and reproduce certain needs, in large part a truism of modern social structures. What is significant is that the glocalizing structures from which these needs arise remain static and beyond democratization and decentralization. As such, the needs they manufacture, even when they are met, do not cease being reproduced. A more concentrated analysis of needs will make these arguments less abstract.

There are many different categories of needs. The first and most basic type consists of those born out of our biological, physiological, and genetic design, things like food, water, clothes, and shelter. These are basic needs and without their satisfaction "at the attainable level of culture," the realization of any other type of needs is impossible.[80] The second type arises from our political-social organization. These are education—political, cultural, communal, and economic. The third type references our "individual" nature. These are psychological, intellectual, spiritual, and creative. These are "sovereign" needs.

This brief typology of needs is insufficient because, like most typologies, as mentioned earlier, it assumes the separateness of the parts, and then assumes the parts as wholes in themselves. For example, economic and political needs correspond in a profound way to psychological and housing needs, just like our need for clothes and food corresponds to the need for community and education. Any attempt to bracket these needs off from one another is impossible. The task then is to undertake a process of mapping, not by discerning one need from another per se, but by understanding the cartography of needs, that is, needs in relation to each other. By looking at needs in relation, attention is brought to the social and political foundations of needs.

Understanding the social and political structures that inform our notion of needs preempts a discussion of needs in and of themselves. In other words, needs are only understood as they exist within and are born out of particular social, cultural, and economic structures. If we understand the dominant structures, we can then begin to understand the function and formation of needs. Neoliberalism, in light of its global practices and policies mentioned earlier, can be characterized by "the rational character of its irrationality"[81] illustrated through a process of political, economic, and social hegemony "*anchored in the new needs which [the society] has produced*" (my emphasis).[82]

For example, we have the need to open up markets in foreign countries for business ventures because neoliberals argue—in the face of facts that show explicitly the brutal consequences neoliberal initiatives have had on nations suffering from poverty—that the deregulation of capital will provide economic opportunities in those societies.[83] Within the educational context, neoliberals in 1999 counseled educational experts, calling for "every state [to] adopt standards backed-up by standardized tests [and] to set up a system of 'rewards and consequences' for teachers, students, and schools based on those tests."[84] This call for neoliberal standards and standardization articulates explicitly with the *need* to train our teachers to be neoliberal technicians as well as the *need* to train our students to think and act within the acceptable epistemological parameters established by neoliberalism (I will discuss this aspect of teacher education at the end of the chapter).

In Marcuse's somewhat oversimplified language, needs manufactured in the service of neoliberalism should not only be considered "false" (i.e., repressive), but their satisfaction must be understood in the context of how it helps perpetuate the repression that their "falseness" signifies. Marcuse's insight into the issue is worth quoting at length:

> "False" needs are those which are superimposed upon the individual by particular social inter-ests in his repression: the needs which perpetuate toil, aggressiveness, misery, and injustice. Their satisfaction might be most gratifying to the individual, but this happiness is not a con-dition which has to be maintained and protected if it serves to arrest the development of the ability (his own and others) to recognize the disease of the whole and grasp the chances of curing the disease. The result then is euphoria in unhappiness. Most of the prevailing needs to relax, to have fun, to behave and consume in accordance with the advertisements, to love and hate what others love and hate, belong to this category of false needs.[85]

True needs, conversely, must be understood both in their "contradiction to the pre-vailing ones" and in the service of meeting "standards which refer to the optimal development of the individual, of all individuals, under the optimal utilization of the material and intellectual resources available to man."[86]

Since Marcuse's time, postmodern thought has upset these easy dichotomies, recognizing the relevance that context and power have on informing notions like truth and falsity. But his ideas, I would argue, are germane, given the structured and organized nature of neoliberalism on one hand and its hostility to collective struc-tures that challenge its hegemony on the other. Although postmodern thought has offered many things to critical social theory by challenging "master narratives," ahis-torical discourses, and decontextualized appeals to truth and beauty, it nevertheless struggles to locate and hold accountable power and authority as they manifest themselves in specific social, political, and economic structures. When power gains strength from its place within "invisible social structures,"[87] it does little at the level of the political and pedagogical to argue that modern structures do not exist. By link-ing false needs to repression and true needs to social justice, Marcuse indirectly brings attention to how neoliberal needs perpetuate repression through competi-tion, greed, and inequity; the destruction of public life and collective institutions; the creation of narrow corporate identities; and an attack on the construction and function of knowledge itself.

The attack on knowledge can be seen in the neoliberal (and neoconservative) need to test our students using positivistic forms of measurement and evaluation, because technological rationality within neoliberal logic deems all other models of assessment inefficient at best and irrational at worst. Neoliberalism endorses what Giroux calls a "culture of positivism." More than a philosophical concern, positivism "must be viewed through its wider function as a dominant ideology, powerfully com-municated through various social agencies."[88] He is worth quoting at length:

> The major assumptions that underlie the culture of positivism are drawn from the logic and methods of inquiry associated with the natural sciences. Based upon the logic of scientific methodology with its interest in explanation, prediction, and technical control, the princi-

ple of rationality in the natural sciences was seen as vastly superior to the hermeneutic principles underlying the speculative social sciences. Modes of rationality that relied upon or supported interpreted procedures rated little scientific status from those defending assumptions
and methods of the natural sciences. . . . The point here is that the culture of positivism is
not just a set of ideas . . . it is also a material force, a set of material practices that are embedded in the routines and experiences of our daily lives.[89]

With the culture of positivism informing the material practices of schooling,
including curriculum development (which I will discuss as length in the next section), assessment, and accountability, neoliberal ideology has affected educational
policy directly by "shifting emphasis from input and process to outcomes, from the
liberal to the vocational, from education's intrinsic to its instrumental value, and from
qualitative to quantitative measures of success."[90] Its power is in its ability to make
these shifts seem like a matter of common sense, a matter of doing what needs to
be done to best meet the needs of the twenty-first century, needs that are self-evi-
dent and beyond critique.

One major sphere of schooling that is directly affected by these moves is curriculum reform and development. Neoliberals have illustrated an acute understanding of the significance of curriculum reformation in the transmission and
acquisition of neoliberal knowledge, the latter acting as "the structuring principle
around which the school curriculum is organized and particular classroom social
relations legitimated."[91] In what follows I will analyze New Jersey's Core Curriculum
Standards, discussing how the ideology of neoliberalism gets rationalized and tran-
scribed through a discourse of needs. Evident in this critique is how the state of New
Jersey has been hollowed out by the state's ideological power as it is made operational by the educational ICA.

New Jersey Core Curriculum Content and Standards: Corporate Authority, Private Needs, and Neoliberal Interests

In the past, critical engagements with the "hidden curriculum" tried to give the
anonymous a name. These critical interrogations attempted to bring attention to
how dominant ideology manifested itself in curriculum and pedagogy generally, and
how it reproduced social, political, economic, and cultural inequality specifically. In
our current cultural and economic climate, the hidden curriculum, as it was traditionally understood in radical educational discourses, is often not so hidden
anymore.[92]

Joel Spring argues that a "peculiar combination of Hayekian and human
accounting ideas" signals the "triumph of corporate thinking over schools."[93] He

comes to this conclusion through an examination of corporate interest in public schooling. In 1983 the Task Force for Economic Growth wrote a report entitled "Action for Excellence," which stated,

> We believe especially that businesses, in their role as employers, should be much more involved in the process of setting goals for education in America. If the business community gets more involved in both the design and delivery of education, we are going to become more competitive as an economy.[94]

Twenty years later, in New Jersey, Maude Dahme, president of the State Board of Education agrees: "Our task, as the State Board of Education, is to provide opportunities for all students to receive an education that will prepare them to be competitive in the international market place of the future,"[95] Or, as Stanley Aronowitz notes in reference to higher education, university's have remained, for the most part, loyal to "Clark Kerr's fundamental philosophy that the university is constituted and must remain a source of knowledge that serves the corporate order and, more broadly, the national interest in economic growth. Indeed, the notion that the university has a critical as well as research function has disappeared from the discourse."[96]

This attention to the "international market place" and corporate needs is troubling in our current economic and political climate. Implied in this formula is the attitude that preparing students for jobs—high level, technical jobs—is, *in the final analysis*, the work of schools. But given, as Aronowitz and William Defazio argue, that we already have "too many workers for too few jobs, and even fewer of them are well paid," this formula for education becomes a contradiction of intentions at best and hypocritical at worst. It ignores the structural shift from an "industrializing era of world capitalist development—a highly differentiated workforce, strong unions, powerful states that guarantee economic security and promote economic growth" to a "scientifically based technological change in the midst of sharpened internationalization of production."[97] By ignoring this shift in the political economy, standardizing frameworks for education, like New Jersey's, become complicit in training students—many of whom will become either unemployed, low-skilled labor, or middle managers—for a "jobless future" or a future in which work and the workplace is increasingly characterized by deskilling, disempowerment, and a highly controlled internationalized system of production.[98]

Given the state's commitment to satiating the needs of neoliberal interests, the critical project today must be characterized not by making the "command and commander" visible per se, arguably visible in many regards by their own admission and interest in public schooling, but rather to understand how their needs and subsequent strategies of satisfaction have become normalized into the discourse of education and schooling to the extent that they represent the standards to which public schools now uncritically aspire. Still, hidden in the corporatist philosophy is an implicit assumption that history has ended and that resistance is futile and dangerous—dangerous to those who are being resisted and (more chilling) dangerous to those who resist. Unwilling to confront the barbaric legacies of colonialism, imperialism, and the hegemony of Western, Judeo-Christian thought, neoliberal ideology makes invisible its own hostility to democratic ideals (namely equity), collective political struggle, and cultural pluralism.

New Jersey's Core Curriculum Content and Standards consists of eight sections: Cross Content Workplace Readiness, Language Arts Literacy, Visual and Performing Arts, Science, Comprehensive Health and Physical Education, Social Studies, World Languages, and Mathematics.[99] These standards are made operational through various pedagogical and curricular WSR frameworks, like *Success for All*, *Put Reading First*, and *Co-nect*.[100] These models must align themselves with local state standards, but, as I will show, the local state educational standards are often trumped by the ICA-nation state complex. This does not mean that the "state," as mentioned above, does not often align itself with business interests. But, as I will discuss in the context of the New Jersey's liberal arts standards, it sometimes veers from the party line. When this occurs, educational ICAs, through the adoption of WSR models that articulate with state power, bypass the "state's" authority. This shift is significant because it reinforces the power of the state while delegitimating the power of the people. By analyzing the (dis)connection between the "state's" educational standards and WSR, we can begin to get a sense of how the state's neoliberal ideology plays out "in" education and not just in debates "about" education.[101] I will keep my comments limited to two sections of New Jersey's standards: Cross Content Workplace Readiness and Language Arts Literacy.

❧ Cross-Content Workplace Readiness

Career education might seem like a straw man for a critique of curriculum and neoliberalism. I would argue, however, that universal notions of "career" and/or "work" do not overdetermine what it means to be educated in the interrelated spheres of management, labor, and entrepreneurialism. As such, the section on Cross Content Workplace Readiness is especially important given that it is the most overt in its ideological alignments with neoliberalism and globalization. These standards, in fact, do not represent a disconnection between the needs of the state, the practices of the educational ICA, and local state government:

> Rapid societal changes, including innovations in technology, information exchange, and communications, have increased the demand for internationally competitive workers and for an educational system designed to meet that demand. Today's students will be employed through much of the twenty-first century and will, therefore, need increasingly advanced lev-

els of knowledge and skills. To obtain and retain high-wage employment that provides job satisfaction, they will also need to continue to learn throughout their lives.[102]

At first glance, the first sentence seems to state a truism; in reality, as Aronowitz and Defazio point out, "The new technoculture in the workplace emerges on the ruins of the old mechanical, industrial culture."[103] Industrialization and the structures that made it go did not simply evaporate, especially when we discuss their mechanisms of production in *cultural* terms. At the level of culture, these forms of management are manifested in the tightened control of workers, panoptic control of time, separation of the product from the workers input, deskilling, and so forth. The "ruins" of industrial culture, like asbestos, might appear benign, but still infect the worker and workplace in dangerous and disempowering ways. "From the perspective of the worker," write Aronowitz and Defazio, "whether in the factory or the office, the second phase of automatic production—computerization—is merely a wrinkle in the long process of disempowerment."[104] In other words, the parameters of neoliberal discourse limit the understanding of technology to a means to concentrate power, exploit labor, acquire more capital, and reproduce the relations of production.

For example, Educational Technologies Group at BNN Corporation established the WSR model *Co-nect*, which has been adopted by Bolger Middle School in Keansburg, New Jersey.[105] It "offers comprehensive school-wide and district-wide capacity-building programs that include planning for continuous improvement, data-driven decision making, and alignment strategies such as curriculum mapping, technology integration, benchmarking, and leadership training."[106] BNN charges each school, at a minimum, $65,000 per year for three years, and must "provide high-speed classroom Internet access for all teachers (at least by the end of the first year of implementation) to take advantage of online training and resources." This is an interesting requirement considering BNN asserts that it is a "forerunner of today's internet."[107] Given the lack of direct information on the potential conflict of interest here, we can only speculate that BNN's interest in education has something to do with the technology it has to sell. By making technology a fundamental definer of the model, as opposed to a tool that might enhance the complexities of teaching and learning, *Co-nect* reveals itself not as a model of responsive teaching, but as a corporate entity that must rationalize its own corporate services in the context of schooling in positivistic terms. But the relationship goes deeper than one characterized by the production, consumption, and rationalization of goods. BNN, as a corporation, accepts by definition the ideology of corporate culture. This acceptance animates their goals of leadership, for example, which must come to mean leadership within the context of corporate norms. Leadership within this context is often defined in hierarchical and antidemocratic terms; it is a kind of leadership that is highly conservative in how it conceptualizes structural change. In short, corporate leadership, like neoliberalism in general, is hostile to collective movements that challenge elite interests.

Moving back to the "state's" standard, the first sentence also suggests that a new demand for "internationally competitive workers" is a result of a dynamic techno-social process. This is not false per se, but it ignores the fact that the competition is driven by the few highly skilled jobs there are and not by an economically potent technological system of production. Is it really the "rapid change" that has increased demand, or the diminishing availability of techno-knowledge based jobs? Given the plunge in technology stocks and the corresponding masses of unemployed technology workers, it would seem that the latter presents a more accurate description of reality than the former. Couple this with the "common sense" reasoning that "labor-changing technologies combined with organizational changes (such as mergers, acquisitions, divestitures, and consolidation of production in fewer plants, a cost saving made possible by technology) yield few jobs,"[108] and we get a troubling vision from New Jersey concerning workers and the economy.

The next sentence asserts that students will "need increasingly advanced levels of knowledge and skills." Again, this seems to be a truism. But what does it mean to suggest that students *need* advanced knowledge and skills? What kind of knowledge will they need? What kinds of skills? If fewer techno-skill-based jobs are available, then why would students *need* technological skills? And finally, what if Aronowitz and Defazio's contention is correct and "skill is no longer central to the labor process?"[109] If knowledge—critical and theoretical—has replaced skills as the primary dimension of labor, with "skills" being handled by technological and computerized machines, what does that suggest for New Jersey's assertion that advanced knowledge and skills are needed? An answer is given in the vision statement:

> Members of the business and industry communities have identified vital career and technical education skills. In 1992, the Secretary's Commission on Achieving Necessary Skills (SCANS) identified productive use of resources, interpersonal skills, information systems, and technology as essential workplace competencies. The SCANS foundation skills included basic and thinking skills as well as personal qualities.[110]

But again, we are confronted with some important absences. For example, "productive use of resources" is a fine skill to have if there are resources to use. There is an assumption that workers have a vast array of resources at their disposal, which in a real sense means that they have power. But we know this to be untrue if measured in the context of equitable power relations and democratic decision making. It also implies a consensus around the word "productive." In the context of capitalism, this of course means "in the service of profit." But how might the meaning of "productive" change given the harsh realities that the technological labor landscape presently represents?

Productive, in this context, might mean being effective in redistributing resources, using technological tools and knowledge as a means to do so. It might also come to mean using resources in the service of protecting workers' rights. It might mean using political resources to regulate business. But, in the end, we know that these are not what "productive" means in the vision statement because the skills that the "state" deems essential are developed by the business community to meet *their* needs, as though the needs of labor and the needs of corporate management are the same. They are not, and although there are correspondences that we must pay attention to, the hard reality is that the needs of workers are often antithetical to the needs of neoliberal globalization. By creating official standards that are guided by this vision, the state has sanctioned neoliberalism by creating a curricular form that satiates its needs, while it ignores the "reality" of labor.

Along similar lines, the first section of the vision statement above states, "To obtain and retain high-wage employment that provides job satisfaction, they will also need to continue to learn throughout their lives." As Spring notes regarding such references to lifelong learning, "The assumption is that unemployment is primarily the result of the inability of workers to keep up with technological change."[111] The onus of responsibility here lies with the workers to change or keep up with changing economic conditions, in spite of the fact that they have very little say as to how economic conditions change. In contrast, the statement might have read that states have a responsibility to their workers to ensure that they are trained, benefited, and secured so that they can directly participate in the labor process. Moreover, the state would ensure that corporate interests do not over shadow democratic needs. As such, standards in career education might be developed around the kinds of knowledges and skills workers might need to confront structures of management that are hostile to those basic needs, as well as to be educated in the politics of work and the work of politics. In this scenario, labor is understood as an asset and not a liability. In the sentence written by the state of New Jersey, by contrast, future workers are perceived as liabilities—to themselves and the economy—while technology is reified, just as it is rationalized as the primary means to economic security and happiness. Finally, and most importantly, labor is never understood *positively* in terms of its economic agency, that is, in terms of its power to shape and influence the economic and political environment in a way that might be more humane and equitable.

The final paragraph in the vision statement reads as follows:

> To compete in this global, information-based economy, students must be able to identify and solve real problems, reason effectively, and apply critical thinking skills. The career education and life skills standards identify key career development and life skills which students must achieve in order to achieve continuing success.[112]

Here again we have a certain level of ambiguity that begs to be addressed. It should be noted that the statement's ambiguity is part of its appeal. It seems a matter of common sense being able to problem solve, reason effectively, and apply critical thinking skills would be beneficial. But it would be false to argue that critical thinking is a static concept. Critical thinking has historically been linked up with thinkers as diverse as Max Horkheimer and Theodor Adorno on one hand and Mathew Lipman on the other.[113] While the former understood critical thinking as a way to reveal the rational irrationalities of Enlightenment philosophy and practices of domination, the latter has theorized critical thinking as a set of logical skills.

To solve "real" problems is another ambiguous phrase. Real to whom? Who gets to determine which problems get solved and which ones do not? For example, if workers have a problem with their salaries and want a raise, is that a "real" problem? Or should we understand the statement to mean that "real" problems are those that must be fixed in the service of capital accumulation? If there is a problem of sexism, racism, or class bias in the workplace, can we assume these things to be "real" only if solving them does not affect the ability of business to reproduce the conditions of production? Is the right to strike a "real" issue or one that is characterized as something less important? So, again, ideology works here to normalize neoliberal capitalism through the creation and sanctioning of need—business needs—and their satisfaction through an uncritical appeal to "reality," as though what constituted the "real" was not contextual and transcended the discriminate needs of labor and corporate management.

Absent in this discourse are the needs that come out of labor's historical struggle against management and, more recently, transnational corporations' global operations. As such, the state ignores the needs of workers, technological or otherwise, to confront, demand, struggle, and resist the hegemony of neoliberal globalization, especially as it desiccates unions and their ability to organize and recruit members. What is at stake is more than the ideological *visibility* of either dominant systems of thought or their counters. What is at stake, finally, is the elimination of alternative subjectivities; it is the homogenization of the individual through the production of neoliberal-capitalist subjectivities that is the biggest threat to independent thought, critical dialog, and freedom. As neoliberal-capitalist ideology produces subjectivities through curricular standards, we can expect that the subjects themselves will demand satiation for needs that have been manufactured. By satiating the needs of these subjects—"reskilling" them through the techniques of corporatist education—the educational ICA functions to normalize and reproduce relations of production.

🍎 Language Arts Literacy

The Language Arts Literacy standard appears to be a progressive, if not radical, illustration of what "state" standards can mean if they are devised outside of neoliberal concerns. The introduction to the standard begins as follows:

> Language arts are the abilities that enable one to think logically and creatively; express ideas; understand and participate meaningfully in spoken, written, and nonverbal communications; formulate and answer questions; and search for, organize, evaluate, and apply information. The language arts are integrative, interactive ways of thinking that develop through reading, writing, speaking, listening, and viewing. Literacy is the ability to think, as well as know how to acquire knowledge for thinking and communicating. Literacy is more than the acquisition of a specific, predetermined set of skills in reading, writing, speaking, listening, and viewing. It is also recognizing one's own purposes for thinking and communicating (through print or nonprint, verbal or nonverbal means) and being able to use one's own resources to achieve those purposes.[114]

The state's perspective on language arts literacy reflects a progressive conceptualization of language development because it focuses not on basic skill development, direct instruction, and/or phonics, but rather highlights the relationship between knowledge and the social practices associated with and constitutive of literacy development. Moreover, it brings attention to the plurality of literacy as well as its contextual nature. Literacies are understood as a way to "represent experience" and "make sense of the world." "Language," the statement reads, "evokes histories, emotions, values, issues, knowledge, and inventions. It is what we share, and what sets us apart." This constructivist view of language arts literacies is made even more explicit through the four stated assumptions of literacy and language development:

1. Language use is an active process of constructing meaning.
2. Language develops in a social context.
3. Language ability increases in complexity if language is used in increasingly complex ways.
4. Learners achieve language arts literacy not by adding skills one-by-one to their repertoire, but rather by using and exploring language in its many dimensions.[115]

These assumptions frame five literacy arts standards: (1) all students will speak for a variety of real purposes and audiences; (2) all students will listen actively in a variety of situations to information from a variety of sources; (3) all students will write in clear, concise, organized language that varies in content and form for different audiences and purposes; (4) all students will read various materials and texts with comprehension and critical analysis; and (5) all students will view, understand, and use nontextual visual information.[116]

But to remain consistent to the assumptions, the authors of the standards insist that they should not be understood or taught as a discrete set of skills or content areas:

> The language arts are interdependent processes that inform and enrich each other, more often than not merging in an integrated act of learning and knowing. The division of language arts into separate standards is merely a method that allows us to highlight the special features of each and to identify developmentally appropriate behaviors among language arts learners. The separation is not meant to suggest hierarchical order, or any linear or sequential approach to literacy instruction. The standards should be construed and applied as integrated aspects of teaching and learning. They are intended not as a curriculum guide, but as a catalyst for curriculum development and revision.[117]

These standards, undergirded by a progressive philosophy on literacy, language, and knowledge resist the conservative thrust that standards often have, in part, because they are suspect of standardization. Standardization, as a pedagogical and curricular practice, is hostile to "context," constructivist views, and revision. As the word implies, standardization attempts to rationalize the homogenization of knowledge and skills, in part, by decontextualizing knowledge, individualizing literacy and language development, and limiting teachers' input into and influence over pedagogy and curriculum development.

It would appear that these "state" standards overwhelmingly contradict and confront neoliberalism's determined march into the schools. And if the "state" controlled the means by which these ends were made manifest, then, yes, the confrontation would be more than just an illusion. Unfortunately, the "state" has handed over, in many instances, the operation of its schools to private interests that operate under the rhetoric of "whole-school reform."

These models often make the "state's" standards secondary to the state's neoliberal mandates. As such, the schools no longer operate in the service of the "state," but rather function as glocal formations that serve the interests of corporate culture, private business, and neoliberal globalization.

For example, *Success for All/ Roots and Wings* is one of the most popular models in New Jersey, with sixty-nine schools adopting it as the best model to meet the "state's" standards.[118] But this model places specific curricular and pedagogical demands on teachers and students, preventing teachers from responding to the needs of their students as well as complying with the objectives stated in the "state's" literacy arts standards. This model goes as far as to put time constraints on various exercises that students must do. The goals for *Success for All/ Roots and Wings* are most notable for how much they contrast with the "state" standards summarized above:

1. Develop independent, confident readers. Provide systematic opportunities for successful application of reading skills within meaningful texts.

2. Increase students' ability to hear sounds within words, know the sounds associated with specific letters, and blend letter sounds into words.
3. Develop comprehension strategies.[119]

In this model, texts are meaningful, whereas the "state" understood that student's make things meaningful through their ability to use language creatively and critically. The divergence is important and more than an issue of emphasis. By advocating for the "successful application of reading skills within meaningful texts," the model implies that texts are meaningful in and of themselves (i.e., outside of language, history, social context) and that if students have the basic decoding skills, they can discover the meaning of said text. The second goal is a thinly veiled reference to direct phonics instruction, which is in direct contradiction to the "state's" focus on literacy development as a social process that demands an exploration of "language in its many contexts." By focusing on phonics at the expense of literacy, *Success for All* sacrifices the dynamic energy that language brings to experience. In this model literacy is not perceived as the ability to think, but represents a discreet skill that will help students to function successfully within this model of schooling specifically, and within the "new" economy generally. Lastly, this model creates a hierarchy of skills and knowledge. Unlike the "state's" emphasis on integration and revision, *Success for All* adopts a scripted developmental model of learning, whereby students advance in stages through different skill sets. By ignoring the relationship between teaching and learning, this model ostensibly makes the teacher obsolete at best and a liability at worst. The teacher is expected to adhere to the imperatives of the model, rather than to the needs of his or her students as they arise out of specific social, political, and cultural contexts. More egregious is the fact that teachers are held accountable to educational outcomes even though they are directed to follow the model's pedagogical and curricular mandates.[120] This separation between teaching and learning has important implications for teacher education, some of which I will discuss in the concluding section.

This example makes evident the disconnect between the "state's" position on language arts literacy and the WSR model, *Success for All*. More importantly, the reform model not only disconnects from local governing bodies, but it connects substantively with the neoliberal objectives of the nation-state. This connection is vital to the perpetuation of state power, as well as to the reproduction of the conditions of international or global capital reproduction. With an emphasis on direct instruction and decontexualized pedagogies and curricula that ignore issues like oppression, racism, sexism, and the reproduction of class relations, knowledge is transmitted to students as though it were not "interested" in perpetuating a particular kind of future, a future characterized by huge global disparities of wealth, education, and health care. As such, what constitutes glocal knowledge is left unexamined. In light of the state's neoliberal role, which according to Bob Jessop is to manage "the process of internalization,"[121] this relationship between the educational ICA and the state is more than an innocent articulation between local and national formations. The articulation is constitutive because it *creates* the symbolic and material reality of "interiorization," that is, the integration of international constraints "into the policy paradigms and cognitive models of domestic policymakers."[122] Moreover, as Jessop argues, "interiorization is not confined to the level of the national state: it is also evident at the local, regional, cross-border, and interregional levels, as well as in the activities of so-called entrepreneurial cities."[123] WSR models, like *Success for All*, and their intrusion into the public schools, even as they contradict "state" standards, signal the successful interiorization of neoliberal globalization, the hollowing out of local governmental formations, the concentration of state power, and the strengthening of the (repressive) state apparatus.

✪ Conclusion: Teacher Education in a Neoliberal Age

The interiorization of neoliberal globalization presents an enormous challenge to teacher-education programs that invest in "progressive" models of pedagogy and curriculum development. The Early Childhood, Elementary, and Literacy Education (ECELE) Department in the College of Education at Montclair State University in New Jersey, in which I am an assistant professor, understands its role in preparing teachers in progressive, if not radical, terms. In two separate documents, the department as well as the college make it clear that their role is to prepare teachers that can function not only in the schools as they are, but more radically, as they could be.

The progressive model of teacher education suggested by these two documents runs against the grain of what is occurring in the glocal school districts. Not aligned with the needs of the neoliberal model of education, Montclair's teacher-education program emphasizes, among other pedagogical and curricular considerations, critical thinking and the needs of a democratic society. The needs of a democracy, as discussed earlier in relation to efficiency, often directly contradict the needs of neoliberal globalization. Ideally, fulfilling the needs of a democracy would entail producing and reproducing the conditions of democratic relations. The production of democratic relations necessitates the reproduction of equitable power relations, as well as a public sphere in which these equitable relations of power can engage in discussion and debate. The ideology of neoliberalism demands nothing of the sort. Equity (or inequality) is not a problem for neoliberalism; nor is the destruction of the public sphere and collectivities.

The question for progressive teacher-education programs like Montclair's, in light of this disconnect between the needs of democracy and the needs of neoliberalism, is which needs should get satisfied? Granted, a rear guard effort can be fought in which progressive programs try to appease the neoliberal ideologues (who also hold the purse strings), while staying true to the institutional mission. But at Montclair it is becoming clear that this rear guard effort is failing to intervene in the hegemony of neoliberalism on one hand and is jeopardizing the progressive nature of the college and department on the other.

The complexity of the problem is enormous. Elementary and secondary schools, under the control of WSR, are demanding that new teachers be trained to function in the highly regulated environment of standardization and high-stakes testing. In the context of educating literacy teachers, the demand is made even more specific, calling for an abandonment of whole-language, critical-literacy, child-centered, and/or balanced approaches to language development in exchange for the drill-and-skill model of phonetic development. Feeling pressure to respond to these demands, the department has, informally, introduced *Put Reading First* and the National Reading Panel's report into its teacher-education curriculum, rationalized by their power to shape reading instruction at the elementary and secondary levels. The inclusion of these materials into the curriculum ideally plays two roles in the program. First, it prepares students to function in the learning environments that are constructed through the influence that these publications have on reading instruction. Second, the materials are subjected to a critique and measured against other models of literacy instruction. The second role is supposed to help future literacy teachers understand that there are other valid models of literacy development available to them as literacy educators. But there are a number of problems with this strategy.

First, the hidden reality behind the inclusion of these publications is the epistemological and pedagogical reduction of the development of literacies to a one-dimensional perspective of reading. Developing multiple literacies and the multiple pedagogies that follow, in this context, are dismissed, at best, as secondary considerations in the reading enterprise. Because of time constraints, as well as competing philosophical commitments from faculty, the reduction of literacy to reading is defended in pragmatic terms. In other words, the needs of the schools must be met *before* the needs of the larger project that the department and college have stated as their goal. The either-or dichotomy that this problem represents is, in the pedagogical context, somewhat forced. Most, if not all, faculty attempt to intervene critically in the hegemony that these publications represent, but the political effect of this intervention is often undermined by the related problem of "deskilling."

In essence, our teachers are being deskilled as they are being educated to meet the manufactured needs of neoliberalism. As such, what is taught *before* has a direct

effect on what is learned *after*. By positioning the development of multiple literacies as a secondary consideration in educating literacy educators, we (inadvertent-
ly) deskill future teachers from learning the kinds of literacies they might need to
transform the conditions in which they will work. The issue is both about what
teacher-education programs teach teachers to teach, as well as what they teach teachers to know. Without a more inclusive conception of literacy driving curricular and
pedagogical considerations, holding "conservative" models of reading development
up for critique will fail, in and of itself, to educate future educators about the politics of structural transformation. Stated a different way, the critical literacies that
educators would need to transform literacy education as it is taking place in many
of our public schools are sacrificed in an attempt to meet pragmatically the needs
generated out of a neoliberal commitment to reducing literacy to the learning of
basic skills, decoding, and basic comprehension of written texts. By pragmatically,
albeit analytically, meeting through teacher education the language needs of students
as they have been manufactured by neoliberal interests, progressive departments, colleges, and universities jeopardize the legitimacy—epistemologically, philosophical-
ly, pedagogically—of their progressive projects. There are many effects of deskilling,
but an important one is its ability to produce both a cynicism and fatalism within
our future teachers.

For example, many education students at Montclair are committed in varying
degrees to the department and college's progressive project. Their problem with the
program is its failure to prepare them to work progressively in elementary and secondary schools where standardization and testing dominate pedagogical and curricular decisions. These students are enthusiastic to make changes, but lack the
strategies needed to confront institutionalized power. Hope soon turns to cynicism
when enthusiastic teachers are disciplined for or constrained from practicing progressive pedagogies after they have been educated to consider that change is needed and possible. Their cynicism is often directed at the progressive programs that
taught them how to think critically and teach in progressive ways *minus* the strategies of unionization, insurgency, and organized dissent. This problem points to an
unmet need in many progressive education programs. That is, if our students are to
avoid becoming cynical, then hope must be more than rhetorical. Hope must
become, in Giroux's language, "educated."[124] Educated hope is rooted in historical
social struggle, informed by a sustained critique of social formations, enlivened by
theory, and driven by a commitment to solidarity.

In my view, one of the most important benefits of such a project is its ability
to make the fatalism of neoliberalism unconvincing. It gives students a sense of
agency by getting them to experience and understand power collectively and productively. No longer are they simply closing their doors so that they might be left
alone to pursue a progressive lesson here and there. They will be prepared to think

and act strategically against those institutions of established power that prevent them from teaching and developing a curriculum that is responsive to the needs of their students, as those needs are defined by the larger projects of social justice, democratic ideals, and liberation.

These larger projects should also drive the leadership of progressive colleges of education to take a stand against ideologically conservative programs like George W. Bush's *No Child Left Behind* and *Success for All* initiatives, just as they take a position that promotes their own progressive ideas. Of course, this takes risk, but these are risky times, and much is at stake if progressive colleges retreat from their own stated commitment to "prepare individuals committed to making life better for citizens in a political and social democracy."[125] In many ways, this statement carries with it the potential for radical work. Preparing educators to work in a social democracy is preparing them to change what is currently in place, while preparing them to participate in a political reality that is yet to come. It implies educating them, in a concrete way, to challenge the state's corporatist hegemony on democratic and social grounds. But without commitment from leadership in pedagogical, curricular, and political spheres, the hegemonic power of these words begins to wane, just as their power to determine which needs of which individuals will be satisfied diminishes.

By naming neoliberalism's ideological authority to manufacture needs, progressive leaders would take a giant step toward transforming the institutions that both produce and satiate those needs. By rearticulating the needs of students and communities in the service of releasing democratic relations from the grip of elite interests, progressive educational leaders can begin to enliven their visions with practices that are consistent with their projects, just as they refuse to satiate the false needs that have been created by oppressive educational apparatuses. In our current climate, where even hiring decisions are being made based upon these false needs, the imperative to take a leadership role against the hegemony of neoliberal ideologues cannot be overstated. If progressive colleges of education have a chance to survive in our neoliberal age, they (we) might want to consider the implications of meeting needs that have been manufactured by elite interests and begin to meet the needs that a socially just and democratic republic demands.

A vibrant democratic culture needs a literate adult population. The unprecedented attention that "the child" has received from local, state, and federal policies has not only left many adults struggling to learn to read behind, but silenced them and rendered them invisible. These older students do not quite fit in with neoliberalism's fetish for human capital. In a world where human value is measured in large part against human productivity, adults who struggle with their print literacy also struggle for their own human validity. It is to these issues that I will now turn.

chapter two

Leaving Adults Behind

The Conservative and Neoliberal Attack
on Adult Learners

From the specific interests of a business-oriented economy to the needs of our present-day democracy, adult literacy education is often argued to be the great elixir of social disease and economic inequality. Unfortunately, in our current context it is safe to say that adult learners continue to suffer at the hands of (neo)liberal and conservative forces, both of which, I will argue, are dangerously out of touch with the needs of learners on one hand and a socially just and democratic society on the other. A strange combination of social, political, and pedagogical influences has created a debilitating environment for adult learners, challenging adult educators to redefine not simply the "how" of adult literacy education, but the "why" as well. This environment is constituted first and foremost by a "white noise" that drowns out the social consequences and political urgency not of adult literacy education per se, but of transforming the "invisible structures" that position struggling adult learners as the cause (and cure) of their own difficulties.[1]

In the field of acoustics, "White noise is a type of noise that is produced by combining sounds of all different frequencies together.... You can think of white noise as 20,000 tones all playing at the same time,"[2] making it extremely difficult to hear anything at all. In the context of literacy theory and practice, white noise is produced by a proliferation of data that, by its sheer size, shape, and source, makes it difficult, if not impossible, to see and hear alternative ideas and findings. Moreover, white noise, because it suggests a diversity of tones, obfuscates the structural homogenization of power that drives the dominant research. More to the point, as conservatives and (neo)liberals manufacture white noise, it becomes extremely difficult to locate and hear the voices of those who are struggling to read to learn. Drowned out by the enormity of what pose as comprehensive studies, adult students' individual and collective realities as struggling readers get lost in the din of "scientific," positivistic, and ideological knowledge, while dominating social structures "hide" themselves within a blanket of white noise.

This chapter examines some of the forces that have manufactured this white noise, the conditions that they have helped to create, and the implications they continue to have for adult learners. Drawing on both the successes and limitations of the Citizenship Schools born out of the work of Myles Horton, Septima Clark, and Esau Jenkins, I conclude by discussing some strategies—pedagogical, political, and curricular—that might help cut through the white noise that surrounds the field of adult literacy education.

🕮 The Politics of Adult Literacy

With the fanfare of *No Child Left Behind* and *Put Reading First,* as well as standardized programs like *Success for All,* it is easy to ignore the overwhelming "silence" that constitutes the subject of adult education generally, and adult literacy specifically, in the United States. The administrations of Bush II and those that came before it have generally stayed irresponsibly silent on issues of adult education and adult literacy. Yes, it is true that Bush I, in 1990, "and the nation's governors, including Governor Clinton, adopted the goal that all of America's adults be literate by the year 2000."[3] It is also the case that in 2001 the National Center for Education Statistics published many studies, including *Adult Literacy and Education in America,* in an effort to better understand the 1992 adult literacy survey.[4] But this is the point of white noise. Under its influence, "silence" must be understood as that which is constructed *against* and *in relation to* the cacophony of voices demanding that no child be left behind and that adults be "trained to read to work" in low-level jobs. But it would be a mistake to assume that this kind of silence is simply relative; it is also productive.

For example, Bush II's "silent" conservatism positions "illiterate" adults as either criminal or immoral or both, making it quite easy to dichotomize the innocence of children left behind on one hand (and deserving of federal aid and "compassion") and the criminality and immorality of adults on the other. Within this ideological frame, adults are the cause of their own problems, whereas children can still be saved.[5] The administration's perspective is manifest in its missionary zeal to employ religious institutions[6] to dole out, as well as to determine who receives, mea-

ger helpings of social aid and services, while its enthusiasm for *continuing* the production of the prison-industrial complex[7] is evidenced by the fact that, according
to the Bureau of Justice in 2002, the "Nation's prison and jail population exceeded
2 million for the first time."[8] Add to the mix that "seven in 10 prisoners performed
in the lowest two literacy levels,"[9] and we begin to get a picture not only of a
moralistic attack on poor people, African Americans and Latinos, but on struggling
readers as well. In short, the disciplinary fetish that informs U.S. prison policy and
its attack on struggling readers, under Bush II, has a decidedly conservative bent in
that it is no longer simply an issue of economic or social welfare, but is now one of
moral justice.

Although it is utterly antidemocratic in nature, the appeal to moral justice by
the "new" conservative right connects adults' reading abilities to their moral worth.
The pattern of moral justice becomes all the more glaring when we realize that major
increases in incarceration are due not to violent crimes, but to drug offenses.[10] As
such, the conservative moralism that fuels this attack on minorities and struggling
readers is nothing more than a thinly veiled initiative to rid the streets and our democratic process of "adult illiterates," drug offenders, poor people, African Americans,
and citizens of Latin American origin.[11]

On the international level, literacy and adult education have also been relatively popular subjects, as in the U.S. domestic agenda, are surrounded by a deafening
white noise. The important difference is that the international agenda is more
(neo)liberal than conservative, changing the issues, although rendering them no less
problematic. As Daniel Wagner states, "The 1990 World Conference on Education
for All (WCEFA) in Jomtien, Thailand included adult literacy as one of its six major
worldwide goals."[12] At this conference, the goal was to cut back illiteracy rates by
half by 2000. Although Wagner points out the difficulty of obtaining accurate sta-
tistical data, it is evident that WCEFA also missed their mark:

> According to UNESCO, there were an estimated 962 million illiterates in the world in 1990,
> 885 million in 1995, and an estimated 887 million in 2000, constituting 27% of the adult
> population in the developing countries. Of these illiterates, the majority are women, in some
> countries accounting for up to two-thirds of adult illiteracy. Regionally, Eastern and Southern
> Asia have the highest number of illiterates, with an estimated 71% of the world's total illit-
> erate population. The Sub-Saharan Africa and Arab regions have about the same (40%) adult
> illiteracy rate, with Latin America at about half this rate. Overall, the geographic distribu-
> tion of adult illiterates has not changed very much over the Jomtien decade (or over the past
> several decades).[13]

These numbers are indeed disturbing, especially given the attention that adult
literacy has been afforded in the international community. There are many reasons
for these stagnating numbers, but generally the responsibility is placed on the
shoulders of those who are struggling to learn to read. Wagner states that although

many reasons were offered as to why these numbers have not moved, such as "inadequate programme quality; lack of time and resources of learners; poor quality of textbooks and pedagogy; lack of social marketing; and so forth," he nevertheless concludes that "there is little doubt, however, that the general factor behind all of these technical issues is that learners, for whatever sets of reasons, do not feel motivated to participate and remain in such voluntary programmes."[14]

His answer to the problem of motivation rests on innovative strategies:

> Innovative ways of meeting learner needs while at the same time enhancing learner motivation include: language policy and planning (e.g., providing more robust methods for introducing mother-tongue and second language literacy), empowerment and community participation (e.g., decentralization of literacy provision through NGOs), learning, instruction and materials design (e.g., better concatenation in materials development and production between formal and non-formal education domains), gender and family (e.g., further growth of intergenerational, mother-child literacy programmes), multi-sectoral connections (e.g., adapting literacy instruction for integration with health education and agricultural extension programmes), post-literacy and income-generation (e.g., integration of literacy with income generation schemes), technology and distance education (e.g., use of multimedia for improved teacher training).[15]

His suggestions are sound and should be part of any literacy initiative, adult or otherwise. Of particular concern here is an issue that articulates with the silence that informs the subject of literacy generally and adult literacy specifically: a disregard for *why* social and economic structures that adversely affect poor adult learners are left in place. By ignoring what might be the most significant variables in literacy development, motivation devolves into a psychological problem, much as illiteracy—when divorced from questions of power—devolves into a matter of cognitive or behavioral skills. In this context, we are no longer dealing with moral degeneracy (the conservative trope) as a primary cause of illiteracy, but rather, we are implicitly pushed to understand illiteracy—and "the illiterates"—as causing *their own* poverty generally, and their own illiteracy specifically, via their lack of motivation.

This position is notable, for it is built upon the absence of a sustained structural critique. In other words, a critique of motivation, or the lack thereof, leaves social structures unexamined for how they construct hierarchies of opportunity, power, and authority. It is a position that supports the belief that with the right motivation adult learners will develop the literacy skills necessary to participate in the information economy. Missing from this critique is the reality, which I will discuss shortly, that a lack of motivation (i.e., resistance) might in fact be a *reasonable* response on the part of those who know the harsh realities of poverty, racism, class exploitation, and gender bias. The knowledge that is born out of victimization/survivorship should not be so easily dismissed; it is an important lens through which to view critically the social formations from which the violence gets its force and legitimacy. In simpler terms, the appeal to motivation is a "blame the victim" perspective concealed in a liberal wrapper. Most damaging for the success of a mass-based adult literacy movement are the socioeconomic structures that position struggling adult readers as a cause of their own illiteracy that this perspective leaves in place.

Wagner's summary of the international literacy initiatives is disturbingly silent about how economic and social structures condition our experiences as literate global citizens. These initiatives ignore the relationship between poverty and illiteracy, failing to consider that poverty might be the cause of illiteracy and not the other way around. Of course, by ignoring this relationship, it is quite easy (and logical) to search out innovative methods of instruction in an effort to affect standards of illiteracy. However, it is not clear that even this kind of critique would offer up definitive answers regarding the relationship between poverty and illiteracy. More importantly, it might lead to the conclusion that if we change the *conditions* of poverty instead of the *structures* of capital, we will change the conditions of illiteracy.

For example, it is far from clear that poor people throughout the world will not remain poor, literate or not. It is true that those who have higher reading levels, in general, make more money than those that do not. But that is not the same thing as saying that adults who are poor and gain a higher level of linguistic proficiency do not remain poor. For example, in the United States, the National Adult Literacy Survey of 1992 indicated that 44 percent of adults who scored in the lowest literacy level lived in or near poverty as defined by 1991 government criteria.[16] This is, indeed, a high number. But what is often not mentioned is the fact that if 44 percent of people who are living in or near poverty are in the lowest literacy level, then 56 percent of adults who scored in the lowest level were *not* living in or near poverty levels.

But as advocates for the poor often point out, "official" levels of poverty are grossly out of touch with real-world demands. For example, the federal government states that a person is living in poverty if he or she makes $8,980 per year, or $172.69 per week. Some measurement standards suggest that people should anticipate spending 10 to 15 percent of their after-tax income on food.[17] That means that a person who makes $172.69 per week would spend between $17 and $25 per week on food. This, it seems, is an accurate accounting of poverty. But what happens when we double the number. If a single person makes $17,960 per year ($345.38 per week), then he or she can expect to pay, on average, $40 a week on food. Is this a realistic amount for a working person to spend on food in order to live a healthy life? It seems highly unlikely. So whether the measurement of poverty changes or not, one thing is certain. Significant numbers of *literate* people in the United States and throughout the world are still struggling under the weight of economic structures that *produce* poverty. Stated another way, literacy is not, nor has it ever been, the means to economic justice. It does mean, however, that a project of economic justice must include the issue of literacy. But only if it is reconceptualized to include many other dimensions of freedom, some of which I discuss in the conclusion to this chapter.

Nevertheless, (neo)liberals push the agenda that literate adults are more marketable (read: useful) than illiterate adults to a neoliberal world order and, therefore, should be trained to read to work. But as many have pointed out, including Glynda Hull, Charles Lemert, Patrick Shannon, and Stanley Aronowitz and William Defazio, the arguments that lower-level jobs demand a high level of literacy and that there are enough living-wage jobs available for those who want them are highly specious.[18] More to the point, as evidenced by the generational reproduction of poverty,[19] if the economic structures that have helped cause poverty are left alone, societies will undoubtedly continue to struggle with the problems of illiteracy on one hand, and a literate, but impoverished (employed or unemployed) workforce on the other. Just as affirmative action gives evidence to white supremacy, the reproductive nature of poverty is most clearly evidenced by the need for welfare reform. Although the conservative model of "reform" did little to alleviate the hardships of poverty and did nothing to change the structures of capital, its presence acknowledged that poverty was being reproduced from generation to generation.

Pedagogical innovations are important, but the pragmatics of such an approach can work against the goals of eradicating illiteracy because innovations in and of themselves do not necessarily provoke structural transformations. And when they are discussed at the expense of structural transformation, they work implicitly to obfuscate the relationship between dominant social structures and their mechanisms of reproduction.

The (neo)liberal intervention into illiteracy finally and most egregiously fails on the basis that it silently invests in the myth of the free market to offer opportunities to those prepared (i.e., literate) to participate. Its refusal to address the market's intrinsic inequities forces its advocates to create endless methodological innovations at the expense of structural transformation. Structures that function on the logic of inequality will always fail to produce "equal opportunities" for people, whether they can read or not. This truism of markets is evidenced by the simple "rational irrationality" that posits higher wages for laborers (the majority of the world's workforce) as a threat to "the economy." Higher wages and low unemployment, as Noam Chomsky and Edward Herman point out, are seen as *problems* for the economy (i.e., the shareholders) as opposed to benefits for workers and society.[20] Who will fill the ranks of the unemployed and poor in this Orwellian scenario? Those who historically have been poor and unemployed, literate or not.

◉ Democracy and Literacy

Taking a somewhat different tack and looking beyond the economic considerations discussed above, many argue that in the United States we must understand adult literacy and illiteracy within the context of civic life, which is best understood ideally as those public practices that regulate power—governmental and corporate—in the service of traditional democratic ideals, such as liberty, equality, and justice. The subject of adult literacy, in this context, is extremely important. The argument posits that it is not only the economic considerations that should drive literacy initiatives, but the needs of democratic citizenship. In this scenario, literacy programs should prepare students to function as democratic agents, assuming a relationship between reading ability and democratic participation. Mainly concerned with people's ability to vote, these initiatives want to teach people, in the best instance, to read to participate in democratic life.

But Richard L. Venezky and David Kaplan's analysis of the relationship between literacy and voting finds that time in school, rather than literacy level, is a more relevant predictor of voting behavior.[21] The question that this study raises, but does not answer, is why? Could it be that those who spend more time in school have been indoctrinated to believe in the viability of U.S. democracy and voting to a higher degree than those that have spent less time in school? The authors suggest that "if increased voter turnout is a national goal, increasing the number of years that citizens spend in school will probably do more to reach this goal than increasing either literacy levels or hard news reading."[22] This is an interesting and seemingly unintended comment on the indoctrinating power of schooling.

It is reasonable to speculate in the face of this research that increased literacy rates do not correspond to an increase in voting for good reason. That is, literate adults and those with low levels of literacy with less schooling might be more "politically literate" than those with more years of schooling. As our major elections are generally between two candidates that campaign on the same ideological platform, namely the "business" platform, we must wonder whether the problem is low voter turnout (i.e., motivation) or a system that offers no ideological distinctions and few opportunities for poor, working-class, and middle-class people to be involved in the local, state, and federal decision-making processes. Complicating these insights, and more to the point, is the fact that the structure of U.S. democracy in 2003 makes literacy and illiteracy, schooling or no schooling, irrelevant in the context of democratic agency.

In support of this assertion we need look no further than the 2000 presidential election, especially as it unfolded in the key state of Florida. Greg Palast reports that 57,700 voters were eliminated from the voting ranks, many of whom would have undoubtedly voted for Gore:

Here's how it worked: Mostly, the disks contain data on Florida citizens—57,700 of them. In the months leading up to the November 2000 balloting, Florida Secretary of State Harris, in coordination with Governor Jeb Bush, ordered local elections supervisors to purge these 57,700 from voter registries.

In Harris's computers, they are named as felons who have no right to vote in Florida. Thomas Cooper is on the list: criminal scum, bad guy, felon, *attempted* voter. The Harris hit list says Cooper was convicted of a felony on January 30, 2007.

2007?

You may suspect *something's wrong* with the list. You'd be right. At least 90.2 percent of those on the "scrub" list, targeted to lose their civil rights, are innocent. Notably, over half— about 54 percent—are black and Hispanic voters. Overwhelmingly, it is a list of Democrats.[23]

The brutal evidence of conservative forces undermining democratic life in this example, unfortunately, is not limited to this specific case. But even if it were, we are talking about the election of the president of the United States here, not of the local school board. Quite simply, in this example, power and ideology operate in a way that implicates corporate media and other "private" businesses, such as ChoicePoint,[24] in the silent overthrow of U.S. democracy.

The link to literacy lies in the fact that it did not matter whether or not those "scrubbed" from the list could read or not. Taking it one step further, we know that many of those who were scrubbed by Secretary of State Harris were literate. The argument could even be made that these citizens would not have been scrubbed from the voting registries if they were illiterate or in jail or both. When antidemocratic forces—forces hostile to mass-based democratic agency—drive the institutional structure of "democracy," teaching people to read to participate in democratic life *as it is* is naive at best.

Moreover, a literate citizenry would not have been able to read about the overthrow of U.S. democracy in 2000 because the story never made it to the mainstream media systems. Although alternative presses like *The Nation*, *Salon.com*, and the British presses carried the story, most U.S. readers and TV watchers get their news from mainstream news agencies. Given that these news agencies often report identical news, suggesting a consensus of truth, the "literate" citizenry's consent has undoubtedly been manufactured.[25] No longer are U.S. citizens getting *investigative* reports, revealing truths that challenge the established order, but instead they are receiving truths *from* the established order. Palast explains that investigative reports are "risky, they upset the wisdom of the established order, and they are *very expensive* to produce."[26] As a consequence, he argues, profit-driven companies like U.S. media conglomerates are highly unlikely to take on a story like the conservatives' overthrow of democracy.

For example, after Palast's story of the list of "faux felons" was reported on the Internet, he states that a CBS TV news producer interested in running the story contacted him. Palast gave him the basic information that he had collected at the time:

I freely offered up to CBS this information: The office of the governor of Florida, Jeb Bush, brother of the Republican presidential candidate, had illegally ordered the removal of the names of felons from voter rolls—real felons who had served time but obtained clemency, with the right to vote under Florida law. As a result, *another 40,000 legal voters* (in addition to the 57,700 on the purge list), almost all of them Democrats, could not vote.

The only *problem* with this new hot info is that I was still in the midst of investigating it. Therefore CBS *would have to do some actual work*—reviewing documents and law, obtaining statements.

The next day I received a phone call from the producer, who said, "I'm sorry, but your story didn't hold up." And how do you think the multibillion-dollar CBS network determined this? Answer: "We called Jeb Bush's office."[27]

An adult's level of literacy (as it's defined by the government), in this context, is irrelevant. Quite simply, you cannot read what's not there. Inversely, reading what's there as unmitigated truth is a significant form of *illiteracy*, but one that is chronically ignored by conservatives and (neo)liberals.

More directly, even if readers possessed a level of literacy that was cognizant of news bias, it is still something very different to understand in whose interests the biases are working. Reading the absences in texts is often the key to this understanding. This is where the work of Chomsky and Herman continues, almost twenty-five years after it was first published, to cut through, in their words, the "propaganda" of brutally irresponsible media systems, specifically commercial systems like the one in the United States. But their "propaganda model" of media critique can be applied to all media systems throughout the world. As I do not want to repeat work that is easily accessed, suffice it to say that the informational filters of ownership, advertising, sources and shapers, and flak are still powerful tools for getting to the roots of media bias. In other words, the propaganda model asks not about intentions, but about expectations. What can we expect from a media system, for example, that is run by a few extraordinarily wealthy individuals with conservative views of the world, that is funded in large part by advertising revenues, that uses "official" experts for its information, and that utilizes highly conservative think tanks and governmental sources to produce negative feedback against those bits of information that challenges elite interests?[28] The answer is that we can expect a media system that systematically leaves out news that challenges the interests of business elites generally and, specifically, in the case of the Florida debacle, refuses to cover the overthrow of a U.S. presidential election.

⊕ Literacies of Pleasure

For some scholars, viewing literacy as power, whether economic or political, misses the point of reading, for reading is the key to pleasure. For example, Harold Bloom writes, "Turgenev's stories are uncannily beautiful; taken together they are as magnificent an answer to, "Why read?" as I know (always excepting Shakespeare)."[29] Although pleasure is certainly a benefit one might get from reading, it does not in itself constitute a total literacy project. More to the point, Bloomian pleasures both pronounce and denounce that which is pleasurable by setting up a high-culture/low-culture dichotomy. Bloom's humanistic idea of "pleasure" is the last bastion, not of a scoundrel, but of one who has conceded to, *and benefited from*, the structures of modern life. For Bloom, pleasure, truth, and beauty lie in what he perceives as a mimetic flow of words, words that sanction the exclusive nature of his subjectivity.

Bloom's idea of "pleasure" is transcendent, beyond the social world and totally exclusive to those sophisticated enough (read: human enough) to "read" it. Language in this discourse is not ideological, but rather an aesthetic tool. Its use transcends itself, poetics as opposed to semiotics informing its critique. This position on literacy then is insufficient to a literacy project that must be responsive to the needs of a population that struggles under the weight of oppressive social structures. Although pleasure plays a part in developing adult literacies and might even be a dimension of liberation and freedom, it is inadequate because it fails to address how language organizes our pleasures as well as the contexts in which pleasurable things are experienced. I do not dismiss the pleasure we might find in texts or the power of language to stir the soul. Rather, my position is a critique of pleasurable texts, texts that have been designated as embodying that which is pleasurable. We bring our pleasures and our fears, our dreams and horrors, to the texts we read. The interaction is dynamic, producing reactions that are historically rooted and arbitrary.

Just as important in developing literacies of pleasure is the role the imagination plays in creating opportunities that might, in reality, be beyond the scope of immediate possibility. The space between what is and what could be is a place of enormous potential. Developing literacies of pleasure along the plane of imagination disrupts the fixed nature that characterizes Bloomian pleasures and releases them into the realm of what I call aesthetic agency. Once again power is introduced into the literacy sphere, but its force is felt at the point where a body, mind, and soul collide with history, knowledge, and the "text" to transform the present, to condition the future.

What all of this means for assessing adult literacy education is that if it has little or no bearing on an adult's democratic agency, economic freedom, or ability to interact with texts in meaningful ways, then it is not meeting the linguistic and political needs of adult learners on one hand and the needs of a democratic and socially just world on the other. The pedagogical implications of the conservative and (neo)liberal domination of adult literacy are significant, challenging adult educators to think about literacy and the struggles of adult learners on radical grounds. What might an adult literacy program look like that both teaches adults to read while working to dismantle the dominant antidemocratic and capitalistic structures that have made, and continue to make, literacy and learning insufficient markers of economic freedom and democratic agency?

❦ Radical Interventions into Adult Literacy

The National Adult Literacy Survey defined literacy as "using printed and written information to function in society, to achieve one's goals, and to develop one's knowledge and potential."[30] As such, the roster of adult education programs is littered with GED and adult basic education initiatives, most of which concentrate on basic skills and job preparedness. The definition fails to take into account the fact that language plays a significant role in how literacy is understood, why students should become literate, and how learning to read and write languages should be taught. Acknowledging language and learning, as linguist James Gee has said, complicates this definition in a way that brings attention to its politics, just as it points adult educators in a new direction.[31]

Its politics can be read as conservative because its definition of literacy fails to consider the complexities of language and teaching/learning on one hand, and the necessary relationship between education and power on the other. As such, it is conservative both politically and epistemologically. In order to understand adult literacy in more radical terms, we must first expand this definition of literacy to incorporate an inclusive notion of language. As Stuart Hall states, "Any sound, word, image, or object which functions as a sign, and is organized with other signs into a system which is capable of carrying and expressing meaning is, from this point of view, a 'language.'"[32] This inclusive understanding of language necessitates pluralizing literacy so that when we discuss what it means to be literate, we include multiple literacies in our assessments. These literacies are often connected to one another, even interdependent, making the project of adult literacy education a dynamic one. For example, ideological literacy is intimately connected to media literacy. Media literacy is connected to computer literacy, which is in turn connected to print literacy. Emotional literacy is connected to psychological literacy, which in turn is connected to workplace literacies, and so on. Competency in these literacies allows people to act against, in, on, and through their worlds. A working familiarity with these literacies paves the way for a critical and meaningful engagement with the social structures of everyday life. But in order to make this engagement "critical," it must be driven by a pedagogy that at its core recognizes the teaching and learning process as always tied up in questions of power, knowledge, authority, and culture. With an inclusive notion of language and a critical understanding of educational praxis as a foundation, the radicalization of adult literacies begins by asking the simple question of why read? The obvious answers historically, such as to achieve economic opportunity and democratic agency, as I have argued above, no longer represent reasonable responses.

So, why read? If democratic participation, economic equality, and the search for truth and beauty are insufficient at best because of their constitutive relationships to dominant social structures, then, in my estimation, a compelling answer is that adult literacy students must learn to read to transform unjust social structures. By making the transformation of antidemocratic, economically unjust, and culturally hegemonic social structures the "project" of adult literacy education, the needs of poor adults on one hand, and a socially just and democratic society on the other, get met. The educational implications of this transformative project are profound, demanding that GED and adult basic education, as they are often taught, be disbanded or radically transformed.

These programs fail because they work on the assumptions of "distributive justice." As R. W. Connell explains, "Questions of 'distributive justice' are questions about who gets what—particularly, who gets how much of some social good."[33] The social good is the education itself, ignoring the large body of scholarship produced throughout the world over the last three decades that concludes that class and cultural interests operate through dominant educational projects.[34] As such, what is good for ruling-class adults is not necessarily good for poor or working-class adults. Connell states,

> A crucial policy conclusion follows. Justice cannot be achieved by distributing the same amount of standard good to children of all social classes. Education is a process operating through relationships, which *cannot be* neutralized or obliterated to allow equal distribution of the social good at their core. That "good" means different things to ruling-class and working-class [adults], and will do different things for them (or to them).[35]

A project of *social justice* is distinct from a project of distributive justice, although it has a mode of distribution embedded in it. In other words, power and other resources are redistributed just as the content of power and resources are reconstituted to reflect the form of new social structures. In this scenario, for example, "individual equality [would be] the condition, not the goal, of a just *social order*."[36] Power and resources do not become meaningless; rather they take on different meanings based on different relations of power. Their redistribution becomes critical only when it works to disrupt oppressive relationships of power and transformative when its content reflects the values of a just social order.

☙ Critical Methodologies in Conservative Times: Literacies for Social Justice

Understanding adult literacy education on radical grounds also has a methodological component that compliments the larger goals of the project. The legacy of critical methodologies is vast, and I will only discuss one that I think is vital (although it is often forgotten or ignored) and provides a foundation upon which to advance new strategies for our contemporary context.[37] With the support of Myles Horton and the Highlander Folk School, Septima Clark and others created the Citizenship Schools, which offer contemporary adult literacy educators a model from which to develop a mass-based campaign for literacies of social justice.[38]

In the early 1950s, Esau Jenkins and Septima Clark visited Highlander and Horton to participate in a workshop on the United Nations. But Jenkins approached Horton, telling him that his concern was adult literacy education and that without it, a workshop on the United Nations remained meaningless for his community in Charleston, South Carolina. He asked Horton if he would consider establishing an adult literacy program "to help them become better citizens."[39] At this time in South Carolina, the political inequity caused by the segregation of schools was complicated and made even more manifest by a state law that said if African Americans "couldn't read the constitution, then they couldn't register to vote." Within this context of racism and poverty, Horton struggled, as many adult educators still struggle today, to understand the failure of state- and federal-supported adult literacy programs. He concluded that these programs were degrading to adults who were being taught like young children. Adults, with years of significant life experience, were being asked to "read sentences of dubious value, even to children."[40] For Horton and others who were concerned about the relationship between adult illiteracy and political power, "what" and "why" the adults read in the course of learning to read was as important as "how" they were taught to read.

Horton recognized the need to establish the school in a place that adults could relate to and feel comfortable in. "Moreover, the work of learning to read must be adult work and work that was a part of the islanders' own lives."[41] As many progressive adult educators know, the setting in which adult literacy takes place is often the first and most difficult hurdle for many adult learners. If adults are asked to enter an elementary school or cold and dank basement for their schooling, the message is clear to them that their learning is not a priority and that their real-world literacies should be left at the door.

When I taught adult literacy, the setting was a cold and ill equipped basement in a youth center. As the basketballs reverberated through the ceiling from the kids playing ball above us in the gym, my students tried to concentrate and ignore the noise as well as the children's reading books that lined the shelves in the room. Leaving the classroom, they would often bump into their children's friends, who were at the center for after-dinner activities. Such encounters are often difficult and degrading to adults who are struggling to learn to read and make it quite easy for them simply to stop coming to class. The question to ask as far as attendance goes in this context is *not* why adults *stop* coming or *fail* to come at all, but rather why they *do* attend when the environment for learning is so hostile to their own knowledges, literacies, and experiences?

The "how" of Highlander is directly connected to the "who." In other words, it became apparent that "the teacher had to be a peer and someone who could teach them to read what they needed to read, in this case, the South Carolina constitution."[42] Drawing from the community, Clark "hired" her niece, who had no formal teaching experience. By utilizing the "human" resources of a community, adult literacy educators would create an implicit degree of trust. The community teaches the community. The Highlander literacy initiative in South Carolina, now called the Citizenship Schools, was a huge success. The community was engaged in the literacy process as it was politically empowered. News spread of the Citizenship Schools and more people wanted to learn to read to participate in the democratic process. Jenkins writes,

> And then the people on Wadmalaw and Edisto Islands found out later the reason for Johns Island was so successful in registering Negroes. They ask me if it's possible to help them to get an adult school. So the next year when I went to Highlander, when it comes time for immediate problem again, I brought in Wadmalaw and Edisto, and they again say they will help if I can find a place and the teachers. I found the place, and today Wadmalaw registered more Negroes than ever registered in the history of Wadmalaw. In the 1964 election, Wadmalaw had about two hundred Negro votes for Johnson. Most of the white folks were voting for Goldwater, but Negroes voted enough to hold it in the democratic column. That's the only area in Charleston County that went for Johnson.[43]

However moving and hopeful this account of the Citizenship Schools success is, it must be understood within the context of its limitations. In other words, this model presents adult literacy educators with a new/old approach to literacy, and one that I believe is a necessary part of a mass-based literacy initiative. A mass-based campaign for literacies of social justice would have to learn from the Citizenship Schools, taking seriously its use of community to teach community, settings of respect, and lessons based in the experience of the adult learners themselves. Also important is the notion of a "project." The schools recognized the needs of the communities as stemming from their political impotence. The project, therefore, was to manifest power in both the individual and community. These lessons I believe "travel" well and should undergird a contemporary social justice literacy project. But to be adopted in our current context and have radical effects, such a project must deal with the structural failures of present-day "democracy" and capitalism. Teaching people to read to vote, as already discussed, would have done little in Florida. Literate or not, "voters" were purged from the registry. Literate or not, poor people often remain poor.

The radicalization of this model necessitates an engagement with, and active transformation of, the structural restraints of dominant power. In other words, using the Constitution and the Bill of Rights as curricular resources, as the Citizenship Schools did, is only "empowering" if their messages of democratic freedom are read against the structural realities of "unfreedom." Using these texts to expose the hypocrisy of the current economic and political systems is the first step toward transforming them. By no longer teaching adults to read to participate in the existing system, but by teaching them literacies of social justice prepares them to read to critically engage and transform the systems. By making the *transformation* of oppressive systems the project of adult literacy, we neither discount the importance of reading nor diminish the need for individual and collective political power. Rather, these things are seen as constituent elements in the fight for social justice.

In Part II, I expand my discussion of neoliberalism and its affects to include the theoretical work of social psychologist Erich Fromm and critical educator and philosopher Paulo Freire. Both critical theorists addressed issues of social justice, human agency, and freedom in a way that brought attention not only to the productivity of political and pedagogical authority, but to the ethical dimensions of using power in the service of social and distributive justice. Both Fromm and Freire anticipated the attack on human freedom that neoliberalism represents, and both sought to transform the conditions of unfreedom that had taken hold of the imaginations of so many of the people they worked with. In the following two chapters, I examine their work for what they say about the relationship between freedom, power, and consciousness on one hand, and the social formations that condition our bodies and minds on the other. Notable (and notorious) for their utopianism, I believe their work is a testament to the power of critical theory and radical practice to critically disrupt and inform transformative social and educational policies.

part two

The Work of Critical Theory in a Neoliberal Age

chapter three

Paths from Erich Fromm

Rethinking Authority Pedagogically

But although foreign and internal threats of Fascism must be taken seriously, there is no greater mistake and no graver danger than not to see that in our own society we are faced with the same phenomenon that is fertile soil for the rise of Fascism anywhere: the insignificance and powerlessness of the individual.

This statement challenges the conventional belief that by freeing the individual from all external restraints modern democracy has achieved true individualism. We are proud that we are not subject to any external authority, that we are free to express our thoughts and feelings, and we take it for granted that this freedom almost automatically guarantees our individuality. The right to express our thoughts, however, means something only if we are able to have thoughts of our own; freedom from external authority is a lasting gain only if the inner psychological conditions are such that we are able to establish our own individuality.[1]

Introduction

Erich Fromm's work is relevant in our contemporary context because it draws attention to the relationship between the political and psychological, suggesting a troubling, but important, relationship between the neoliberal construct of individualism and cultural hegemony on one the hand and our ability to question authority and our potential to transform our consciousness on the other. In this context, there is a need to understand the fascist implications of atomization as manifest in the disconnect between social autonomy and individualistic ideologies. In the face of this disconnect, I attempt here to develop a theory of pedagogical authority that situates it as a force for creating a transcultural disruption of consciousness that shifts the cognitive, affective, and ideological relationships we have to each other, to nature, and to social structures in the direction of *freedom towards*. Fromm's critical psychology brings explicit attention to the importance of confronting authoritative structures politically and *thinking authority pedagogically* as necessary steps in authorizing a new consciousness, one that locates individuality within social groups and understands dissent as a principle of freedom.

In what follows, I argue for a productive notion of pedagogical authority that crosses the theoretical borders of modernism, feminism, and postmodernism.[2] Out of the postmodern comes a concern with "difference" and the histories, languages, knowledges, memories, and experiences of those that are all too often excluded from political decision making. Out of feminism comes a commitment to transform patriarchal and authoritarian practices of power. Out of the modern is a radical concern with human solidarity, equity, and social justice. It is "radical" because it demands not only a critique of power in understanding human relations, but also its redistribution. Together these ideas suggest a critical postmodernist feminist paradigm in which to link the personal to the global, identifying a basic universal ethic against which human suffering—regardless of race, class, gender, and sexual orientation—can be confronted and transformed. In the context of Fromm's work, the critical postmodernist feminist paradigm is appropriate because it calls attention to the dynamic convergence of identity, experience, and the politics of representation with ideological systems, structures, and cultural formations.

Lastly, I will discuss some of the critical paths—political and pedagogical—that lead from Fromm's work on authority and power. Reflecting upon the relationship between individual thinking and hegemony, Fromm's work provides an important pedagogical challenge to educators and other political workers. His thoughts provoke a consideration of the hegemony of individualism in the context of democratic life. As the epigraph that opens this chapter suggests, shadows of fascism do not necessarily reflect the lockstep of jack-booted soldiers. Rather, shadows of fascism sometimes stretch out from the feet of an atomized and "free" constituency.

● Background on Erich Fromm

Rethinking authority in pedagogical terms necessitates a critical analysis of both the psychological and ideological. The work of critical psychologist and theorist, Erich Fromm, adds an important dynamic to the notion of authority because, like other critical theorists from the Frankfurt School, he wanted to "reconcile" Marx and Freud. Although inarguably a humanist, Fromm's work, such as that on matriarchy and history's effect on the psyche, anticipates some of the complexities and political impulses of postmodernist and feminist discourses. By wanting to reconcile Freud and Marx, Fromm's work "naturally" crossed and merged the theoretical borders of the psychological, societal, and political. Fromm believed that "psychoanalysis could provide the missing link between the ideological superstructure and socioeconomic base. In short it could flesh out materialism's notion of man's essential nature."[3]

According to Martin Jay, Fromm "understood man's nature as something created through relatedness to the world and interaction to others."[4] In this way, Fromm affirmed the idea of a human nature, although it was not a fixed notion. Rather, it was an "idea of man's potential nature."[5] One major advancement Fromm made in integrating Marx and Freud was using "psychoanalytic mechanisms as the mediating concepts between the individual and society—for example, in talking about hostility to authority in terms of Oedipal resentment of the father."[6]

This led to his developing a social psychology, that is, a way of understanding social and psychological processes as deeply interrelated. As Jay explains, "The task of an analytical social psychology was to understand unconsciously motivated behavior in terms of the effect of the socio-economic substructure on basic psychic drives."[7] Fromm argued that societies had unique libidinal structures; that is, each society contained a combination of "human drives and social factors."[8] How this libidinal structure was affected by changing socioeconomic conditions and the disjunction that this change could cause should be, Fromm argued, the subject of social psychology.

Importantly, some of Fromm's strongest critics were his colleagues in the Frankfurt School, namely Theodor Adorno, Max Horkeimer, and Herbert Marcuse. Specifically, they criticized Fromm's revisionist social psychology by arguing that it mistakenly tried to "psychologize culture and society," thereby ignoring Freud's notion that "psychology was necessarily the study of the individual."[9] For Adorno, this was a serious mistake because it jeopardized the libido, which under Freudian influence "implied a stratum of human existence stubbornly out of reach of total social control."[10] In his effort to critique Freud's patriarchal and libido theories, Fromm and other revisionists, it was argued, had embraced a conformity that "smoothed over social contradictions."[11] At a time when the brutalities of the Holocaust informed all of the Frankfurt School's work, Fromm's optimism was considered by some to be as dangerous as it was naive. Nevertheless, Fromm's work is important because it stubbornly reclaims a psychological perspective that resists positivistic impulses, just as it struggles to understand the relationship between the individual and larger social and political structures.

🎵 Notes on the Crisis of Authority in Critical Educational Discourse

I will take up the issue of authority in the context of the late 1980s in which post-modernist and postcolonial theory were taken up in feminist educational theory, critiquing authority—especially as it was developed in critical pedagogy—for its authoritarian implications.[12] Many educational theorists who were excluded by critical pedagogy's neo-Marxist framework of the 1970s and early 1980s found an important ally in these theories of difference, identity, discursivity, and power. These theories offered a new language to critique Marxist universal declarations and ideas overburdened by a language of emancipation and utopian promises. The "post" theories brought to the fore the exclusions of modernity, the problems of progress, the rational irrationalities of modernism, the scientism of Marxism, and the hegemony of patriarchy. It was a period in the (de)construction of knowledge in which the "posts" and feminism were extremely valuable in bringing attention to the normalizing discourses embedded within modernity's master narratives. In the context of education specifically, Debra Britzman writes that as a consequence of these new theoretical discourses, educational theorists began to understand that

> pedagogy is not just about encountering critical knowledge, but also about constructing contextually dependent relations that recognize the power of lived experiences and of ideology. Methods of specifying one's pedagogy, identifying one's interests and investments, and resisting totalizing claims of transcendence are the contributions of this new scholarship. Equally important is the admission of the limits of the teacher and the contradictory desires she holds.[13]

More generally, Ihab Hassan cites postmodernist theory as part of a "culture of 'unmaking' whose key principles include: decreation, disintegration, deconstruction, decentrement, displacement, difference, discontinuity, disjunction, disappearance, decomposition, de-definition, demystification, detotalization, delegitimation."[14] Both Britzman's and Hassan's characterization of postmodernist feminist theory draws attention to its penchant for the "negative"; that is, it often occupies a certain negative function, producing critiques that unravel what is, as well as what could be. Ironically, the "post" prefix is one of the only "positive," or productive, moves in an otherwise "negative" theory. This is not a critique of postmodernist work as pessimistic, like that which Richard Rorty famously unleashes against postmodernists; rather, it is an observation about the negative functions of a theoretical paradigm that exists primarily in the realm where the prefixes "de," "un," and "dis" draw the map of inquiry and, as such, diminish the link between critique and possibility.[15]

Nevertheless, the postmodern feminist challenge is important because it begs us to ask, what might it mean for educators to *think authority pedagogically* in the face of the inevitable instability and partiality of experience and knowledge? As cultural theorist Susan Bordo suggests in relation to what we can and cannot know, it is true that

> we *cannot* know with certainty. But this merely means that we are fallible, our assessments provisional, our actions subject to revision. It should not be taken as a cause for fatalism or passivity.... To act responsibly and with hope, it's not necessary that we know the final outcome of our actions.[16]

In other words, how might we construct a pedagogical project that encourages us to act with passion and commitment in the face of partial understandings, while forcing us to forge alliances and combat social atomization as part of a larger commitment to democratic concerns, such as liberty, equality, and social justice?

❦ Erich Fromm and the Productivity of Ethical Authority

The crisis of pedagogical authority is essentially an ethical crisis, because it positions teachers outside the scope of "encouraging human [and political] agency."[17] Moreover, it discourages teachers from recognizing the interventionist nature of pedagogical work. This places both students and teachers in the unfortunate position of struggling to achieve freedom *from* authority. Fromm called this type of freedom "negative freedom" because it imprisons individuals within a social matrix of isolation, fear, and anxiety.[18] As such, negative freedom undermines political agency because it attacks individual spontaneity, the pinnacle of positive freedom.[19] Negative freedom creates the conditions for a fear of authority by positioning authority as the opposite of freedom, while offering itself as the only hope for escape.

Instead of escaping into a world in which individual creativity, political agency, and social responsibility guide the creation of democratic formations, people escaping from negative freedom find themselves dependent on a new type of bondage: "Thus freedom—as freedom from—leads into new bondage."[20] The repercussions of this cycle—negative freedom, escape into new structures of domination, dependency due to isolation and the denial of the spontaneous self, then a renewed escape from negative freedom into new bondage—cause a crisis in the educational sphere by delimiting political agency to those actions that denounce political power in the name of freedom, negative freedom.

Unfortunately, students are seriously affected by this crisis of authority in three specific ways. First, they are made to succumb to the power of the university-corporate complex regarding what and how they are to learn. Second, those who are marginalized by dominant social, cultural, and political systems are rarely taught, and are rarely allowed, to see authority and power used in any way other than as an instrument of oppression and domination. This is no small matter. Teachers who retreat from authority help to perpetuate systems of oppression by teaching their students, by example, that there is no productive or oppositional way to employ authority without becoming authoritarian. Third, a crisis of authority often motivates a pedagogy that is first and foremost about "instill[ing] humanistic values in a nonrepressive way."[21] Safety and security become the dominant factors in creating a "liberatory" classroom. As Fromm's work suggests, this only helps perpetuate a condition of "negative freedom"; that is, it works to establish a strategy of "first, do no harm."[22]

By presenting politics as a *hindrance* to freedom, the conditions for democratic self-institution are threatened. As Hannah Arendt argues, "We are inclined to believe that freedom begins where politics ends . . . [even though] the raison d'etre of politics is freedom and that this freedom is primarily experienced in action."[23] Freedom outside an apparatus of authority moves us "outside the sphere of human action, intervention, or struggle."[24] Moreover, freedom understood outside the authority of political action and social engagement devolves into "unfreedom," that is, into a system of governance in which people are free to suffer economic injustice and cultural oppression without institutional interventions on one hand, and minus political agency on the other. For example, people in the United States enjoy the freedom to choose a private health care plan, but without personal resources or social intervention that freedom devolves into unfreedom; that is, they are free to be sick. For another example, African Americans are free to go into any bank and apply for a mortgage, but regardless of their economic resources, if a racist culture dominates, the applicant will most likely be denied that money. In this case, the freedom to apply is made meaningless without political guarantees. These guarantees are realized through people's ability to act in and upon the world. Echoing Bordo, this does not mean that we always know the outcomes of our participation. It simply means that political participation is necessary for freedom to mean more than, to quote Janis Joplin, "having nothing left to lose."

In the context of pedagogy and schooling, a productive pedagogical authority would be responsible for interrogating, unsettling, and displacing the authoritative forms of negative freedom that have been legitimated through dominant ideological apparatuses. As Fromm recognized, the ideological authority that educators must displace is not so much "internal authority" or the internalized expression of external authority, which can appear as "duty, conscience, or super-ego," but rather they must unsettle and displace what he called "anonymous authority."[25] Anonymous authority's pedagogical function is to remove any visible signs of social and political systems of thought to make the ideological a matter of common sense.[26] As Fromm's research revealed, "conscience rules with a harshness as great as external authorities, and, furthermore, that frequently the contents of the orders issued by man's conscience are ultimately not governed by demands of the individual self but by social demands which have assumed the dignity of ethical norms."[27]

Breaking into this hegemony is made even more difficult given that the language of conscience and sociopsychology has been somewhat lost in critical educational discourses. As a consequence, the celebration of "freedom" outside of its dialectic to authority has normalized itself into our common sense.[28] "Instead of overt authority," Fromm argues, "'anonymous' authority reigns. . . . It seems to use no pressure but only mild persuasion."[29] Moreover, he finds that anonymous authority works effectively to hinder political agency by removing a concrete object for resistance. The "moral courage" and "personal independence" that comes from fighting against an oppressive and unjust authority—internal or external—is severely diminished as both the "command and commander have become invisible."[30]

The hegemony of anonymous authorities demands that teachers and other political workers rethink authority in pedagogical terms. That is, if we begin to think authority pedagogically, not only do we complicate its role in the development of counterhegemonic practices, but we also situate it as a principle of insurgency and critical thought. In this context, naming the anonymous provides a viable object of resistance.

Fromm's work suggests a number of conditions and capacities that inform a critical postmodern feminist notion of pedagogical authority. This pedagogical authority must recognize its own relationship to conditions of established power, while attempting to disrupt those conditions. This view of authority rejects the notion of repression as power's only dimension. As Foucault writes, repression is

> quite inadequate for capturing what is precisely the productive aspect of power. In defining the effects of power as repression, one adopts a purely judicial conception of such power, one identifies power with a law which says no, power is taken above all as a wholly negative, narrow skeletal conception of power, one which has been curiously widespread. If power were never anything but repressive, if it never did anything but to say no, do you really think one would be brought to obey it?[31]

Fromm agrees, but moves beyond the "how" to theorize the "who" and the "what" of power as well. Foucault asserts the productivity of power, but fails to complete the hermeneutical gesture. Without the "what" and the "who," the "how" of power is left circulating like wind through the leaves. Neither repressive nor liberating, power creates and destroys, but in the end is not thought of as constituted by ideology and the people who legitimate it as common sense. Power is faceless, bodiless, and mindless, creating instead faces, bodies, and minds. This is certainly an important discursive aspect of power, but it tends to negate the specific location of power, once, in fact, it has been embodied, inscribed, and localized. At the point of localization, one way power becomes manifest is in authority, suggesting in concrete terms a "what" and a "who."

A critical postmodern feminist authority understands the "what" of power as the authority of the institution, the classroom, the desks and chairs, the texts, the division of labor and time, and the various methods used in the schooling enterprise. These things combine to create a *collateral regime of authority*, for it is in the reified materiality of school life that power often functions in a disciplinary way. Rarely is the legitimacy of these constructs challenged. The life of the school is, in part, conditioned by these seemingly innocuous and inorganic elements. Textbooks claim legitimacy based upon their inclusion in the curriculum and the appearance they give as complete, as opposed to partial, ideological, and power-driven, knowledge domains. The school itself is poised as the operative mechanism of behavioral constraint, with its tiled corridors, sectioned rooms, and panoptical surveillance. Collective learning-teaching, action-based learning/research initiatives, interdisciplinary studies, and team teaching, to name but a few strategies, are made inconvenient at best, and impossible to initiate at worst. But these things, in and of themselves, do not guarantee repressive *or* progressive systems of schooling. As important a consideration is the production and utilization of knowledges and the realities they legitimate and delegitimate.

Disciplinary "knowledge," as opposed to the contexts of the students and teachers often drives curriculum and pedagogies. Disciplinary knowledge is understood as relevant regardless of whether it responds to the social realities of teachers and students. Knowledge is no longer something that needs to be produced; rather, it is bought and sold, with the teacher acting as seller and the students as consumers. But it is the teachers who are also consumers in this transmission model of schooling, for they must invest in the value of disciplinary knowledge (if not the knowledge itself) to be good sales associates. Perhaps more significant (and troubling) is the anonymous authority of these disciplinary knowledges to name and legitimize what is appropriate to teach and learn. In effect, they often discount what they cannot address and celebrate what they can.

Within a critical postmodern feminist paradigm, the "who" of power is characterized and animated by both resistance and hegemony. Students are amazing examples of this dynamic. As teenagers, they often have a "natural" inclination to rebel, resist, and question authority. Too often, these "democratic" skills are purged through the dominant ideologies that institute school life. Against these dominating ideologies, students, it must be admitted, have little recourse. That is different from saying, however, that they have none. Students continually engage in acts of resistance, sometimes to their detriment. Nevertheless, from rallies against sweatshop labor to personal initiatives that challenge assignments, grading, and syllabi, student rebellion debunks the myth of false consciousness. Theirs might be called a *dearticulated consciousness*, that is, a consciousness felt at the level of the affective, but not yet linked to a critical vocabulary.

Teachers, principals, and other administrators are, for the most part, the second significant "who" of power. Quite often, these professionals are at odds with each other. Nevertheless, some important connections among them must be addressed. Mainly, their presence within the manifestations of official power situates them at the precipice of liberatory action on the one hand or becoming complicit in oppressive systems of schooling and education on the other. Although their positions and practices are more complex than this dichotomy suggests, I think it is important, through simplifications, to understand directly how some practices play out materially in a way that produces winners and losers. For example, how these professionals utilize their authority—what they authorize as legitimate knowledge, behavior, pedagogy, and curriculum—situates them as engaging in a *freedom toward* or a *freedom from*. Liberatory teachers and administrators who authorize power in the service of redistributing power, as well as reconstituting what counts as powerful, operationalize their authority in the service of liberation. They are conceptualizing freedom in terms that project it forward. These educational workers no longer use the relationship between politics, education, and schooling as an escape from the political, but as a doorway into the mechanisms of teaching and learning. Teachers and administrators who authorize power only in the service of critique tend to diminish power to the level of repression, thereby denying its productive elements. Lastly, teachers and administrators who retreat from the political in order to find freedom have only found a negative freedom, that is, a freedom that hides from social responsibility and political participation in the name of neutrality and autonomy.

❦ Thinking Authority Pedagogically in an Age of Terror/ism

The "war on terrorism" presents educators with modern images of global power. This "war" not only brings attention to the overwhelming role the media play in constructing the conditions to exercise or constrain what Donaldo Macedo calls "literacies of power," but also legitimizes these conditions as necessary in the fight against terrorism.[32] Not historically unique, self-censoring as well as governmental and corporate censoring play a major role in what gets reported, how it gets reported, and when it gets reported. In this context, freedom of speech and other civil liberties are now considered luxuries of peace. For example, the U.S. government, as a means of protecting national security, now sanctions racial profiling. Searches of private residences no longer have to meet previously defined notions of just cause. Wiretapping and surveillance of religious and political organizations are considered useful and legal practices for defending national security. Dominant representations of terror and terrorists, and the policies that follow, present educators with the challenge of using their authority to create what Henry Giroux and Peter McLaren have called a "pedagogy of representations."[33]

In this context, pedagogy of representations intervenes into dominant representations—pedagogically, politically, semiotically, and epistemologically. Because representations teach us about ourselves, while legitimating certain behaviors and attitudes, they are powerful forces in constructing our commonsense notions of social reality. By using the word "teach," I do not mean to suggest that this process is as much conscious as it is effective in conditioning our thoughts and imaginations. Undoubtedly, people learn from media and representations. It therefore goes to reason that representations, in part, function pedagogically. Representations often simplify social and political events, making what is right or wrong seem obvious. Or, they make what is real "appear to be so enormously complicated that only a 'specialist' can understand [it], and he only in his limited field, actually—and often intentionally—tends to discourage people from trusting their own capacity to think about those problems that really matter."[34] A teacher who engages in a pedagogy of representations complicates these oversimplifications and deflections by providing, and encouraging students to undertake, a more complex accounting of the represented event and acknowledging that "experts" and "specialists" are not the only voices that have important things to say. Resisting relativistic thinking, teachers must *think their authority pedagogically* by intervening into the "postmodern" slide of meaning and recognize how dominant power restrains our interpretive and creative capacities.

To develop a critical position concerning the war on terrorism, representations should, in part, be addressed structurally by linking them to power/knowledge and authority. As Fromm writes, "The particular difficulty in recognizing to what extent our wishes—and our own thoughts and feelings as well—are not really our own but put into us from the outside is closely linked up with the problem of authority and freedom."[35] As though free from the mechanisms of the church and state, we have conceded to the rule of capital and live as though it does not function authoritatively. Believing, for example, that corporate media's control over the majority of representations we see has no effect on the quality and complexity of those representations seems to have infiltrated mass consciousness to the extent that suggesting otherwise provokes disdain. Recognizing the authoritative rule of capital accumulation is to acknowledge, at the least, media censorship as the rule as opposed to the exception.[36] But how does the rule of capital normalize itself, making anonymous its mechanisms of control? One partial answer is through the saturation and repetition of a one-dimensional worldview that poses as a totality. This strategy has the ironic effect of fracturing social reality and fostering a dislocated sensibility, just as it obfuscates the specific ideological structures out of which the representations are born.

The authority of capital to condition our freedom is, in part, concealed by a concerted appeal to individuality and difference. "In the name of 'freedom,'" writes Fromm, "life loses all structure."[37] Thus, it would not overstate the case to say that making linkages between the individual and the structures in which that individual has come to know her- or himself *as an individual* is a pedagogical imperative. Contrary to neoliberal dogma, to reconstitute a "structuralized picture of the world" is to enhance our individuality and creative capacities, not to diminish them.[38] This is so because we only know ourselves through our relationships to each other. In turn, our relationships to each other function, in part, as an affect of the structural realities in which they exist. This is not to say that our relationships do not then have an effect on the structures themselves. But the power of social structures to construct identities is, in the end, more forceful than an individual's ability to transform social structures. By drawing attention to the structures that inform the postmodern aesthetic, we are one step closer to transforming those structures through *collective action* rather than individual effort. Solidarity provokes a sense of security as opposed to the alienation and anomie that an investment in the "individual self" often exacerbates because it locates individuals in relation to each other and the physical world. Assuredly, one of democratic capitalism's greatest tricks is to mask its hegemony through the seductive guise of commodified difference and individuality, a trick that has decimated community and democratic life in exchange for the market and glory of hyperindividualism.

The dominant media's representation of the bombings of the World Trade Towers and the subsequent call by the U.S. government for "patriotic" consensus illustrates this hegemonic process. Generally speaking, we are compelled to consent and, in so doing, are encouraged to demonize and criminalize the authority of dissent. In this context, dissent is no longer a principle of democracy and a free society. Rather, it comes to signify an "anti-American" (read: antihuman) attitude and a counterpoint to unity. Through the imposition of unity, we are supposed to ignore the pervasive disunity of power in the United States and around the world, and fighting a "common" enemy replaces the project of addressing the concerns of the least advantaged.[39] Interestingly, the best advantaged are often designated as our common enemy. This hegemonic process manufactures a common sense about power and nation by constructing dissent and dissenters as a potential threat to national security. In a disturbing dichotomy articulated by the Bush administration that states that you are either with us or against us, political dissention and terrorism come to occupy the same *discursive* location. In other words, democratic principles have been replaced by totalitarian ideals, in which subversion is no longer understood as that which makes democratic life, at one and the same time, both difficult and viable. Rather, it is to be criminalized and demonized in the name of freedom. Political philosopher Cornelius Castoriadis calls this conception of freedom "degraded" because it presupposes the individual as both a threat to dominant power as well as its potential victim.[40] In either case, "power (and even of society) [is understood as a] necessary evil."[41]

🌐 Pedagogical Challenges in Troubling Times

Troubling our capacities as teachers and political workers to authorize a politically critical social imaginary, our present neoliberal condition promotes an erosion of public space and the rapid privatization of public institutions, exacerbates a tangible sense of despair and cynicism, exiles private troubles beyond the domain of public concerns, and effectively dismantles our social autonomy and the democratic guarantees that it implies. Technologically advanced modes of surveillance, such as Internet probes, hidden cameras on public streets, and satellites that silently and invisibly witness the movements of daily life, intervene unmolested as a consequence of the privatization and commodification of public life, which, as Stanley Aronowitz argues, follows from the same "principle of atomization" that guided the Nazi's organization of the masses both in production and civil society.[42] Consequently, these molestations upon civil society have become normalized as the rule of capital's subordination of the rule of law becomes a matter of common sense.

The irony is that while conservatives and liberals advocate for individualism, the free market, and smaller government as a way to ensure privacy and individual freedom, we have a diminishing sense of privacy, as well as less authority to resist capital's incursions. Unlike George Orwell's infamous portrayal of government incursions into private life in his book *1984*, we struggle for autonomy under the atomizing gaze of corporate power, which is always on the lookout for more "efficient" ways to accumulate capital. Only through public involvement, the expansion of the public sphere, and a reaffirmation of our common concerns are our individual rights, our ability to fight for particular concerns, and our social autonomy guaranteed. Interestingly, the inverse is not true.

A concentration on individualism under the guise of autonomy, minus the social referent of equitable power sharing, leads not to the need for publicly oriented discourses and practices, but instead informs a politics of individuality outside the sphere of social responsibility. The autonomy of capital accumulation, in this instance, becomes the snake eating its own tail. Sooner or later, freedom in the name of capitalistic individuality, minus the social referent of equitable power sharing, will eliminate vital forms of autonomy and freedom. In this scenario, modern capitalism appears more like fascism, when, as Aronowitz quoting Marcuse writes, fascism is the "consummation of competitive individualism. [As such] the regime releases all those forces of brutal self-interest which the democratic countries have tried to curb and tried to combine with the interest of freedom. Social groups are replaced by the crowd."[43]

The crowd then becomes an object to control. It must be disciplined and restrained, or it will rage out of control. Social groups, on the other hand, demand the rights and necessary guarantees to participate in social and political life. We need to look no further than the recent World Economic Forum in New York City to see how dominant power represented dissenting social groups and thereby transformed them into a riotous crowd needing to be controlled. Once social groups are transformed in the public consciousness and become a crowd that threatens the power/knowledge of dominant institutions, the autonomous project becomes a threat to those in power. This process is characterized not only by a lack of civic agency, but also by a disincentive towards social autonomy. Dependencies get created through an appeal to power's ability to "know" what is right, what social and political pursuits are worth taking, and what is up for contestation and change. In the face of this heteronomic power, dissent is no longer a principle of a viable democratic project; rather, it is a threat.

✿ Conclusion:
Activism as Pedagogical Praxis

In order to confront the increasingly entrenched ideological force of atomization, I will briefly recommend several curricular projects that I believe can, at least, make hope concrete and authority pedagogical. In practical and pedagogical terms, an "activist" curriculum could take any number of forms. For example, students could be introduced to the history of insurgent struggles and then asked to rearticulate those struggles in contemporary terms. Students might be asked to do an analysis of power as it exists in the schools, and then to research different kinds of power-shifting strategies. Students might be encouraged to research different coalitions that are struggling to bring about structural change. They could be educated in the practices of civil disobedience, understanding the risks and benefits of such action. Students might learn to identify allies so that they can form collective and unified power blocs in the schools that they will work in. They could be educated in the practices of public address, so that they will feel comfortable addressing large audiences about contentious issues. Students might be educated to defend their own progressive practices in historical and democratic terms and to think out strategically their implications in political terms. Students could be educated in legal policy and citizenship. They might be taught about the union and its role in history generally and its role in education specifically. They might be educated in the practices of unionization and democratic relations. Obviously, I could go on.

The point, finally, is to develop a socially and politically engaged pedagogy, one that not only works from a progressive methodological position, but one that invests in a radical curriculum driven by a theoretically defensible project. By making the fatalism of neoliberalism—with its penchant for atomization and hyperindividualistic capitalism—unconvincing, it is possible to initiate both a psychological and socioeconomic transformation, two constituent dimensions in the human struggle *toward* freedom.

Paulo Freire, as secretary of education, did this is concrete ways in São Paulo. His work as secretary brings attention not only to the practical nature of his theoretical work, but raises a number of important questions about the role of the intellectual in a leadership position, structural transformation, curricular development, and the democratization of officially sanctioned power. It is these issues that the following chapter explores.

chapter four

Secretary Paulo Freire and the Democratization of Power

Toward a Theory of Transformative Leadership

Introduction

Within critical circles of education, engaging the *possibilities* of pedagogical and political leadership often falls through the cracks of conversation because the idea of leadership carries with it legacies of patriarchy, "governmentality," hierarchal administrative practices, authoritarianism, and domination—all things that critical educators generally want to avoid or change.[1] Correctly suspicious of the legacies of oppressive power that leaders often impose upon those that they lead, critical educators have been in a bind to figure out how to instigate the institutional and ideological transformations that they advocate for, without also developing a theory of leadership that moves beyond the problematic legacies of the past.

Antonio Gramsci's theory of hegemony—not so much a theory of domination as of the manufacturing of common sense—offers a way to break into the myth of leadership as always already tied to practices of domination.[2] His theory leads him to reason that "the formation of the collective will and the exercise of political leadership depends on the very existence of intellectual and moral leadership."[3] His complex accounting of leadership's *necessary* relationship to the pedagogic and hegemonic constitute an important contribution to a theory of leadership by understanding that leadership is not only an element in the pedagogical project of forming a consensus of common sense, but also is an important dimension of oppositional work. That is, leadership can provide a productive force for *breaking into* dominant formations of common sense. His ideas concerning the link between leadership and hegemony provide an important theoretical referent for developing a theory of transformative leadership.

Transformative leadership is an exercise of power and authority that begins with questions of justice, democracy, and the dialectic between individual accountability and social responsibility. Paulo Freire's educational administration in São Paulo, Brazil, from 1989 until May 27, 1991, offers a concrete example of the risks and possibilities inherent in adopting transformative strategies of leadership. In this chapter, I discuss the responsibility of transformative leadership to instigate structural transformations at the material level that reflect a new hegemony, in addition to the ideological work that is done at the pedagogical level. In truth, these things must happen simultaneously, and performing one without the other fails to complete the transformative gesture. I conclude by discussing the social, pedagogical, and political strategies of transformative pedagogical leadership, working loosely within Henry Giroux's critical theory of pedagogy and politics, summarily described as the intersection of culture, pedagogy, and power with civic responsibility and radical democratic struggle.[4]

◉ Paulo Freire and the Politics of Transformative Praxis

Freire's stint as secretary of education was undergirded by his educational philosophy, which formed the backbone of his administration. His ideas are markedly different from those of many who write and practice "critical" pedagogy in that his contributions are not strictly "theoretical" or methodological additions to the existing work that links pedagogy and politics to power and knowledge. Rather, his ideas taken as a whole present, as Stanley Aronowitz states in his introduction to *Pedagogy of Freedom*, conceptual principles for mapping a new educational project, as well as what it might mean to live a radicalized life.[5]

In brief, Freire's philosophy of education, as discussed in his many books, rests on the belief that autonomy is a condition arising from the ethical and responsible engagement with decision making; that we are "unfinished" in our development as human beings; that conscientization—the development of a critical consciousness—is a necessary condition of freedom; that curiosity, both ontological and epistemological, is the keystone of the educational process and the vocation of the human condition; that hope must be understood as a weapon against the fatalism of neoliberal ideologues; that we are conditioned and not determined; that we must not reify knowledge, but critique it; and that an ethics of respect, solidarity, and authority must inform all critical practices of pedagogical intervention. These philosophical concerns root the educational process in the radical democratic sphere, while offering routes—theoretical and practical—toward a political, social, individual, and spiritual horizon not yet known. His philosophy of education cannot and should not be separated from what it means to live as powerful, disciplined, and free individuals, who are ethical because of our "capacity to 'spiritualize' the world, to make it either beautiful or ugly."[6]

Freire's radical principles of unfinishedness, ethics, conscientization, and hope are extremely dangerous to neoliberal ideologues who advocate the end of history, make a claim of determination against that which is only conditioned, and understand ethics only in as far as they function to maintain the domination of corporate ideology and the rule of capital.[7] The major transnational forces that continue to "teach" top-down capitalism and neoliberalism as the only way to evolve as a global community contradict his philosophical principles of freedom, power, individuality, and success not because they do not include these ideas, but because they are given meaning and influence from within the logic of the market. Freire, by contrast, situates these ideals within the spheres of democratic authority, social justice, and political action.

Aronowitz notes that Freire's investment in radical democratic principles, such as "democracy from below," in the face of his understanding of the failures of revolutionary regimes situates him as a strategist of pedagogical and structural transformation.[8] These skills, along with the capacity to limit his personal power through democratic processes, make his work as secretary of education in São Paulo, Brazil, so important to consider in developing a theory of transformative leadership. In the context of "democratic revolution," structural transformations, the limitations and constraints of institutional authority, and the authority of transformative leadership to plant the seeds of personal and collective emancipation, Freire's work in São Paulo offers a geography of leadership within the terrain of democratic struggle.

Freire's administration was responsible for more than 691 schools with 710,000 students and 39,614 employees, and ended in 1993, although his appointment as secretary ended in 1991[9]: it was a monumental responsibility, to say the least. Adding to the pressure was the fact that Freire now had the opportunity to "put into practice" all the "theoretical" ideas concerning pedagogy and politics that he had written about so prolifically over the years. Moreover, Freire's move into a position of power—institutional power—not only infused his words with a certain kind of authority, but brought into relief the political tension between authority and freedom, articulated clearly by Hannah Arendt when she states that authority "implies an obedience in which [sic] men retain their freedom."[10]

As an exiled radical, Freire benefited from the kind of insight that Edward Said has argued comes from the conditions of exile; that is, Freire "sees things not just how they are, but as they have come to be that way."[11] Transformative leadership, on the other hand, must have one foot in the dominant structures of power and authority, and as such become "willing" subjects of dominant ideological and historical conditions. As a force for transformation, Freire had to get inside the operations and apparatuses of administrative power. So what happens when the exiled intellectual is invited back to his place of origin? Does he lose the edge that Said argues is necessary for oppositional or critical work? Does he become an accommodating intellectual, consumed by feelings of gratitude that he was let back in? Do the forces of governmentality play on the oppositional agent, transforming his visions into a blurry acceptance of what is? Does he become a commissar for the status quo? Is there a way to maintain a "consciousness of exile," after one has physically returned into the folds of the dominant culture? That is, is there a way to combat the seduction of official power and knowledge, maintain a critical stance, and disrupt the hegemony of dominant cultural formations when one is partially inside the circle of established power?

In Freire's case, the formation of the administration that he adopted needed a significant overhaul if his philosophical ideas were to have any chance of implementation. He recognized that the social formations that he now occupied as secretary came with a sedimented history built on the authoritarian regimes that came before him. Therefore, he had to "democratize" his power as a first step in transforming the structural formations of the schools. This move, rooted in both the theoretical concern for the relationship between knowledge and power and the practical concern of needing and wanting to involve all branches of the educational workforce, including parents and students in the administration and dissemination of school policy, began a process of transformation that cut through the existing curriculum and the political ideology of the teachers and bureaucrats.[12]

He initiated the transformative process by including "principals, coordinators, supervisors, teachers, janitors, cooks, students, parents, and community leaders [because] one does not change the 'face' of schools through the central office."[13] His commitment to the democratization of power moved his administration to close the space between the leadership and those that it led by "diminishing the distance" between what is said and what is done.[14] As such, his administration advocated for popular public schooling, a concept of education that "arises from political and social analysis of living conditions of the poor and aims at engaging these groups in individual and collective processes of critical awareness and action."[15]

Part of the development of popular public education, in addition to the content of schooling, was the management of the institution itself. As such "autonomy in planning, management, and control of school operations" offered a strong critique of top-down management models and got at the heart of what it means to be a transformative leader. As a transformative leader, Freire had to make sure he was not simply imposing his own ideological agenda on the community, but rather was instigating an alternative democratic project that was rooted in the ideals of liberty and freedom. To this end, he established grassroots organizations within the schools so that the seeds of freedom and democratic unity that his administration planted would not be so easily washed away when power changed hands. Part of the grassroots effort was to "transform values, attitudes, norms, and even organizational culture"[16] by incorporating what was to be called the "Inter Project" into the curricular maps of teachers and administrators.

The Inter Project was an "interdisciplinary curriculum via the generative theme" that attempted to make the learning and teaching process an extension of the social, cultural, and political activities of daily life. It hoped to formalize a major tenet of critical pedagogy that states the importance of experience in the development of pedagogical strategies. Of course, the acceptance of this theoretical assumption was not without conflict. Some teachers and administrators were extremely resistant to this notion, understanding that it took their normal top-down power away, leaving them at the discretion of a more democratized body of influence. This was an essential difficulty, one that Freire and his administration never fully resolved.[17]

Nonetheless, his stint as secretary offers some interesting examples of the intersection of theory and practice in the service of a more democratized educational model of schooling. His administration formalized the notion of transformative power by closing the gap between the leaders and the led, ostensibly altering the structural makeup of São Paulo's educational system. For Freire, transforming the "face" of schooling meant material concerns such as fixing the physical structures of the school buildings themselves, as well as more ideological concerns such as the transformation of authoritarian social and political formations in which the notions of autonomy and democracy were not only foreign, but impossible even to introduce. This is why as Freire states

> [W]e started by making an administrative reform so that the Secretariat could work in a different way. With administrative structures that only made authoritarian power viable, it was impossible to develop a democratic administration that was in favor of school autonomy and recognized that being public the school also belonged to the classes.[18]

This is a great example of what it means to be a transformative leader; that is, by reorganizing the political spaces of power and developing the material structures, Freire was able to rearticulate the political power of the secretariat so that it reflected the possibilities embedded within his critical pedagogy. Without these (de)(re)articulations, the transformative authority of the secretariat would have been overwhelmed by existing social formations that articulated with authoritarian structures of government. As Freire explains, "Without the transformation of these structures, there was no way to think about community or popular participation. Democracy demands structures that democratize, not structures that inhabit the participatory presence of civil society in the command of *res*-public."[19] Additionally, Freire could be said to have maintained a "consciousness of exile," giving him a critical sensitivity to oppression and injustice regardless of where he might be. From within the borders of government, Freire's work as secretariat formalized the relationship between transformative consciousness and structural transformation. Not a subject of governmentality, but rather its opponent, Freire illustrates how transformative leadership bridges the gap between freedom and authority, while reaching through what is on its way toward what could be.

◉ Transformation of Social Formations and Social Formations of Transformation

As Freire's administration and position as secretariat suggests, leadership's authority and power become transformative when they are directed in the service of emancipating systemically entrenched attitudes, behaviors, and ideas, as well as instigating structural transformations at the material level. This means that under the authority of transformative leadership, structures of government, education, business, and health care become the objects of democratic intervention and innovation. Transformative leadership must be intent on "formalizing" its innovations and interventions by establishing democratized structures that reflect its leadership.

For transformative leadership this presents a number of challenging concerns. As actors inside dominant structures, transformative leaders must always make problematic the institutional power they wield. Of course, part of their power comes from the institution itself, but as my phrase "consciousness of exile" is intended to suggest, this does not automatically necessitate the seduction and cooption of critical perspectives. Many disagree.[20] Borrowing from Foucault's discussions of "governmentality," some progressives, like Ian Hunter and Elizabeth Ellsworth in the context of schooling, have argued that any association with dominant social formations, like public schools and government, automatically inoculates opposition, making it impossible for any "radical" work to be done in those sites. Their position effectively closes down all sites of formative power to oppositional pedagogies and political practices, reasoning that all opposition when placed in dominant ideological spheres gets coopted by the dominant power structure. As Giroux correctly argues, "Self-reflexive dialogue drops out of [this] argument, as does the possibility of teachers and students to become critical of the very institutional forms, academic relations, and disciplinary knowledges and regulations that constitute the complex and varied spaces of schooling."[21] From this perspective, the notion of transformation becomes impossible, while the only available politics are the extremes of revolution on one side or domination on the other.

Against this discourse, there are many examples of effective oppositional power that takes place from within dominant social formations, from radical teaching practices that bring about a greater sense of awareness about the oppressive conditions of both the scholastic and the vernacular worlds, to student organizations that use civil disobedience and other means to disrupt the power structures of injustice and inequity, such as the recent nationwide sit-ins and rallies against sweatshop labor. Students protesting their university's likely union with Sodexho-Marriot, which is not only "the largest campus dining hall management company in the world," but also "a 17 percent share holder in the Corrections Corporation of America," making them "the largest investor in the U.S. private prison industry,"[22] provides another example of resistance within the borders of dominant institutions. As such, it would be wrong to argue that opposition within the borders of dominant power is impossible. On the other hand, it would be accurate to suggest that oppositional and resistance movements and pedagogies are struggling for survival in this ideologically conservative time.

Although these examples do not point directly to *structural* transformations, we need to be aware that structural and ideological transformations take time. Because the relationship between democratic opposition and structural transformation is not positivistic, either to evaluate the effectiveness of opposition that takes place inside the walls of dominant ideological structures based on the immediacy of *observable* change on the one hand, or to discount that opposition completely because it is located within dominant formations on the other, is to ignore the subtle effects of transformative politics. A romanticized notion of revolution in which "revolutionaries" institute sweeping structural changes to existing ideological formations, while deposing the accommodating intellectuals and administrators of the dominant regime, often drives this type of positivistic critique. The limitations of this critique for a politics of democratic transformation can be characterized in two distinct ways. First, "revolution" is never a democratic process, and even when something like a "democratic revolution" is discussed, "revolution" takes on a very different hue. In this context, revolution does not connote an antidemocratic process; rather, it connotes a revitalization of human agency and political citizenship. Second, "the direct exercise of popular power is short-lived, whether it succeeds in its immediate goals or not. . . . Direct popular power cannot itself be institutionalized."[23] As such, democracy is not a movement of popular power, in the manner that it used here[24]; nor would it want to be. Rather, it is an institutionally sanctioned set of practices and methods that push society toward the horizon of liberty and equality.[25] In short, the critique leveled against democratic transformation, as a practice or method, on the basis of "governmentality" fails on the grounds that it understands

institutional power and human agency in one-dimensional terms.[26] As a consequence, the extremes of revolution on one hand and facilitation or accommodation
to power on the other obscure the dynamic of democratic struggle as a means
toward lasting structural transformation within both the political and cultural
domains of public and private life.

Political struggle within a democratic context signifies an institutionalized
condition of liberty, equality, and freedom, whereas revolutionary actions signify the
overthrow of existing authority. Revolutionary transformations often lack an ethical component, leaving them open to dictatorial takeovers, professionalism, and
demagoguery amid the confusion that arises in between regimes.[27] Radical democratic struggle, on the other hand, rests on the imperative of liberty and equality,
offering transformative agents (relatively) stable ground on which to develop new
economic, legislative, and social policies. Of course, the ultimate paradox in democratic theory is that through the practice of democracy, democracy itself can be disbanded. "There is indeed a constant danger in a democratic system," writes John
Keane, "that party competition, freedom of association, the rule of law and other
democratic procedures will be used to defeat democracy."[28] This is why parliament
must have the power to check undemocratic forces within democratic ranks. But the
"paradox" is not a reason to abandon democracy; nor is democracy's slow swagger
a reason for its dismissal as a viable means of social transformation. Rather, these
elements demand a more rigorous engagement with democracy through the "radicalization" of democratic and nondemocratic formations.[29] In short, it is a call for
a kind of democratic politics driven by an ethics of social justice.

The critics of democratic transformation (after all, that is where the deployment
of "governmentality" takes us in the twenty-first century) need to consider that the
destruction, creation, and transformation of social formations take time, tradition,
power/knowledge, organization, discipline, and authority to establish new kinds of
common sense, or, in other words, counterhegemonic ideas about the world. A society's shared common sense is one of the most solidifying elements in the maintenance of its traditions, norms, and memories.[30] When common sense is challenged
and changed, society also changes. These changes take place at both the macro and
micro levels. In the context of transformative leadership and structural transformation, understanding the collision between common sense and oppositional ideas is
one key to rearticulating political trajectories and transforming the social formations
that give structure to our thoughts, hopes, and imaginations. When acts of rebellion, opposition, and activism are discounted—either because they did not immediately transform social formations and discursive regimes, or because they were
partially obscured by the constraints of the institution that they were fighting—we
do a great disservice to the complexity of social change and the power that memories of subversion have in guiding oppositional and even revolutionary practices.

By forgetting acts of resistance, we not only devalue the work of activists, but we erase some of the most poignant moments in the history of resistance and rebellion. John Brenkman, writing about Raymond Williams's intense interest in memories of uprising, says that "such historical moments are filled with meanings without which our own search for social justice would be lost."[31] Some of the elements of meaning that are important in such historical excavations refer to the complex and often painfully slow processes of democratic structural transformation. In practical terms, this means that *creating* "forms of democratic participation," more than the simple reformation of democratic institutions or encouraging democratic participation, must be the sine qua non of transformative leadership.[32] Granted, actions of *innovation, reformation,* and *participation* present a vital map of radical democratic participation, but in the end, the *creation* of new democratic formations must be one of the main responsibilities of transformative leadership's authority and power.

⚓ Strategies and Effects of Transformative Leadership

As I have been discussing it, transformative leadership—pedagogical, political, ethical, and spiritual—rearticulates a conception of leadership beyond paradigms of oppression, domination, repression, and suppression; beyond rigid hierarchal models of power and management; and with more complexity than a recipe of characteristics that make for an appealing person who is able to attract attention and "lead" people.[33] Although these are all aspects of contemporary conceptions of leadership, rearticulating leadership in terms of strategy, function, and effect—ethical, political, social, cultural, and pedagogical—allows teachers and other political workers to direct their authority and power productively, self-reflexively, and critically by opening up a space of "continuous reenactment"[34] that offers a "provisional" place to deploy pedagogical strategies of social engagement and transformation, while remaining critical of the function of leadership and its effects.

My thoughts about transformative leadership as a social and political category build upon and work within a Girouxian critical theory of education, politics, pedagogy, ethics, and power in four significant ways: (1) leadership is developed within the political rubric of democratic freedom and action; (2) a politics of the "vernacular" is positioned as both a linguistic, performative, and pedagogical strategy of engagement and transformation; (3) personal accountability and social responsibility are conceived as ethical imperatives; and (4) pedagogical experimentation and creative production are deployed in an effort to link the ideas of politics and "spirit," which are commonly regarded as separate.

First, for transformative leadership to make any sense, it must be understood within the context of democratic thought. In this context, leaders are led, just as those who are led are leaders. This relationship, although confusing at first, upsets traditional conceptions of leadership in that it understands the relationship between the leaders and the led dialectically as opposed to hierarchically. Within the field of critical education, Freire suggests an axiom that captures this kind of relationship, although his thoughts describe the relationship between learning and teaching: "Whoever teaches learns in the act of teaching, and whoever learns teaches in the act of learning."[35] In the same way, transformative leaders lead by and through the leadership of those that they lead. This conception of leadership runs against the grain of top-down models of leadership as well as more progressive, "egalitarian" models, in which there are no "leaders" and everyone occupies a space of unreconcilable "difference," leading consequently to a politics and pedagogy of immediacy, minus a political vision.

A fundamental function of transformative leadership must be to ask itself questions such as, Opportunity for what? Schooling for what? Power for what? The answers to these questions help delineate a project and therefore a horizon of possibility. Make no mistake, these questions are almost always being asked and then answered by the neoliberal and socially conservative right wing. As such, they have articulated a project dominated by the rule of capital, the logic of the market, and the morality of Christian fundamentalism. Education's role in the context of their project should be to provide workers who can perform in the New Economy and citizens restrained not by an obligation to democratic values and secular models of governance, but by an obligation to a hollow moralism, illustrated so powerfully when John Ashcroft's overt homophobia and racism were defended on individualized moral grounds. Critical educators who distance themselves from the responsibilities of leadership miss the opportunity to confront such hypocrisy. If they were to contextualize their notions of pedagogy politically, instead of their politics pedagogically, they would find it necessary to formulate a project that confronted the Right's domination of nothing less than the country's political and social imagination. In this sense, transformative leadership, to be transformative, must confront more than just what is, and work toward creating an alternative political and social imagination that does not rest solely on the rule of capital or the hollow moralism of neoconservatives, but is rooted in radical democratic struggle.

Transformative leadership also troubles the liberal critique of leadership as patriarchal and power as domination on the grounds that freedom needs always to be understood, in some sense, in relation to political action.[36] Political action exists as an organizing force, instilling the notion of liberation with freedom, that is, the organization of private and public life that reaches toward the horizon of equitable and just economic and social conditions through democratic participation. As

Arendt argues,

> Freedom needed, in addition to mere liberation, the company of other [people] who were in the same state, and it needed a common public space to meet them—a politically organized world, in other words, into which each of the free [persons] could insert himself [or herself] by word and deed.[37]

As a functionary of this kind of freedom, transformative leadership is a vital social category in the development of a theory of radical pedagogy because it gives democratic force and direction to the terms, conditions, purpose, and future of teaching.

Second, for the political to have meaning as a representation of democratic life, for the notions of freedom and liberation to become meaningful in the political and pedagogical sense, the transformative leader must embrace what I call a politics and pedagogy of the vernacular, that is, a language and praxis of social responsibility and personal accountability that gets articulated through the public and private (dis)(re)organization and (de)(re)articulation of daily life. It is in part a response to the negative effects that "the insulation of the social theoretical 'discourse' from the language of the everyday" has had on separating intellectual work from public concerns.[38] Transformative leadership uses the vernacular to bridge the private and the public in a way that undercuts the contemporary trend to publicly display "private agonies and anxieties which, however, do not turn into public issues."[39] It transforms public concerns into personal responsibilities on one hand and private troubles into public concerns on the other. Moreover, it is an attempt to draw attention to the need to translate what are often inaccessible, but important, discourses instead of ignoring them or mobilizing against them simply because of their difficulty.

By utilizing the vernacular, in the simplest sense, transformative leadership makes itself understood across "discursive" borders; that is, it "speaks" in multiple discourses to multiple audiences. This seems like such an obvious imperative for democratic leadership. But leadership is often bamboozled by its own inability to speak to those whom it most wants to lead. From inaccessible academics and the drone of political candidates who speak at an eighth grade level, to leaders who confuse speaking simply with simplistic speaking, those who miss the vernacular as the discourse of transformative leadership fall to the wayside, drowning in their own incoherence.[40] Dr. Martin Luther King Jr., Malcolm X, Jesse Jackson, Michael Moore, Greg Palast, and Bob Dylan, to name only a few, embrace(d) the vernacular with great success. Their work reaches into the material of life—experience, power, yearning, passion, struggle, suffering, hope, joy, love; these are the things that, when engaged in the vernacular, make people move, reflect, dance, cry, sing, rage; these are the building blocks of the political as well as the pedagogical; *this is the grammar of daily life*; this is the space and place where knowledge becomes meaningful, possible, transformative, historical, and powerful. It is absolutely true, as

Henry Giroux and Roger Simon have argued, that it is not enough simply to have voice; the conditions to be heard must be established.[41] It is equally true that when the conditions to speak and be heard have been established, those who are speaking must be understood, or more accurately, make themselves understood and take responsibility for what they say. This is the responsibility of transformative leadership; it implies the need to link not only the private and public, but also the empirical and theoretical, the everyday and the future, the imaginative and the real, the past and the forgotten, history and tradition, power and knowledge, and learning and life.

But we must not understand a pedagogy and politics of the vernacular simply as a linguistic function as the term *discourse* used above implies. The vernacular is also a tool of the performative. It must be understood as a link between the cerebral and the corporeal. To work within the vernacular is to reestablish the body as a site of social connection and political contestation, as a place of intimate, interdependent relations. We interact, move against one another, smell perfume and cologne. Energies pass among and through us collectively, organizing and reorganizing the social landscape, and this is part of transformative leadership.

It is being able to tap into the power of that messy grinding of bodies in the delineated space of social struggle: the urbanity of iron and glass shooting upward, making a facile gesture to the endless expanse of heaven, cool shadows stretching west, then east; the cramped and jagged concrete space of ghettoized America, from Los Angeles to New York, stained with the blood of young brown and black men as poverty paces up and down, wearing the memories of history and pleasure thin—persistently dismantling dreams and possibilities with the rusting tools of repression and domination; the rural space of agribusiness, combines grazing, like corporate behemoths on public life, against the uninterrupted horizon of grain, straight lines cut away the messiness of farm life; and the suburban space of minimansions, strip malls, gourmet coffee, elegantly prepared to-go-food in plastic containers, and chrome bathroom and kitchen accessories, resonating with the emptiness of private life, with the commodification of social values—providing ample evidence of Ernst Bloch's provocative insight into capitalism's "swindle of fulfillment."[42] This is the realm where the pedagogical conjoins with freedom and authority; it is where we not only learn ourselves socially, where we locate (or do not locate) ourselves systemically and institutionally, but also where we begin to understand ourselves individually, as autonomous social beings trying to discern our capabilities amongst a heap of discarded promises.

It can be said, truthfully enough, that freedom and authority converge metaphorically in the space of the subway; the autonomy of all and sociality of each is no more apparent than in the move of bodies, the bustle of suits and high-heeled shoes, the sheen of silk and shock of pink Lycra, combat boots threatening

patent leather, torn stockings and sweat-stained arm pits, racing somewhere, probably late, while the patter of wealthy feet move above ground, out of sight, although,
generally, not out of mind. Ride a subway in New York City at rush hour from Union
Square in Manhattan to Atlantic Avenue in Brooklyn, and the energy concretizes
the self-in-relation, individuality as the social; giant iron organisms, rushing head-
long over bridges, through the darkness of tunnels that only rats, spiders, and the
homeless dare (or are dared) to navigate, moving along tracks that the subway car
wants to jump, freedom from the grid-locked traffic on Flatbush Avenue, impris-
oned by capital's brutal delineations. But outside and up the urine-splattered stairs,
you wander up Union Street, feeling the late afternoon light cheat the edges of your
dark sunglasses. The air feels cool, and there seems to be no one, anywhere. This is
the vernacular also. It is the material of transformative leadership; the responsibility of its authority and power.

Third, transformative leadership must link the notions of personal accountability and social responsibility by making more than a gesture to democratic ideals.
Following Chantel Mouffe's notion of equivalences, transformative leadership must
place democratic *relations* at the center of its social and pedagogical project.[43] By
doing so, social responsibility—democratic responsibility—gets pulled through a
notion of personal accountability, making the latter a condition of the former.
Teachers as transformative leaders can begin this process in the classroom by taking a position on a socially relevant subject. Taking a position does not automatically situate her/him in a position of domination or close off the possibility for a
reenactment of the position given a new set of determinants. Instead, it makes him
or her accountable to the partiality of his or her ideas and subsequent actions that
the position suggests. Pedagogically, it offers both the students and teacher a way
to "perform" the dialectic between personal accountability and social responsibility by offering up a topic that will be private for some and public for others. This
strategy recognizes the classroom as a site of struggle in which the transformative
teacher helps organize and connect personal opinions, experiences, and concerns to
larger contexts on one hand, while rearticulating the larger contexts back into private concerns on the other. This type of strategy offers an object for critique while
also presenting an argument for a particular point of view that must be rooted in a
human ethic that is not afraid to condemn oppression, violence, and brutality in all
their forms.

From this human ethic, the transformative leader creates the conditions of her
or his classroom around certain ethically defensible criteria. For example, slavery as
a topic for discussion would not automatically necessitate the teacher including a
defense of its "economic benefits" because the ownership of one person by another person would not be a consideration within the ethical parameters of democratic education. This does not mean that the ideology of racism and how it functions

historically as both an exclusionary force and as a modern principle of colonization should not be taken up.[44] It means that transformative pedagogical leadership is antiracist, antisexist, antihomophobic, and responsive to class exploitation. These positions should be understood as ethically defensible on democratic grounds, and it is the responsibility of transformative leadership's authority to make this known both in and outside of class. This kind of leadership, rather than closing down or censoring discussion, allows for the possibility of freedom through the organization of the social space. For example, it combats the censoring effects of standardized curriculum, testing, and pedagogy by opening up the educational sphere to agonistic struggles, socially responsive pedagogies, and contextually relevant curricula.

Fourth, transformative leadership in the classroom is characterized by a willingness for experimentation and creative production. This means, in many senses, being capable of learning enough about history and tradition to begin new projects that learn from the past and are conditioned by tradition, but trapped by neither. It also means being able to reach around and tap into different cultural notions of learning and teaching. Western pedagogues have a lot to learn from traditions, from Shamanism to Taoism, that extend much farther back than Socrates and Plato. Part of making the familiar strange and the strange familiar[45] is engaging different ways other cultures have understood knowledge, power, hope, spirit, and energy.[46] Transformative leaders have a responsibility to themselves and their students not simply to teach against the grain, but to make the pedagogical a holistic principle, that is, to make teaching and learning part of the process of spiritual understanding so that the dichotomy between politics and the spirit(s) of humanity are not thought of separately. Spirit is both a collective and individual phenomenon and, like the political, needs the authority of leadership, that is, seers, shamans, medicine men, teachers, and the like, to help with the organization of social and political space so that, as individuals and a society, we can live to the fullest of our abilities.

This is not a digression into New Ageism, but rather an acknowledgment that as humans we are, as Freire has commented, in a "permanent process of searching" and "our being in the world is far more that just 'being' . . . it is a 'presence . . . that is relational to the world and to others."[47] In light of this, transformative leadership advocates for what I have termed a pedagogical culture of "concrete dreaming" and "transcendental praxis." Concrete dreaming occurs within the spaces of oppositional cultural spheres. It is a moment of possibility that stays fully aware of the struggles and realities of the present moment. It involves a dimension of "escape"—not *from*, but *toward*. It remains an aspect of the political by representing a dimension of "knowing" and "being" not yet known.

By using the phrase "transcendental praxis," I hope to suggest a reflective and active state of intense spiritual, emotional, and "political" discovery. It is a departure, of sorts, from what is easily accessed, implying a state of being that reflects a moment of creative intensity; that is, a state of awareness in which we are able to imagine, without constraint, our relationship in and with the world, while going beyond it. It works loosely within the logic of creativity, which depends upon moments of chaos through the authority of freedom. As such, "transcendental praxis" suggests a relationship to a kind of power that is wholly "other." Within the sphere of culture and imagination, it is the link between this "otherness" and reality that provides a trajectory for the political as it has yet to be known.[48]

In popular culture, this notion was recently represented in the movie *Shine* about the concert pianist David Helfgott. During a competition at the Royal Academy of Music, Helfgott experienced a moment in which he was both connected and disconnected from his playing. This moment of transcendental praxis pushed him beyond what he knew, but allowed him to perform, in concrete form, more brilliantly than he had ever performed before. The important aspect of transcendental praxis is how it suggests both a departure and engagement with a specific object simultaneously. Through this congruous, albeit paradoxical moment, the student should find an intense clarity to his thoughts and actions; the clarity and intensity of the moment provide material for contemplation and action after the moment has passed. As such, transcendental praxis is momentary, although the rippling effect of its occurrence suggests a process—a pedagogical process—that is not easily forgotten or discarded. In this way, it must be thought of as part of the process of Freire's well-worn notion of *conscientization*, or critical consciousness.

Lastly, teachers as transformative leaders need to insert an ethical as well as a political discourse back into the language of education, confront the discourse of reactionary ideologues, and make visible to students and others alternative viewpoints, as well as the mechanisms of power and domination that structure the corporate-government complex and the dismantling of democratic institutions. In the university, tenured faculty are poised to play a major role as transformative leaders in higher and secondary education because they are somewhat protected from the kind of unfettered abuse to which nontenured faculty are vulnerable. Tenure must come to mean more than just the "freedom" to publish (or not to publish); it must be used as a political tool in the dismantling of corporate power and the radical democratization of school and everyday life. But more than that, transformative leadership must create linkages between school, home, work, and family. As Mouffe argues, by drawing alliances between different spheres of power and identity, solidarity can become the mechanism within the chain of democratic equivalences that connects different political considerations with common concerns.[49] Additionally, transformative leaders must also play proactive roles in curricular decisions by subverting the legacy of the canon, without instrumentalizing the discourse of schooling. Poised at the crossroads of knowledge and power, transformative leadership must be prepared to traverse the immediate and the teleological with equal aplomb. This is both an impossible goal and a necessary strategy: impossible because pragmatism taken to its illogical conclusion is the enemy of political vision; necessary because the struggle for social justice, the expansion of political agency, and the deepening of democratic relations demands people who are prepared to take risks, form strategic alliances, learn and unlearn their power, and reach beyond a "fear of authority" toward a concrete vision of the world in which oppression, violence, and brutality are transformed by a commitment to equality, liberty, and democratic struggle.

In the following two chapters, I explore, within a pedagogical context, how transformative leadership can function critically in the classroom. Through curricular and methodological development, I illustrate the power and possibility in using authority ethically and rigorously. In the age of neoliberal hegemony, a teacher must be prepared to use his or her authority not only to make the learning process meaningful for students, but to make it part of a larger project that is committed to reclaiming the dream of equality and hope that animated the thoughts and actions of great leaders like Dr. King.

part three

Critical Pedagogies and Literacies for a Neoliberal Age

Beyond Remediation

Ideological Literacies of Learning
in Developmental Classrooms

[R]emedial education is one of the thorniest issues in higher education today. Many students sail through their K–12 education and arrive confidently on campus, only to find that they are academically unprepared. Universities provide costly assistance to these students, only to face internal and external pressure to tighten standards. And parents and community members everywhere are left bewildered: How could the public education system have shortchanged these students so completely in the past, and how can it fail them now?[1]

But, of course, we know perfectly well that people can know how to read, in the sense of decode and engage in word recognition, and even achieve basic comprehension, and still not know how to read to learn.[2]

The illiteracy to which we refer can only be addressed in the context of social movements that wish to make serious social changes. The other model of rapid learning for whole populations is the *ideological* model. In a country lacking the conditions for rapid economic growth or the motivating force to accept a highly militarized educational process as grounds for learning, the only alternative is to argue for literacy on radical foundations.[3]

Introduction

In the neoliberal age, remedial or developmental academic programs generally, and reading/literacy programs specifically, in colleges and universities are on the one hand in high demand, while being threatened on the other by a number of different social and political forces. From the call to privatize remedial services and billing high schools for the cost of remediation for their students who need it,[4] to passing the buck to community colleges and blaming teachers for their students' struggles, remedial education and those whom it serves are under siege. Striving to survive in an academic climate dominated by a discourse of high-stakes testing, standardization, and "excellence," remedial programs have felt the pressure to respond to these demands, regardless of whether or not it is in the best interest of the students, democracy, or transforming society's inequities. In New York City, "Mayor Rudolph Giuliani . . . threatened to withhold millions from the City University system unless steps were taken to privatize remedial education training for incoming students and to hire a private company to review testing standards."[5] Charles B. Reed, chancellor of the California State University system argues, "eliminating the need for remedial education begins not in high school or elementary school, but with the preparation of high-quality classroom teachers. Understanding that the quality of students we receive depends on the quality of teachers we prepare."[6]

The problem with Reed's approach is that it embraces a debilitating contradiction; that is, while he claims to want to better prepare teachers to teach, he embraces the logic of standards and testing, two of the major conditions that prevent teachers from teaching and students from learning. To teach is more than managing prepackaged curricula, overseeing practice tests, and drilling students on material that might or might not have any meaning to their lives. Likewise, to learn is more than rote memorization and the regurgitation of information. Stating the devastating effects of standardized testing, Barbara Miner writes, "It leads to a dumbed-down curriculum that values rote memorization over in-depth thinking, exacerbates inequities for low-income students and students of color, and undermines true accountability among schools, parents, and community."[7] In the face of Miner's research, to subject remedial studies to the logic of standardization and testing is to doubly bind the teaching and learning process within a catch-22. Given that many of the students who need or are placed in remedial classes come from low-income backgrounds and are cultural and linguistic minorities, the ability of remediation to close academic inequities is seriously compromised given the exacerbating effects that standards and testing have on socioeconomic and cultural inequities of power.

In this context, the discourse of "accountability" so prevalent in the conservative view of schooling and evident in Giuliani's and Reed's approaches to remedial education, as well as the ways strategies of remediation are deployed, obfuscate the social, cultural, and economic conditions that have at least as much to do with failing schools and academically struggling students as any other variable.[8] Obviously, both Giuliani and Reed want to intervene into remedial education so as to limit its need. But without acknowledging and acting to palliate the vast inequalities that plague our cities and schools, we will fail to alleviate the need for remediation. As a consequence of this absence in the conservative critique of remediation, the most vulnerable in our society, as well as the most victimized, are made, on some level, responsible for their own "substandard" conditions. As such, the need for remediation (and the monies that it necessitates) is seen as an effect of a personal or cultural failure, as opposed to a systemic failure or a natural outcome of an educational system that is racist, sexist, and class biased.[9] Ignoring, as Alfie Kohn points out, "the very real obstacles [that limit learning and teaching opportunities in schools] such as racism, poverty, fear of crime, low teacher salaries, inadequate facilities, and language barriers"[10] increases the likelihood that those suffering are blamed for their own predicaments. From this perspective, "standards of outcome rather than standards of opportunity"[11] become the register of accountability. In the context of remedial literacy education, this is especially true.[12]

Unfortunately, as more high school students enter college ill prepared to tackle the kinds of literacies they are expected to master, more universities and colleges have offered remedial/developmental reading and writing classes that are guided by the assumption that literacy is a singular skill that can be mastered through methodological proscriptions and high-stakes testing of decontextualized generic texts. This is a mistake. On the contrary, *literacy* is a term that signifies an investment in a complex matrix of language, learning, culture, identity, knowledge/power, and political ideology. At the minimum, then, to be literate means, in James Gee's terms, to develop "control over secondary uses of language."[13] As such, to become literate in the multiple discourses of the academy, students must be introduced to an array of texts and the politics that inform them, while being exposed to the theoretical tools that can help them link these discourses to larger formations of power. Most importantly, literacy in this context would be linked to social action and engagement, making, for example, the "savage inequalities" that Jonathan Kozol speaks about both a text and context to read, engage, and transform.[14] In other words, the conditions that Kohn describes as exacerbating schooling would be taken up as texts to be read, understanding that to be literate, going beyond Gee's definition, is to be able to learn about, engage, and transform the oppressive conditions—social, economic, and cultural—that have exacerbated social inequities and sanctioned ideological illiteracy.

Although advocates of traditional remediation would most likely balk at this approach to literacy, believing it either too rigorous or outside what it means to teach people to read, in what follows I argue, through an interpretation and discursive analysis of my experiences teaching developmental reading, under the direction of the College Assistance Migrant Program (CAMP) at Pennsylvania State University's main campus, and my work with developmental readers at Montclair State University, that this kind of literacy project not only teaches students multiple literacies, but radically intervenes into the debilitating effects that the standardization and testing movements continue to have on economically, culturally, and linguistically marginalized populations. I discuss how remediation can be more—must be more—than phonetic decoding, literal comprehension, and generic engagement with language and written texts. I will also discuss how strategies of critical pedagogy can help break down the boundaries of traditional remediation and the methodologies that support it. Neither a method nor a technique, critical pedagogy provides a theoretical map of power relationships, curricula, and ideology in which to develop culturally and politically responsive practices that encourage ideological literacies of learning and social engagement.

Teachers should always remember and begin with the understanding that students who need remediation are not stupid and have an array of literacies to draw upon that can help them interrogate, interpret, and revise dominating discourses—those same discourses that have often been at the heart of exacerbating retrograde social and economic policies. In CAMP and at Montclair State University, I felt it was my job to learn what these literacies were and how to utilize them in the service of a project of possibility.[15] I created remedial projects that taught *ideological literacies of learning*. These are literacies that prepare students not only to read the word and the world, but give them the tools "to read to learn"[16] and *transform the world*. Those who read to learn to transform are social agents, students and citizens of the word and the world, teaching as they learn and learning as they teach.[17] As such, they act upon the world, transforming it, just as they are transformed themselves.

🦉 Developmental Reading and the Politics of Literacy: Moving beyond Basic Skills

CAMP—a federally funded educational initiative—originated in 1972 to provide students of migrant and seasonal farm workers access to postsecondary education. At Penn State University, CAMP offers its students academic, personal, and financial support. A large part of the academic support comes in the form of two "developmental" reading classes: LLED 05 and LLED 297A. Before I became involved in the CAMP program, these classes were undergirded by an investment in generic language learning, a back-to-basics program that resulted in the students scoring worse on reading tests than before they took the classes. In this context, I was asked to develop a literacy project that did not disrespect students, taught them how to read, and prepared them for a successful university career at Penn State. It should be noted at the outset that from my personal conversations with many CAMP students, the acronym "CAMP" has some unfortunate effects on their sense of themselves as university students. Students who are accepted into CAMP sometimes feel that they are not part of a vibrant intellectual experience, but are rather "going to camp." The association can be demeaning simply because of its name. Moreover, as Donaldo Macedo has pointed out on numerous occasions, the tag "migrant" connotes negative images and is an ideologically loaded word. As an example, he correctly points out that European immigrants are never referred to as "migrants," but are called "settlers."[18]

CAMP students must take LLED 05 in their first semester and LLED 297A in their second semester. Together, I wanted these two courses to offer CAMP students the opportunity to read more effectively across the many different academic disciplines that they would encounter at Penn State. Working on comprehension and critique to interpretation and interrogation, these two courses were designed to prepare CAMP students for the rigorous reading and research schedule that they could expect from a Research I university.

At Montclair State University, students are tested before entering the university as freshmen. Those who do not fair well on the test are required to take READ-053, a course that has traditionally been taught by adjuncts and non-Ph.D. faculty members. Whole-language and phonetic practices have been used, as has the Nelson Denny Test as a measure of students' reading ability. My students are African American, white, Latino, Asian, and Arab. All are from working-class or poor neighborhoods, facts that trouble the widely held belief that schools are providing equal opportunity and access for all students. My approach to these classes diverges considerably from the norm and is rooted in the belief that, as Macedo writes, "We must first read the world—the cultural, social, and political practices that constitute it—before we can make sense of the word-level description of reality."[19] Troubling our efforts to read the world, as I have discussed in previous chapters, is an established antidemocratic ideological system of indoctrination that "teaches" our students in a way that consistently privileges dominant knowledge in an effort to reinforce dominant power. In order to break into this debilitating system of schooling, I introduce students to different academic and social texts, offering strategies for ideological comprehension and interpretation. This is quite different, and more difficult, than reading to memorize or reading to pass a reading test. It suggests that there is a relationship not only between the world and the words that help construct our understanding of it, but also between our relationship to language—written, oral, visual, and technological—and the ideological systems that, in part, structure our ability to participate in a democracy. Students are challenged to engage academic and social texts critically, which means that they learn to situate texts *ideologically* and in terms of race, class, and gender, while they are introduced to a number of different theoretical tools that encourage them to question how these texts link up with the political assumptions of larger social and cultural institutions, such as schools, the workplace, home life, and the media. Reading critically also means being able to discern what these texts teach us about ourselves and the world we live in, while being able to register the implications—social, cultural, political—of their pedagogical lessons. Lastly, students are asked to produce new knowledge in light of the various literacies that they have learned to exercise throughout the year.

Framing both of these programs is a concern with critical inquiry and the responsibilities of citizenship in a public democracy. Critical inquiry is the ability to mediate, interrogate, interpret, intervene, and revise multiple texts. Students educated in the art of critical inquiry are less likely to be victimized by exclusionary practices and more likely to be the authors of their own experiences, histories, and ideas. Having critical inquiry skills will help prepare students to govern thoughtfully and effectively in a multicultural world and to be responsive to a rapidly evolving economic environment. Critical inquiry will assist students in negotiating the challenges of a rigorous academic schedule, while remaining cognizant of the extracurricular messages embedded within the social, written, and oral texts that they will be asked to read and learn. Given that developmental readers often come from communities that have struggled to be heard in political and academic life, they will sometimes find that the texts they are assigned in their classes do not represent their experiences, memories, or social realities. Critical inquiry affords them the opportunity to acknowledge not only what is in the texts, but maybe more importantly, to be aware of what is absent. Reading the absences—historical, cultural, and economic—offers developmental readers the opportunity to interpret and "revise" these texts so that their invalidating absences become potent presences. As such, through critical thinking/reading/writing, they can begin to, as Homi Bhabha says, use "interpretation as intervention, as interrogation, as relocation, and revision."[20] In these terms, critical inquiry is a key principle in the development of democratic citizens prepared to govern.

My approach to ideological literacies of learning is rooted and informed by a central premise (and promise) behind a social or public democracy, which states that each citizen must not only be governable, but, more importantly, be prepared to govern. A government by and for the people demands a "people" competent in certain skills and abilities, possessing certain attributes and capacities, and committed to a value system undergirded by a commitment to equity, political struggle, human rights, and social justice. Building upon the work of Jefferson, Dewey, and Rousseau, David Sehr, an English teacher to new immigrants and former director for educational change at Brooklyn College, maps out five major elements of a public democracy that inform this literacy project. A public democracy "sees people's participation in public life as the essential ingredient in democratic government. Public participation arises out of an ethic of care and responsibility, not only for one's self as an isolated individual, but for one's fellow citizens as co-builders and co-beneficiaries of the public good."[21] In the context of a literacy project, we might also add as "coauthors" as well as "cointerpreters" of public texts.

Beginning with "an ethic of care and responsibility," Sehr suggests that social citizens must value and accept the view that we are "individuals-in-relation." As such, we neither give up our individuality nor deny our social responsibilities. In this formulation, it is quite possible to see how our sense of ourselves as individuals rests, in part, on how we see and treat others. Second, a public democracy demands "respect for the equal right of everyone to the conditions necessary for their self-development." In this context, a notion of difference is not linked simply to a notion of democratic tolerance, but rather articulates with the "fundamental equality of all social groups," not including those that threaten the rights of others. Third, he argues for the "appreciation of the importance of the public." The creation of public spheres where citizens can go to debate and discuss the most pressing social issues of our times must be developed with as much abandon, if not more, than the proliferation of strip malls and designer coffeehouse chains. In these public spheres, the public nature of certain private troubles can become manifest, illustrating what it means to be individuals-in-relation, conscious of our responsibilities as social citizens. Fourth, a public democracy demands a citizenry capable of "examining underlying relations of power in any given social situation." The connection between literacy/language and power is profound, undergirding these literacy projects, while providing trajectories of inquiry for both the students and teacher to explore. Lastly, citizens should be able to "learn more about any issue that arises" through either public disclosure or self-guided research.[22] These points provided markers that did not so much dictate curricular decisions as influence my pedagogy and the responsibility I feel to construct a classroom environment that encourages a range of literacies in the service of bringing into being democratic institutions and a sense of social responsibility.

🌀 Critical Strategies and Generative Themes

Two important curricular inclusions set up these literacy projects. First, I introduce my students to the approach to reading and language discussed above through what I hope is a provocative description of literacy as a process—cultural, ideological, political, and pedagogical:

> This is a course designed to help improve your reading. But unlike many other literacy courses, we are going to learn about reading in many different ways: We will talk about reading in relation to books, magazines, newspapers, and scholarly articles; we will learn what it means

to "read" films, television, advertisements, murals, art, and music videos; we will learn what it means to "read" the culture of this university, U.S. culture, and the culture of academia; we will learn what it means to "read" political events, such as the presidential election and political commercials; we will learn what it means to "read" and do research on the Internet. In short, we will discuss and learn what it means to be literate in the 21ˢᵗ century.

This approach to literacy will help you develop cross-disciplinary reading skills that are invaluable in college. From literature and philosophy to biology and physics, this literacy strategy will help prepare you for a successful college career.

In addition to reading these "texts," we will be writing about them also. We will write "essays," "compare/contrast" papers, "critiques," "summaries," and "discussion" papers. We will be writing about these texts in a way that asks them questions and responds to their messages.

How do their messages relate to our personal experiences? What do their messages say about the role of schools? What do they teach us about the world that we live in? How do they influence us to think in particular ways about each other? How are women portrayed differently than men in music videos? Should we care? How are non-native speakers of English represented in movies, television, and news reports?

All of these different "texts" provide us as a class and individually with challenging and timely material. We will find, I think, that we might "read" the same text differently. Because of our different experiences, we often have a different understanding of the same text.

Second, I include a somewhat lengthy "letter" to my students, which I read aloud. In summary, it talks to them as intellectuals and future leaders. This means that I speak with them about the importance of their experiences and interests in the development of the course. I speak with them about their limitless capabilities. I speak with them about how they deserve to be at Penn State or Montclair State University and how reading ability has nothing to do with intelligence. And lastly, I speak with them about their own personal and community literacies and the significance of those literacies within an academic context. It is of utmost importance that these students understand that their experiences and their reading of those experiences matter.

Following this introduction, my syllabus is designed to be open enough to respond to my student's needs and experiences, at the same time that it is used to shape the direction of our literacy project. For example, every two weeks we read a different text. In the CAMP program, the first two weeks focus on Penn State. Beginning in the library, the students are introduced to the "official" culture of Penn State via an overview of the collections, databases, scholarly journals, and the like.

On one occasion, quite unexpectedly, they was also introduced to the "unofficial" culture of Penn State via racist attitudes expressed "innocently" by the white, southern woman who was conducting the workshops. Two examples will suffice. As my students made their way into the library—baggy jeans, bandannas, and a determined swagger—this woman said cheerfully, "Wow, ya'll look like you're in a gang." My students just looked at her, aware of the comment, but unsure what to do in the face of it. The second incident occurred moments later while we were in the computer lab. "Ya'll have such difficult names to pronounce," she drawled, proceeding to mispronounce names, as though it was my students' fault that she must now contend with names other than Michael, Robert, and Jennifer.

Back in the classroom, I simply asked my students whether they thought the woman's attitudes were problematic. They did not hesitate to speak of her attitude as "racial," demeaning, and hurtful. I tried to move this "reading" of her attitude into a discussion about racism. Moving the conversation from the personal to the public means, in part, drawing connections between larger formations of power and privilege and the attitudes and ideas that they reward and legitimize. In other words, it is often the unofficial discourse that gives us insight into the underlying logic and ideology of the official discourse. If the responsibility for the dissemination of the official discourse is conveyed by people who embody a discursive position that, for example, is racist, then we must be diligent in our interrogation of the *relationship* between the two. It complicates matters that my students must feel comfortable not only going to the library, but also asking for help when they need it. In the face of this experience, it was a real challenge to get my students back into the library, even though they had engaged in a complex and critical reading of the culture of Penn State along racial lines.

But it would be false to suggest that all of my students came to the same conclusions about the racist discourse that they had experienced at Penn State. Not to be misunderstood, they all "read" the situation as racial, but their feelings about the implications of that discourse varied. For example, one student said he understood that the woman was prejudiced, but he did not believe that her bigotry was articulated institutionally. Another student was concerned that by naming racism as a hindrance to opportunity, he was making excuses for himself. Rather than suggesting racism as a *reason* for the difficulty many students of color have in places like Penn State, he was thinking of it as an excuse. Both of these comments provoked a conversation in which I wanted my students to make a distinction between opportunity and capability on one hand and cause and effect on the other. In the context of a dialogical pedagogy, it is less important that students are convinced or persuaded by my arguments (and vice versa) and more important that they are provoked to interrogate ideas, attitudes, and institutions that have become normalized under the influence of established power. In the end, the strength of this practice is not in its immediacy, but in its relevancy; that is, it provides an environment for students to develop more complex understandings of the world and the word, while also honing their ability to defend their ideas in a public forum.

Another two-week section was titled "News and Perspective: Reading between the Lines." I picked the *New York Times* as the primary text for three reasons. First, the students receive it for free. Second, I felt it offered a more advanced reading level for my students to engage with. Third, it deals with international and national issues in an authoritative and seemingly objective manner. The combination offered a pedagogical opportunity to, as I wrote in my syllabus, "discuss layout, photography, design, advertising, content, context, perspective, and tone."

Many of my students had never read a newspaper and brought to the class the dominant assumptions that "news" meant unbiased reporting of an event. As we began to discuss the paper, I depended heavily on Gee's notion of discourse to begin interrogating what the newspaper represented. He writes, "By a 'discourse' I . . . mean a socially accepted association among ways of using language, of thinking, and of acting that can be used to identify oneself as a member of a socially meaningful group or 'social network.'"[23] Some of the questions I asked my students to consider regarding the newspaper articles that we read were, What group did the newspaper represent? What ways of thinking and acting did the newspaper's messages articulate? What future does the newspaper's discourse imply, and how can we begin to break into the dominant meanings that the "text" connotes? What relations of power are legitimated in the texts? These questions were difficult for my students to understand at first. It is not that they failed to get the "right" answer (as I will discuss later in this chapter), but rather, the very politics that drive these types of questions were, for the most part, foreign to my students, which made them difficult to grasp. By beginning with my students' experiences, we slowly began to make some headway into considering the *implications* of these questions for making meaning, producing knowledge, and disrupting the consensus of common sense that news often manufactures and legitimates.

In more strategic terms, when we had a text that we were struggling to read and understand, I would not begin with the text. Rather, I would begin with my students' experiences and then pull them, *and be pulled by them*, through the text. In this way, we can begin to see how reading is a political process of translation, explication, interpretation, and construction. We can then begin to link the products of these processes to larger social formations, revealing the intertextual nature of reading, and on a much larger scale, of life itself. On the other hand, if I were to begin with the text as an isolated moment, as a product to be reified, as an objectified fact, I would be privileging not only text over context, but I would be reinforcing the validity of dominant social structures that teach us to believe that language is nonideological, history is singular, and facts are meaningful outside of our interpretation of them. Even if I were sensitive to my students' experiences and at some point wanted to address them in relation to the text, if I did not begin by understanding the text as meaningless outside of a particular social and political discourse, then I

would simply reproduce the dominant traditions of those who privilege the importance of the text over the context that gives it meaning in the first place.

A couple of examples will make these ideas more concrete. Because African
American and Hispanics are often portrayed in the news as criminals, the commonsense assumption is that most African Americans and Hispanics are criminals. In
my CAMP class, a Hispanic male student argued that this portrayal was accurate;
after all, he reasoned, if you rounded up the drug dealers he knew in New York City,
they would be primarily black and Hispanic men. For him, the representations that
he saw and read in the media were *reflective* and not *constructive* of a reality that he
knew all too well. But more to the point, his critique failed to consider that the representations and their immediate source constituted a network of cultural practices
that are "always linked together with specific social formations and have specific
effects."[24] As Carl Boggs writes, using data from the Sentencing Project,

> while blacks constitute only 13 percent of the total population and 13 percent of regular drug
> users, they account for 35 percent of those arrested for possession, 55 percent of those con-
> victed, and 74 percent of those jailed. ... As Diana Gordon argues, U.S. drug policy is at heart
> an attack on poor urban minorities.[25]

As such, my response was that he should measure the percentage of representations
that he sees in media of African Americans and Hispanics as criminals against those
who are not portrayed as criminals, and the percentage of the African American and
Hispanic population in New York City who are drug dealers against those who are
not. Pedagogically, this intervention is meant to instigate a political economy of representations that focuses not just on what we see, but (maybe more important to the
literacy project) on what we do not see, why we do not see, and the political, social,
corporeal, and pedagogical implications of those absences. It is vital that students
begin to recognize that "what is 'out there' is, in part, constituted by how it is represented."[26]

At Montclair, a student discussed his experiences with racial profiling, and from
there the class began to interrogate the recent profiling of Muslim people in the
United States. Reading articles from different news sources like the *New York
Times* and *The Nation*, students were able to identify the different logics that
informed the news articles that they read. Seeing one's own experiences similarly
articulated (read: validated) in alternative news sources throws into relief not only
the ideological perspective that informs such perspectives, but also presents the dominant discourse as ideological. No longer invisible behind the veil of truth and
objectivity, dominant news is read as a cultural practice, that is, as an ideological
activity that inscribes and legitimates specific relationships of power, cultural norms,
and economic practices.

As a final example, at Montclair we were reading about the September 11 bombings of the World Trade Center. In an effort to provoke my students into thinking about the construction of meaning, even in relation to such a horrific event, I assigned them a writing/research project that asked them to find two news sources—mainstream and alternative—that discussed some aspect of the bombings. This was immediately a problem for my students because most did not know what "alternative" news meant. How do you speak about ideology when one of its major principles is hegemony? Mainstream news I described as that which we have easy access to, such as the *New York Times*. Alternative media I described as that which is not part of the popular media and that often takes a very different view from the mainstream. Most students came back the next class and said they could not find any alternative news sources in the library. Part of this, of course, was the fact that they were not looking in the right places. But more significantly, it says something about the almost complete domination through saturation of dominant media. In response, I told them to find articles in *The Nation*, given that it comes out every week and is also available online. As students compared the different reports of the same event, they began to get an idea of how meaning gets constructed through our interpretations of facts. Many students also found articles from other countries, some of which addressed questions that had not even been posed by the U.S. media at that point. Although we were not speaking about these differences as ideological per se, the students were being introduced to a major principle of ideological literacy; that is, they were being made aware of the power of language to construct reality. As I will discuss shortly, we eventually took up issues of power, presenting a more complete picture of how these constructions become truths and common sense.

🎧 Honesty, Respect, and Accountability: Three Principles of Pedagogical Engagement

I conduct my classes as seminars, dialogical as I mentioned, and as such, reading assignments are relatively short, although our discussions of the texts read are intense and rigorous. But for this process to be effective, we need to develop a sense of trust and respect. It is these issues of trust and respect that are often overlooked as major barriers to radical pedagogies. In my class, I have found that a combination of blunt honesty, holding students accountable for what they say, and a process of questioning that stays consistent with my project of expanding political agency through ideological literacies begins to establish a modicum of trust and, eventually, a level of mutual respect. As Noam Chomsky and other progressives suggest, we must speak *with* our students, not *to* them.[27]

A few examples will suffice to illustrate how this process developed. My "blunt honesty" was exemplified by both an intellectual and emotional commitment to take a position, however contestable and provisional, about something that I might have heard on the radio or seen on television. When a telephone strike had paralyzed many students' phone service at Penn State, I was not hesitant to voice my opinions about how the management of the company had presented the conflict as a "labor problem." I suggested to my students that I felt that with the overwhelming profits and mergers that big corporations were enjoying unmolested by antitrust laws, it was unfair that labor was being blamed for the problems. As Freire and other critical pedagogues have argued, it is unethical for a teacher to try and hide her perspective, just as it is unethical to "deny others the right to reject it."[28] Freire goes on to say,

> In the name of respect I should have toward my students, I do not see why I should omit or hide my political stance by proclaiming a neutral position that does not exist. On the contrary, my role as teacher is to assent to the student's right to compare, to choose, to rupture, to decide.[29]

Because this strike was being reported in the *New York Times*, we were able, as a class, to interrogate the written reports as a cultural practice. Of course, many of my students did blame the workers for their lack of phone service. Why wouldn't they? But as we read through the articles, and I filled in some of the epistemological gaps with relevant labor history, referencing Marx, whom many students had never heard of, the "discourse" of the *New York Times* began to come into relief. When students are offered even a small bit of a secondary discourse, like labor history, the dominant discourse looks a little different than it did before; it makes the invisible visible, desublimating a discourse, ostensibly revealing it as a discourse.

But what is the role of the teacher in this kind of literacy project? It should be to lead her class through the articulatory relationships of these discourses in an effort to reveal their associations and disassociations to larger social formations. Discourses need to be rubbed up against each other in an effort to reveal what they teach, the history that they imply, and the future that they suggest. In this way, students begin to get a sense of how discourses create subject positions for them to inhabit that are part of a social network. It is less important that students agree with my beliefs than they have the discourses and the power to disagree.

Whether they agree or not, I find that holding them accountable for what they say establishes a certain amount of respect by showing them, on one hand, that what they think matters and, on the other, that what they think is always already caught in the web of social and political relations. Too often I hear of teachers who agree with everything their students say, simply because they want to validate their experiences, avoid confrontation, and divest themselves from decision making. This makes no sense to me. How does offering students facile validation for the thoughts they have and the experiences they draw upon do anything more than create docility and apathy. If it is all just about having an opinion, then what is the point of teaching? This is not to say that as critical teachers we should deny the validity of students' experiences; it simply means that we complicate them, move them out of the domain of the private, personal, and psychological and into the arena of the systemic, political, and sociological. By validating experiences without linking those experiences to larger social formations, we do a great disservice to students. By failing to show how experience is inevitably caught up in a web of power relationships, we help perpetuate a discourse of individualism and self-blame. It is incorrect to assume that students will not make the connection between what it means to be validated individually as well as blamed individually. In other words, if a student's experiences are not seen as part of a larger network of beliefs, attitudes, behaviors, and expectations, that student will learn that her struggles and failures are also hers, and hers alone. This does little to advance the student's political agency and only reinforces what it means to make the mistake of thinking that private accomplishments as well as "private agonies and anxieties . . . turn into public issues just for being on public display."[30]

🐚 A Pedagogy of Critical Questioning: Bridging the Gap between Acquisition and Learning

In the service of these literacy projects, I have taken up a strategy, as I illustrated above, of critical questioning. These questions attempt to organize what Ernesto Laclau would call a new discursive field,[31] developed to motivate counterhegemonic ideas, attitudes, and actions. Whether my students have answers to these questions matters little. In fact, some of the questions are strictly rhetorical in that they are advanced to highlight absences in texts, contradictions in experiences, and possibilities that lay dormant at the bottom of the epistemological barrel. But do not misunderstand—these questions are not innocent. They are leading (although not Socratic, because I do not necessarily know where they are going), designed to make my students think about the relation of things and, as Foucault has shown, the order of things as well. Sometimes I'll attempt to answer my own questions if I find that they have failed to stir the curiosity of my students. Sometimes I will try to pose my questions differently. I do not always know the answers to the questions I ask. It is the indeterminate and contingent aspect of this strategy. Depending upon my students' experiences with the topic that we are discussing, or the text that we have read, the answers to my questions and the questioning of my answers are always caught in the web identity, ideology, and power/knowledge. They are attempts to engage my students in a critical dialog, to get them to think creatively about the topic we are discussing, and, eventually, to get them to create linkages between what is said, what they see, how they understand the network of discourses that locates them as bodies and minds, and the identifications they make ideologically. In the final analysis, one central goal of critical literacy and pedagogy "that wishes to force a shift in ways of seeing, feeling, and perceiving [must] begin by questioning established power."[32]

This pedagogy of questioning is aligned with Gee's important distinction between acquisition and learning. "Acquisition," he writes, "is a process of acquiring something subconsciously by exposure to models and a process of trial and error, without a process of formal teaching."[33] On the other hand, he states, "Learning is a process that involves conscious knowledge gained through teaching, though not necessarily from someone officially designated a teacher."[34] By initiating the strategies mentioned above in my literacy classes, I am trying, in a sense, to create a hybrid pedagogy of acquisition and learning. This hybridity, if held up against Gee's definitions, would appear not as a hybrid at all, but as an example of "learning." But by loosening the definitions a bit, I think that it is possible and fruitful to conceptualize and enact a pedagogy that attempts to make the relationship between learning and acquisition more porous.

For example, when I ask questions of established power in class, I employ a pedagogy that begins in the domain of learning. When students struggle to respond to these questions based upon their experiences and the texts being read, either with answers or more questions, they are making a transition from learning to acquisition. When they respond with questions of their own, they are advancing their ideas from the domain of acquisition. Again, these distinctions are analytical. In the context of the classroom, it would be impossible to make any clear distinctions between one and the other. But it is helpful in beginning to think more critically about what schools and teachers can do to disrupt, validate, and complicate knowledges that have been strictly acquired or learned and that have come to occupy the realm of common sense. Hybrid pedagogy blends the knowledge domains of acquisition and learning, attempting to make the classroom an extension of the world and the world an extension of the classroom.

In both programs, creating a hybrid space of acquisition and learning means asking and addressing some fundamental pedagogical questions. First, how can "critical" authority, that is, the authority of a teacher who is responsive to the link between social formations and power/knowledge, be made operational in a way that subverts the sedimented mistrust that students, especially students from oppressed classes and cultures, generally have of educational institutions? Second, how can counterhegemonic knowledge be presented so that it disrupts and disturbs without terrorizing and disrespecting students' vernacular understanding of the world? Third, how can teachers begin to conceptualize the literacy process as it functions as part of a primary and secondary social network? In other words, not only do teachers need to address the distinction between acquisition and learning, but they also need to pay attention to the distinction between what it means to know or to be knowledgeable in different sociopolitical contexts. Pedagogically, the implications of recognizing such distinctions lead toward the realization that knowledge whether it is acquired or learned often means two or more entirely different things depending upon where and when it is deployed.

For example, when a working-class student has acquired the knowledge that he is outside the domain of "official knowledge," that is, outside the discourse of capital, both cultural and material, at the same time that he is victimized by it, he can still deploy that knowledge in his own neighborhood in a way that gives him some power. As Paul Willis has shown, from a working-class kid's perspective, to be in the elite is to be weak and unknowing in the things that count in working-class life.[35] But in the context of the elite, working-class knowledge is not only subordinated, its resistant functions work against working-class people's own political agency. The point here is that critical teachers must be responsive to how "secondary discourses" and "primary discourses" are taken up *inside* the classroom because they often act on and in the social reality outside the classroom in unexpected ways.

For another example, if I incorporate rap music or a popular film into my curriculum, I must be aware of how the school might be seen as a threat to the resistant functions of popular culture. For students, this can be an affront to their sense of power. If they get some of their power from acts and products of cultural subversion and resistance, then bringing the subversive material into the classroom as part of the curriculum is to say that nothing is sacred and that the power of the institution can reach even the most intimate places. Don't misunderstand—I think it is imperative to include popular culture into the literacy classroom because it does often necessitate dealing with the intimate and affective investments people make. As Stuart Hall remarks,

> One should not forget why one went to the popular in the first instance. It's not just an indulgence and an affirmation; it's a political, intellectual, pedagogical commitment. Everybody now inhabits the popular, whether they like it or not, so that does create a set of common languages. To ignore the pedagogical possibilities of common languages is extremely political.[36]

The role of the literacy teacher would be to include these materials in a way that complicates them and holds them accountable to the worlds they imagine and the language they use and to recognize the power they have in mobilizing desire and passion. By complicating these materials, the teacher de-reifies them, while respecting their power. The combination of effects illustrates what it might mean to be conscious of the pedagogical fusion of acquisition and learning in regard to secondary and primary discourses.

It is important to understand two things about acquisition and learning as they get taken up in the service of an ideological literacy project. First, acquisition, as Gee says, is a powerful force in the learning process; it is a conditioning of the intellectual, subconscious and corporeal dimensions of social and private life. This includes deeply sedimented myths of the human condition, history, and knowledge and the invisible or normalizing power of the social formations that mythologize these conditions in the first place. When conditions are sedimented in the subconscious as traditions, they move into the mythological sphere of determined outcomes. A pedagogy that hopes to dislodge ideas stuck in the fatalistic sphere of determination must attempt to harness and understand the "differential sources of power"[37] that learning and acquisition represent.

Second, the relationship between teaching and ideological literacy is indeterminate. This means that there is not going to be a necessary or immediate response to pedagogies that attempt to dislodge what has been acquired. Dislodging or transforming acquired knowledge is like removing the color blue from a complicated, multicolored weave. It is not impossible, but it takes perseverance, dedication, and the understanding that the weave itself will be unlikely to call attention to the nooks and spaces in which the blue has been spun. Unlike advocates for standardized testing who believe that the relationship between learning and teaching can be measured, critical literacy educators must be aware of the indeterminancy of their pedagogies and, hence, the inability of their pedagogies to create a *direct* trajectory of literacy and ideological consciousness. In light of this, creating multiple trajectories of possibility by leading students through the complex associations of learning, doing, knowing, and understanding should be, strategically, the broadly conceived goal as it relates to teaching and learning in the remedial literacy classroom. In effect, an ideological literacy project prepares students for a life of learning and political participation, minus the oversimplified certainty that standardizing outcomes promote.

On the other hand, indeterminacy does not mean that the contingent nature of knowledge/power and experience should be discarded for a laissez-faire pedagogy in which all relationships are seen as arbitrary or all meanings relative. What might it mean pedagogically to say that contingency is a force that contextualizes and, hence, politicizes the indeterminacy of teaching and learning? It means that teachers must take seriously the experiences of their students and that they need to occupy the space of leadership in their classrooms; that is, teachers must take back control of their classrooms from administrators and neoliberal overseers so that they can be responsive to their students' needs. It also means that social formations have a powerful effect on how individuals think about their experiences and the world around them. Social formations must be linked historically, epistemologically, and politically to the experiences students have. Moreover, it suggests that the formation of political agency is a consequence of indeterminancy in that political agents must be able to respond to the unexpected in a manner that is empowering, ethical, and effective. In this context, political agency represents a condition of humanity that is antithetical to the standardizing effects that standards-based education has on students, when standards education is understood as an essentializing process of teaching and learning that separates knowledge from power and politics from education. This notion of political agency celebrates diversity and difference and thrives on the indeterminancy that must obviously follow.

🎵 The Praxis of Political Discriminations: Literacy of Ideology

In my literacy classes, I try to encourage my students to engage structures of power by first suggesting that they exist. The most powerful thing about structures and systems of power are their invisibility. My students had acquired an understanding of language in its most one-dimensional form; that is, they understood language and reading as a way to describe and explain reality—what they observed and thought as *individuals*. But even after my introduction to literacy, it was still very difficult to enter into a dialog about discourses and the knowledges that they produced. As far as my students were concerned, there was only one "discourse," that being the words, images, and ideas that circulated through dominant society everyday, although "dominant society" was not a concept anyone was prepared to accept easily. It was not that they did not know that many of their experiences and opinions, as I have said before, were inconsistent with a certain societal logic. Rather, they did not have a language that could begin to make ideological distinctions between discourses. Having a language of critique and a *language of discrimination* is more than being aware of and fluent in primary and secondary discourses. If a language of critique suggests the critical function of theoretical discourses on one hand and the potency of inquiry to disrupt the normalizing processes of dominant ideological formations on the other, then a language of discrimination suggests the need to make distinctions between ideological spheres as part of the literacy process.

Having a language of critique and discrimination at the earliest stages of literacy is to be able to *ideologically situate* discourses. In short, this process reflects a *literacy of ideology*, a powerful first step in the reading-learning-transforming process. Moreover, becoming ideologically literate entails more than students' learning to discern ideologies from each other; it also means that ideological spaces open up for them to inhabit *consciously*.

One way I tried to instigate a literacy of ideology was to teach students what it means to be on the political "left" or on the political "right." Although these political designations float freely within the theoretical discourses of academia, especially within educational and cultural theory, my students in both institutions did not know what it meant to be on the right or on the left. I found Derrida's distinction between the right and the left particularly helpful in getting students to think about ideological perspective in relation to the meaning of the texts they read. He writes, "On the left there is the desire to affirm what is to come, to change, and to do so in the greatest possible justice. ... . [The right] never makes justice the first resort or axiom of its action."[38] In our present conjunction, the right affirms the rule of capital and the market to determine fairly the social and political outcomes of daily life. Moreover, the right tends to celebrate individual competition while denying the value of social and political struggle. Lastly, the right can be discerned by its mistrust of government outside of its role as handmaiden to corporate activities. As such, material values more than social values take precedent in its political imaginary. In Noam Chomsky's famously direct language, the right generally puts "profit over people," with the implication that a free market is the same thing as a democratic republic.[39]

Using these guideposts, my students had a "language" with which to begin critiquing what they read. This is not to say that they immediately knew whether they were on the right or the left, but at least they were able to begin a process of discrimination in which issues of power as well as meaning were part of the learning process. By offering them the admittedly simplistic dichotomies of right and left ideologies, the notion of perspective moved from a quality and an effect of character and individuality to one that suggested a condition of power. These broad political designations acted generatively in the service of political classification which is "the basis for all social discrimination, and discrimination . ... is no less a constituent element of the social realm than equality is a constituent element of the political."[40] These political discriminations offered students a vantage point from which to build a vocabulary of distinctions. From there, they were able to rub "texts" against each other, measuring the limitations and possibilities of their truths within the parameters of power.

For example, I first gave the CAMP students an article to read in *Newsweek* entitled the "The New Face of Race in America."[41] After a week of discussion, I gave them an article from *The Nation* by H. Jack Geiger entitled "The Real World of Race."[42] In retrospect, I should have assigned the articles together because they so explicitly present two different ideological perspectives about race and power in America. The *Newsweek* article argues that we are in an "Age of Color" and that the "ancient divisions of black and white" are no longer relevant in a time when "an entire generation [of youth of color] have grown up in prosperity, attending schools with people of mixed backgrounds and set out to work in the New Economy, where there are few walls and little hierarchy."[43] The implication is that we are in a state of integration in which opportunity does not discriminate, power is perfunctory, and, although "there is no question that African-Americans still bear heavy burdens, disproportionately suffering from poverty, imprisonment, and racial profiling," "old dualities have given way to a multiplicity of ethnic forces."[44] The article seems to suggest that multiculturalism has replaced the white/black dichotomy, and as such, power can no longer be delineated in racial terms. Power is not mentioned in the article, but the implication is that it now runs along multiple trajectories of color, deflecting attention away from the unequal power whites have over all other ethnic minorities. On one hand, the article makes whiteness invisible, declaring a laissez-faire multiculturalism in which opportunity exists outside the sphere of power; on the other, it admits to power struggles within the ranks of ethnic minorities. This strategy is effective in a pedagogical sense because it addresses the visibility of the multicultural "other" in the New Economy, while making invisible the formations of white power that limit the opportunities for the other. Half-truths are always more convincing than complete lies.

In his review of David Shipler's *A Country of Strangers*, Geiger begins by outlining the right-wing ideology of reactionary intellectuals like Dinesh D'Souza and Jim Sleeper, who announce, resonating with the dominant public discourse on race, "Racism is dead!" "How then," Geiger writes, rhetorically responding to this conservative declaration and the one ostensibly articulated in the *Newsweek* article, "to explain the overwhelming realities of desperate inner cities, soaring back unemployment, crumbling housing, failing schools, increasing segregation and family disintegration, crime and drugs if white racism is not their root cause?"[45] Again echoing the right's response, "Black people did it, did it to the country, did it to themselves. Black behavior, not white racism, became the reason why Blacks and whites lived in separate worlds . ... the failure of the lesser breeds to enjoy society's fruits became their fault alone."[46] At the heart of Geiger's review of Shipler's book is the notion that "true integration means power sharing," an absence in our present multicultural conjunction, often ignored by the right and one that [should] define the struggle of the left.

Because I had assigned the *Newsweek* article by itself, my students had no language to discriminate this perspective from any other and, therefore, no language of critique to interrogate the parameters of power that informed such a reading of the world. When I gave them *The Nation* article to read, even before our discussion of left and right, they not only recognized a difference of perspective, but almost all were incredibly "jazzed" about the perspective itself. One woman who had not yet spoken in class enthusiastically yelled out when I asked what people thought of Geiger's article. She said that she liked it much, much better than the *Newsweek* article because it described the way she had experienced race in America. In short, by providing a counter text, they not only began to read intertextually, they began to conceptualize what it means to make distinctions and discriminations between texts.

But, again, it would be misleading to suggest that all of my students agreed with Geiger's statements. In fact, when asked to engage these ideas at the level of their experiences, many of them shared stories of interethnic racism. My students had been victimized by other ethnic minorities, just like the *Newsweek* article suggested. This provoked me to address the issue of whiteness. It also provoked me to ask them about their experiences with white people. As I came to find out, they had plenty of experiences with white racism, but because I was white, they felt hesitant to share their experiences with me. To digress for a moment, this is why trust and respect must be seen as principles of pedagogy that are under constant negotiation. That a level of trust was established under one set of circumstances does not automatically mean that it will carry over into another set of circumstances.

As I gained their trust anew in the context of white racism, namely by discussing white privilege, we discussed both the validity of their experiences with interethnic racism and its limitations to address the invisible and often anonymous power of white racism. In other words, we discussed how when ethnic minorities participate in racist ideologies, it pushes them down and lifts the white race up. Likewise, whites are elevated under the regime of white supremacy, while ethnic minorities (the majority) are pushed down.[47]

Moving beyond the texts toward an engagement with the political and social formations in which these texts articulated was a small step. Concrete examples taken from the material of the urban landscape provided sufficient illustrations for my students to begin interrogating the texts. The CAMP students' questions dug at the roots of poverty by beginning in the fields of migrant workers, shedding light on how *Newsweek's* portrayal of race and ethnicity victimized the victims of poverty and racism by failing to consider how "social power and transforming discourses, institutions, and social practices of privilege" normalize whiteness in a "liberal swirl of diversity."[48] As Geiger asks rhetorically, how else to explain overwhelming poverty and urban decay in minority alcoves, if one does not consider formative structures of racism and oppression, than by blaming those who live there? My students began to understand that reading the word did in fact mean reading the world. How, they asked, could *Newsweek* print such an article? This question completed the hermeneutical gesture not only by acknowledging the authority and power that the text had to teach and persuade, even when the lessons contradicted the experiences of my students, but also by initiating a relational process of reading in which the link between source, message, social construction, social formations, and pedagogical implications were understood as interrelated parts of the "literacy" whole.

The CAMP students also began to make connections between the politics of the *Newsweek* piece and personal interactions they experienced at Penn State regarding their status as CAMP students, which is, in effect, an affirmative action program. If every thing is equal and opportunity has nothing to do with resources, if integration rightly means diversity and not the democratization of power, then what is the defense of CAMP and programs like it? The defense, if it comes at all, is that minority students are incapable of succeeding without help due to their own individual problems or character traits and not that we live in a racist society in which the distribution of wealth is iniquitous, and power and white privilege are made invisible. As Geiger writes, "Affirmative action is such a threat because it challenges unseen and unacknowledged privileges of whiteness,"[49] thereby exposing the symbolic violence of "white" power in the form of a pedagogy of invisibility and normalization. Moreover, programs like CAMP are identified as giving minorities an unfair advantage over whites, tipping the scales in favor of the "other." My students had been subjected to this kind of racism at Penn State and had felt defeated and diminished by it. After reading these two articles against each other, they were better able to articulate a defense of their right to an education on the basis of social justice.

At Montclair, I gave my students an article to read in the *New York Times* entitled "Counterpoint to Unity: Dissent" by Richard Bernstein.[50] We first discussed any personal experiences that my students had with dissent. One was involved in a class in which students were discussing school tracking, and he was the only person arguing against the practice. Another student found herself quietly dissenting from the ideas of one of her professors. Interestingly, after speaking with her classmates, she found solidarity. This generated a conversation about the notion of dissent and power, for if dissent is defined as a "minority" opinion, then could this student's dissent actually be dissent? After all, she and her classmates outnumbered the professor. Students began to question power's ability to ignore or create a consensus, or a perceived consensus.

I then asked the students if "dissent," as it was situated in the title of the article, indicated the opposite of unity. They said yes. I then asked them how they understood unity. They responded with phrases like "coming together," "unified," and "agreeing." I then asked them what Americans were coming together around. Answer: the war. Yes, but what larger principles were being discussed in relation to the war? What unifies Americans politically, whether one is on the right or the left? A commitment to what? Some said "freedom." Freedom of what? I asked. "Freedom of speech," many said because earlier in the class we had discussed free speech and access to media. And why is free speech important? We struggled and eventually found "democracy." We are unified to a greater or lesser degree around the tenets of democracy, the most urgent, some would argue, being free speech. Is dissent a necessary outcome of free speech? If so, why is it set up as a counterpoint to "unity"? In this context, would not dissent be a natural and necessary element of a democratic republic unified by its commitment to free speech? Is there a commitment to free speech given the unequal access to media and the public ear that the wealthy have in this country and around the world in comparison to the poor? Is there a commitment to free speech given the recent call to ban certain songs from the radio? Is there a commitment to free speech given Bush's displeasure at the media for allowing the Taliban to communicate their ideological position on the ideology of the United States? Does a commitment to free speech demand a free press? These questions were posed and discussed. Again, answers varied. But the point is that we created a pedagogical space in which these questions could be asked and grappled with.

As a consequence of these questions, the Montclair students began to interrogate the very notion of unity in relation to difference. Some questioned why people were not asking why so many countries "hated" the United States. Others challenged their fellow classmates when they presented the popular view, becoming dissenters in the process. In the face of these interactions, I again, brought attention to the "unity" of the class in spite of the dissension. This unity is established by a belief and corresponding pedagogy that encourages dialog and critical engagement. They also began to ask why the dissenting opinions did not get as much coverage in the mainstream press, leading them to further problematize the relationship between knowledge and power. They then began to make linkages between power and right and left ideologies, understanding quickly that, as the article states, the dissenters are on the left, minus significant power and access to the mechanisms of public disclosure. It should be made very clear that this whole process is a *literacy process*, one in which students are learning about language, power, ideology, and their place in the world. As such, they are being prepared to act upon the world, to govern, to have power, to lead.

❦ Conclusion

What has become evident for me in these classes is that, in the end, when we talk about the relationship between pedagogy and knowledges, and especially when we talk about ideological literacies of learning, we are talking about "relations of power, not relations of meaning."[51] These relations of power, lived out pedagogically in the literacy classroom through the battles between acquired and learned knowledges, suggest that educators must be aware, as Foucault has argued, of how "power produces knowledge."[52] Certainly in the context of expanding political agency and democratic relations, destructive knowledges, both acquired and learned as products of a "'general politics' of truth,"[53] must be interrogated as part of the literacy process if learning how to read means, in part, developing a "critical" stance toward society's dominating discourses. As Foucault states,

> Each society has its regime of truth: that is, the types of discourse which accepts and makes function as true; the mechanisms and instances which enable one to distinguish true and false statements, the means by which each is sanctioned; the techniques and procedures accorded value in acquisition of truth; the status of those who are charged with saying what counts as true.[54]

In other words, literacy education must be involved in not only a pedagogical process of "translation," but it must also encourage an engagement with structures of power and the knowledges that they produce. This is one of the reasons why a "critical" pedagogy is not, in fact, an indoctrination, but at its best is an intervention into oppressive regimes of truth. When the accusation of indoctrination is applied to "critical" practices, it is often the case that a critique of power relationships is missing. Although certainly beyond the scope of this discussion, it is nevertheless important to realize that without a critique of power relations and the knowledges that they legitimate and invalidate, an analysis of pedagogy as either indoctrination or intervention will lack substance.

Educating people to read and act upon the world is quite different from training them to pass a test. The former produces citizens prepared to govern, while the latter has the real potential to produce students "who have successfully passed basic reading tests by the third grade and yet cannot use language (oral or written) to learn, to master content, to work in the new economy, or to think critically about social and political affairs." Considering the overwhelming need for remediation and the catch-22 (discussed at the beginning of this chapter) that binds traditional remedial programs, ideological literacies of learning provide a comprehensive and effective alternative. Moreover, their general principles of evaluation are well tested in other progressive literacy projects of the past, including Dewey's experimental schools, Highlander Folk School, the Citizenship Schools, and the Quincy schools, to name only a few.[55] But it would be wrong to suggest that to improve the conditions in schools, remedial reading programs, and impoverished neighborhoods, we only need to teach ideological literacies of learning. Without a significant redistribution of power in our schools, neighborhoods, and governmental institutions, without a commitment to democratizing our most important social institutions, progressive projects and the citizens that they produce will continue to exist at the margins of political and educational discourses; or worse, their ideas and practices will disappear into the shallow grave of history that established power and privilege quietly dig.

The next chapter enlivens many of the strategies and theoretical ideas discussed above by linking literacy and critical pedagogy to cultural studies. Cultural studies is a potent theoretical force in the struggle to reclaim a sense of intellectual clarity in a world increasingly characterized by a commonsense acceptance of neoliberal ideology. By teaching students how to do cultural studies, critical teachers provide an invaluable service in civic responsibility. The knowledge that develops from such cultural critiques and pedagogical interventions has the potential to cause critical disruptions in the fabric of political and social thought. Through the development of conceptual "tools," powerful hegemonic forces are made visible and, consequently, more realistically resisted.

chapter six

Beyond "Doing" Cultural Studies

Toward a Cultural Studies of Critical Pedagogy

The media exercise an influence on public consciousness. In that respect they are more akin to education than to industry, and their offerings should be as much a matter of public concerns as the quality of our education.

—Michael Parenti

One should not forget why one went to the popular in the first instance. It's not just an indulgence and an affirmation; it's a political, intellectual, pedagogical commitment. Everybody now inhabits the popular, whether they like it or not, so that does create a set of common languages. To ignore the pedagogical possibilities of common languages is extremely political.

—Stuart Hall quoted in Julie Drew

What [the idea of permanent education] stresses is the educational force of our whole social and cultural experience. It is therefore concerned, not only with continuing education, of a formal or informal kind, but with what the whole environment, its institutions and relationships, actively and profoundly teaches.... For who can doubt, looking at television or newspapers, or reading the women's magazines, that here, centrally, is *teaching*, and teaching financed and distributed in a much larger way than is formal education.

—Raymond Williams

Introduction

As the quotes suggest, popular culture is one of society's most effective devices for categorizing our affective and thinking capacities, teaching as it entertains and entertaining as it teaches. The relationship between entertainment and educational capacity suggests that films and other popular cultural media are as pedagogically effective as they are *because* they entertain. In this context, popular culture is entertainment, but it is not *only* entertainment. It has extraentertaining capacities, one of which is its pedagogical and hegemonic capacity to produce what Nelson Goodman calls a "rightness of rendering,"[1] which refers to media's pedagogical capacity to normalize representations so that they appear correct and seem consistent with our common sense. Infiltrating the market at near saturation levels, these hegemonic representations severely limit our ability to break critically into their implied assumptions about the world and its social, political, and cultural ordering.[2]

A return to a concentration on the pedagogical aspects of popular culture without denying the political and cultural aspects of pedagogy brings us closer to developing pedagogic strategies that encourage social engagement and fuse the affective and intellectual dimensions of learning.[3] Pedagogy, in this discourse, is not relegated to the language of schooling or teaching techniques and strategies. Rather, the scope of pedagogy is extended to include the hegemonic strategies of popular culture specifically and media generally. Relevant here is Antonio Gramsci's insight concerning the hegemonic function of pedagogy and the pedagogic function of hegemony. In this context, pedagogy indicates a circuit of social and political ordering and the *normalization of that ordering*. In other words, we are "schooled" in the logic of dominant formations through a subtle and not so subtle barrage of cultural stimuli. From commercials and sitcoms to Hollywood blockbusters and school curricula, we both learn and acquire the knowledges that help perpetuate the dominant social order.[4] For example, neoliberal hegemony is, in part, a result of pedagogical strategies that mobilize public desire, construct common sense, and restrain our sociological and political imaginations, narrowly defining public life in consumerist terms, just as it relegates the notion of democratic struggle to the periphery of social discourse or criminalizes it in the name of civility (i.e., see mainstream reporting of the L.A. uprising and Seattle protests against the WTO and IMF).

Although a growing body of literature makes up and takes up the "theoretical" and historical side of cultural studies[5] and an increasing number that "do" cultural studies,[6] there is little that takes up what it means to teach people "how to do" cultural studies. The importance of this absence cannot be understated. As Stuart Hall explains, cultural studies ideally must work on two fronts: the theoretical and pedagogical. If the latter is overwhelmed by the former, "you get an enormous theoretical advance without any engagement at the level of the political project."[7] This imbalance is not due to an incompatibility between cultural studies and critical pedagogy. Henry Giroux points out that although cultural studies and critical pedagogy are two "critical traditions . . . that rarely speak to each other,"[8] they nevertheless share similar concerns:

At the risk of over generalizing: both cultural studies theorists and critical educators engage in forms of cultural work that locate politics in the interplay among symbolic representations, everyday life, and material relations of power; both engage cultural politics, as the site of the production and struggle over power, and learning as the outcome of diverse struggles rather than as the passive reception of information. In addition, both traditions have emphasized what I call a performative pedagogy reflected in what such theorists as Lawrence Grossberg call the act of doing, the importance of understanding theory as the grounded basis for "intervening into contexts and power . . . in order to enable people to act more strategically in ways that may change their context for the better." Moreover, theorists working in both fields have argued for the primacy of the political in their diverse attempts to produce critical public spaces, regardless of how fleeting they may be, in which popular cultural resistance is explored as a form of political resistance.[9]

This intersection provides intellectuals/teachers both in cultural studies and education a new theoretical framework for analyzing the pedagogical implications of cultural practices, the cultural implications of pedagogical practices, the social and political effects of representations, and the articulations between knowledges and formations of power.

✱ Cultural Studies in a Neoliberal Age: Giroux, Kellner, and Kincheloe

According to Grossberg, there are two major pedagogical trajectories of cultural studies.[10] First, there is the kind of public pedagogies that media and other cultural formations utilize. Giroux's most recent work, for example, engages the complex pedagogical processes at work in media, especially film, between power and knowledge on one hand and representations of difference on the other.[11] But, Giroux has been involved in this cultural studies/critical pedagogy project for more than twenty years.[12] Drawing connections between public pedagogies and the larger formations of power in which they are a part, Giroux makes a powerful argument for returning to the pedagogical dimensions of popular culture in cultural studies projects. By doing so, we necessarily move from a critique of text to the relation between context and text. Beyond deconstruction, this type of engagement is explicitly political because it approaches discussions of meaning as struggles over power. It is also explicitly critical because it demands an engagement with the objective implications of domination in an effort to transform conditions of oppression.

Giroux's insurgent cultural pedagogy offers a unique opportunity to enliven the classroom and relieve both teachers and students from the intellectual shallowness and social irrelevancy that standardized curricula and high-stakes testing often promote and enforce.[13] Giroux's insurgent cultural pedagogy orients cultural studies toward the interventionist project of critical pedagogy, making the theory and practice of articulation—the "methodological" practice of cultural studies—more than a banal exercise in linking "texts" normally observed and understood as disconnected.[14] It also liberates theories and practices of teaching and learning from the burdensome legacy of "practicality," a code word that implies the sublimation of theory to the instrumentalization of teaching through the privileging of methodologies, techniques, and practices. Lastly, it draws theoretical validity and social relevance by accepting the intrinsic partialities of knowledge and experience without denying the "broader features of social organization and conflicts."[15] As such, Giroux's insurgent cultural pedagogy recognizes, as Steven Best and Douglas Kellner put it, "that while it is impossible to produce a fixed set and exhaustive knowledge of a constantly changing complex of social processes, it is possible to map the fundamental domains, structures, practices, and discourses of a society, and how they are constituted and interact."[16]

Giroux's insurgent cultural pedagogy de-reifies popular culture, while respecting its power to teach, just as it provides a theoretical framework for interrogating popular culture as a "commodity that must be examined as a source and effect of supra-individual relations."[17] In this way, cultural material as curriculum offers the teacher an opportunity to use her authority to link cultural "artifacts" with social formations of power, while constructing oppositional knowledges that challenge the moral legitimacy of dominant social formations. For example, what might it mean to link the production of gansta rap to white, corporate America without denying the resistant function rap sometimes plays in urban life? How does thinking about popular films and other modes of cultural production as "teaching machines" present teachers and students with the challenge of asking what, how, and why they teach us what they do? By respecting the power of these teaching machines to mobilize desire, to instigate anger, fear, and lust, to whitewash history, and to validate certain ways of being in the world, teachers can begin to make learning meaningful, just as they disrupt hegemonic representations without totally dismantling a student's power investments in popular culture.

To illustrate this project, we can look to Giroux's recent critique of *Fight Club*, a film that he sees as articulating with the "politics, ideology, and culture of neoliberalism."[18] As such, he argues that the film is driven by an investment in individualism, a construction of masculinity that relies on violence and misogyny for its sense of agency, and a total disregard for "social, public, and collective" responses to the increasing callousness and alienation of market-driven social policies.[19] Posing as a socially engaged film, *Fight Club* "ends up reproducing the very problems they attempt to address."[20] By utilizing a transgressive aesthetic, films like *Fight Club* romanticize violence, racism, and sexual abuse, among other antidemocratic practices, in the name of creative freedom, progressive politics, and entertainment.

Generally denying any relationship between entertainment and public pedagogy, Hollywood mystifies the role it plays in encouraging the affective investments we make, our occupation of narrowly conceived subject positions, and our individual and collective attitudes and behaviors toward "difference."

Demystifying Hollywood's discourse of innocence and entertainment, Giroux critiques a film's public pedagogy by mapping its sociopolitical "lessons" to larger public discourses. In the context of *Fight Club*, taking a detour through the film's public pedagogy exposes the paradoxical relationship between its transgressive aesthetics on one hand and its conservative politics on the other. Because teaching is never divorced from the context in which it occurs, a focus on the film's teaching strategies and capacities and the lessons it promotes leads to an engagement with the sociopolitical context of the film. As such, a film's pedagogy takes on relevance outside the limited scope of the film itself. In the case of *Fight Club*, once its transgressions are articulated to the discourse of neoliberalism, they are, in fact, no longer transgressive. Rather, the film's transgressions are employed in the service of a highly conservative discourse, one that critiques consumerism along misogynistic lines, just as it advocates for a construction of masculinity and agency through an appeal to violence, atomization, and social eruption.

Giroux's insurgent cultural pedagogy is unique in the field of cultural criticism because he not only deals with the pedagogic aspects of popular culture, but he engages and wants to transform the political structures that, in part, are given purpose through a highly refined system of public pedagogies. Recognizing the historical importance of other work, Giroux nevertheless distinguishes himself from other social critics, such as the deconstructionists or those that read films diagnostically. Giroux's interpretive practices reflect a concern with how films "function as public discourses that address or at least resonate with broader issues in the historical and socio-political context in which they are situated."[21] As such, the natural slip and struggle over textual meanings, although never stopped, is significantly shaped given how dominant discourses inform and limit our choices and imaginations. For example, *Fight Club* could easily be taken up diagnostically, that is, taught against the grain of its politics. This interpretive/pedagogical practice, like the method of deconstruction, is not without its benefits, but it often reproduces a decontextualized method of interpretation that shies away from an engagement with systems, institutions, and discourses of pedagogical/political consequence. In other words, although deconstruction and diagnostic approaches to film and other cultural practices have offered a great deal of important interpretive insights into the organization of "signs," they have generally shied away from engaging the political apparatuses in which those texts are situated. Again, these strategies are not wrong per se, but they do, on an important level, miss the point of a critical pedagogy.

Never claiming that his critiques are the "last word," Giroux does want to engage the public pedagogy of films and other cultural practices in order to "shed critical light on how such texts work pedagogically and politically to legitimize some meanings, invite particular desires, and exclude others."[22] For educators and other social critics, this means mapping "discourses, everyday life, and the machineries of power," just as they attempt, through an understanding of these maps, to transform oppressive geographies of power democratically.[23]

Delineating Giroux's insurgent cultural pedagogy are five organizing axioms. First, traditional academic disciplines "cannot account for the great diversity of cultural and social phenomena that has come to characterize an increasingly hybridized, post-industrial world."[24] By making students more attentive to popular culture as a site of "pedagogical and political struggle," we can address the epistemological demands of a multicultural community, just as we attempt to disrupt those common-sense "representations of the real" that draw their legitimacy from hegemonic formations of power.[25]

Second, culture and power are key concepts in understanding the dynamic political processes of daily life. Not only has this concern with culture and power opened the door on the relationships between "knowledge and authority, the meaning of canonicity, and the historical and social contexts that deliberately shape students' understanding of accounts of the past, present, and future," but it also has disrupted the commonsense understanding that the only texts that deserve critical attention are print media.[26] As such, research on films, advertising, television, and other visual texts has proliferated in the academy, drawing scorn from both academics on the left and right. Never suggesting that books are not important and valuable artifacts, it is vital to understand their axiomatic and symptomatic relationship—both in form and content—to power and knowledge.

Third, political insurgency must be informed by a commitment to, in Stuart Hall's words, "the vocation of intellectual life."[27] The vocation of intellectual life, as Giroux understands it, suggests four separate but interrelated points. Pedagogically, it suggests a rejection of a banking philosophy of education, where intellectuals make deposits of what they consider vital information into passively awaiting students. Ethically, it suggests that "intellectual work is incomplete unless it self-consciously assumes responsibility for its effects in the larger public culture, while simultaneously addressing the most profoundly and deeply inhumane problems of the societies in which we live."[28] Politically, it points to the issue of the redistribution of power both within and outside the schools. Strategically, it implies a dialogical as well as a dialectical consideration of the teaching-learning rubric. This means that a teacher who is committed to the vocation of intellectual life must take seriously "how dialogue is constructed in the classroom about other cultures and voices by critically addressing both the position of the theorists and the institutions in which such dialogues are produced."[29] A dialectical awareness of the teaching-learning rubric exposes the partiality of knowledge without giving up the political effectiveness that provisional closures afford. As such, dialogic exchanges, in order to be critical, must also be, in part, dialectical.

Fourth, society's representations signal a register of social, economic, and political health. Representations help construct our social and political reality and, as such, must be taken seriously. For Giroux's current project, this means paying close attention to how media plays "a part in the formation, in the constitution, of the things they reflect. It is not that there is a world outside, 'out there,' which exists free of the discourse of representation."[30] Not content simply to acknowledge that the world is "socially constructed," Giroux pushes the hermeneutical envelope by asking what the pedagogical/political implications of those constructions might be and who or what is to be held accountable for the material and psychic effects of those constructions.

Fifth, theoretical work, or theorizing, is part of the critical and transformative process. Breaking away from education's fetishism with practice, where "methodological issues [are abstracted] from their ideological contexts and consequently ignore the interrelationship between the sociopolitical structures of a society and the act of reading and learning."[31] Giroux believes that theory can provide a link between social formations, knowledge/power, and the practices of education and teaching. Moreover, theoretical work is understood as *doing something*. I like to call this process a "pragmatics of theorizing," that is, a practice of doing theory in which the act of theorizing is understood as real work.[32] I believe Macedo is correct to argue that the subordination of theory to the pragmatics of method creates an abstraction between the interconnection of social formations and knowledge. To avoid this abstraction, theory should be taken up, or "desubordinated" in a way that utilizes its ability to create linkages between what we do, why we do it, and the future possibilities that we hope to create through our pedagogical practices. At the same time, our practices must not be thought of as disconnected from the social formations of which they are inevitably a part.

Douglas Kellner's work is another example of this kind of cultural studies, albeit not as direct as Giroux's in linking the constraining forces of larger public discourses with the interpretive process.[33] Additionally, although he does not necessarily discuss the pedagogical implications of films per se, he does address the intersection of symbolic forms with dominating political and cultural formations of power as part of the hegemonic process. Kellner's work implies that there is pedagogy operating in this intersection that finally provides the means both to understanding how meanings are produced as well as how to troubling those meanings. Taking up texts diagnostically, Kellner creates articulations that "use history to read texts and texts to read history."[34] His methodological approach to cultural studies is "multiperspectival," avoiding any one particular "read" of a film. This risks a relativism that Kellner, for the most part, avoids by deploying his practices "within a critical social theory that attacks a system of domination and that struggles for a more democratic and egalitarian social order."[35] Kellner, like many critical theorists, struggles to reconcile the modern and the postmodern in a way that neither denies the vitality of social structures to limit or expand our political and psychological capacities nor denigrates the multireferential realities that are born and bred out of the personal and social identifications that we make or that are made for us. His critical process is important because it moves beyond a critique of the textual to "diagnose social trends and tendencies," revealing the fissures in hegemonic circuits.[36]

Joe Kincheloe's approach to cultural studies is animated, in large part, not through a critique of media formations per se, but through a hermeneutical interrogation of cultural structures and symbols, most recently McDonald's.[37] Kincheloe critiques McDonald's "symbolic capital," constructing articulations between the "competing signs of the burger" that characterize its semiotic power throughout the world. This is not to say that Kincheloe's critique lacks a political referent; it simply means that his critique is neither polemical nor one dimensional. He points out that in many countries McDonald's is a symbol of wealth, whereas in the United States it is not. He also points out McDonald's symbolic association to U.S. nationalism and the significant inroads it has made into the educational sphere. As Kincheloe points out, "taking advantage of [neoliberal ideology], McDonald's has produced advertisement-laden curricula for almost every academic subject, including language courses in Russian, Spanish, French, and German."[38]

But McDonald's power to "produce and transmit knowledge, shape values, influence identity, and construct consciousness" goes far beyond its influence in schooling. McDonald's, argues Kincheloe, is an educative structure, teaching consumers not only about its special brand of consumption, pleasure, and entertainment, but more significantly, teaching the world the legitimacy of capitalist relations of production, distribution, and consumption, even as McDonalds is complicated within a global network of neoliberal policies. Kincheloe writes, "McDonald's operates on both a Fordist and post-Fordist economic plane in the context of premodernist, modernist, and postmodernist cultural logics; it functions as a highly rationalized and as a transrational/affective organization, depending upon the goal."[39] Kincheloe's hermeneutics is not unlike Stuart Hall's famous exposition of the Walkman. It is a creative project driven by the need to understand how cultural formations possess symbolic capital that have the power to shape and normalize the dominant structure of everyday life. The power of cultural studies in all three examples is its capacity to bring attention to the cultural pedagogies that are at work, theorize their implications, and hold accountable the "teachers" of these sociopolitical lessons.

🌑 Cultural Studies of Critical Pedagogy

The second trajectory of cultural studies, which has been almost completely ignored, takes up the kind of pedagogical practices that constitute what I call cultural studies of critical pedagogy. These are practices that are deeply implicated in teaching educators and other political workers how to participate in the articulatory process. By doing so they engage in the production and disruption of knowledge/power and in a cartographic process of mapping what might appear to be disparate cultural practices. These pedagogical projects and strategies are meant to instigate and provoke, just as they are meant to give students the tools needed to critically break, and break into, the continuity of dominant and established representations. From questioning common sense and identifying dominant social formations to interrogating identity constructions and the normalizing discourses of established power, students are involved in working in the spaces of political, social, and cultural *relations*. This means that students are asked to make articulations between texts and contexts, examining power's ability to normalize the strange, obfuscate social processes, and depoliticize knowledge.

This is not to say that articulation is the proscribed method or theory of cultural studies, although when understood correctly, it provides a powerful tool for the study of culture. As J. D. Slack writes, articulation has often mistakenly been appropriated as *the* tool—methodologically and theoretically—of the cultural studies theorist.[40] This has led to both an oversimplification of the meaning of theory and method in the context of cultural studies. Rather than see theory in a formal sense, that is, rather than using theory in a positivistic way or as a science, cultural studies understands theory as a "'detour' to help ground our engagement with what newly confronts us and to let that engagement provide the ground for retheorizing."[41] Similarly, methods are understood not as stagnant "ways of doing" outside of changing contexts. Rather, they are understood as practices that must be responsive to changing historical realities.[42] In this context, the articulatory process is an engagement with the

> concrete in order to change it, that is to rearticulate it. To understand theory and method this way shifts perspective from the acquisition or application of an epistemology to the creative process of articulating, of thinking relations and connections as how we come to know and as creating what we know. Articulation is, then, not just a thing (not just a connection) but a process of creating connections, much in the same way that hegemony is not domination but the process of creating and maintaining consensus or of co-coordinating interests.[43]

The complexity of such a project is daunting, and it often seems that articulation is both the key and gatekeeper of a radical discourse meant only for those who understand its intricacies. However, I think it is possible to teach a rudimentary understanding of this process in a manner that allows students to begin "doing" cultural studies in such a way that neither takes away from the political nature of the project, nor reduces articulation to the deconstruction of texts. By fostering an understanding of a few important evaluative markers, students can begin to do cultural studies just as they learn to complicate their understanding of what they are doing. In the end, cultural studies of critical pedagogy must provide an *underdetermined* theoretical and methodological framework so that students can think creatively in the face of newly emerging cultural realities on one hand and hegemonic social forces on the other.

Consistently with the work that has been done on critical pedagogy in the past, which I have discussed at length throughout this book, cultural studies of critical pedagogy initiates the teaching and learning process through dialog, the democratization of authority, and a critique of established power. Briefly, dialog is generated between the teacher and the student so that experience and the contexts that it implies become part of the teaching/learning process. By creating the environment for dialog to take place, the teacher/student and student/teacher are no longer situated outside of the learning process, but rather are directly implicated in it. By having to listen to and learn from the students, the teacher not only legitimizes students' experiences, but also opens herself up to critique and contestation. Moreover, dialog in the context of critical pedagogy means that both students and teachers are held accountable for their ideas and beliefs.

The democratization of authority occurs in part through dialog, but is made more concrete by a writing and public speaking activity that I give to my students. Borrowing from Giroux,[44] I have my students write response papers to the assigned readings. The writers for each given day bring in enough copies for the rest of the class, and then present their papers, as though they were on a panel. This practice further takes away the centrality of my authority, just as it provides many of the themes that we will discuss during class. The public speaking aspect of this assignment helps turn the classroom into a public sphere in which the speakers are held accountable for their ideas by me and their peers.

Lastly, a critique of established power and its social, cultural, and pedagogical implications helps to delineate exactly what is at stake in cultural studies of critical pedagogy. By recognizing the normalizing effects of established power, we can begin to reveal its existence, as well as hold it accountable for its practices. This is no small matter. Students, whether they are graduates or undergraduates, often have a difficult time acknowledging the existence of dominating power formations. Through a critique of its implications, its anonymity is eventually given a name.

In what follows, I want to describe and critically reflect on a specific "project" that I use in my undergraduate classes that illustrates what a cultural studies of critical pedagogy can look like. The strategy is an attempt not only to link theory and practice, but to understand/learn the practice of theorizing through a concrete pedagogical exercise. It would be a mistake to devalue the political implications of thinking theoretically, especially as it pertains to teaching some of the "practices" associated with cultural studies of critical pedagogy. Unfortunately, thinking theoretically as a political practice has been denigrated by those on the right and the left and must be relegitimized as a form of pedagogical praxis. On the right, the logic of the bottom line encourages thought primarily as it applies to accumulating capital. On the left, the production of theory is seen as both a luxury of privilege and an excuse for "real" political work. Forgetting that there is a difference between doing and understanding, critics of intellectual work on the right and left fall prey to the same hegemonic forces. Common sense tells both that meaningful "work" is constituted by the production of materially oriented things and is essentially pragmatic.

Contrary to these perspectives, my "lesson" is undergirded by both an understanding of what I above called "evaluative markers" and their utilization. These are ideology, hegemony, identity, power/knowledge, and representations. In an important sense, they help form the theoretical skeleton of the articulatory process specifically and of cultural studies of critical pedagogy generally. These five evaluative markers open doors into historical reality, just as they function as tools of revision. Obviously, there are other evaluative markers that we could take up in the service of this critical project. But these five are important because they create a theoretical framework that is underdetermined, freed from the constraints of any one particular school of thought, such as Marxism, feminism(s), critical theory, postmodernism, and the like. In what follows, I will elaborate on these markers and their underdetermined nature in the context of the pedagogical project. In other words, I will discuss different ways to engage students and get students to engage these evaluative markers in the service of cultural studies of critical pedagogy.

ⓐ A Pedagogy of Theoretical Engagement

Although each of these evaluative markers has its own logic, they are somewhat interdependent. Nevertheless, it is important from a pedagogical perspective to teach each separately before complicating them. As any seasoned teacher knows, the key to teaching/learning is making the process meaningful. One way to do this is to draw on the experiences of the students. These different experiences—cultural, political, social, familial, and the like—act to create a "context of differences" in which to develop illustrative examples and construct provocative arguments. But it is less about defining contexts and more about developing a "common language" in which to understand these contexts of difference. In this sense, objective contexts are delineated through our relationship to experience and language. As Hall argues,[45] building upon the work of V. N. Volosinov, "language is the medium par excellence through which things are 'represented' in thought and thus the medium in which ideology is generated and transformed."[46] This is so because language has a "multireferential" capacity to construct different meanings from the same historical set of circumstances. *Language gives perspective ideological significance.*

Although ideology is a contentious word in the history of epistemological studies and its relevance in "postmodern" times is sometimes questioned, I would argue that it is still a fundamental marker of social relations generally and of relations of force specifically. As Hall argues in response to Foucault's critique of ideology as an insufficient marker of relations of force

> as soon as you begin to look at a discursive formation, not as a single discipline but as a *formation*, you have to talk about the relations of power which structure the inter-discursivity, or the intertextuality, of the field of knowledge. I don't much care whether you call it ideology or not. What matters is not the terminology but the conceptualization.[47]

Taking up ideology in the context of cultural studies of critical pedagogy means that it must be understood "not merely as a system of values and beliefs inculcated from above. Rather, the job is to help students see ideology as lived experience in literature, music, painting, and social interaction, without regard to distinctions between great canonical literature and the art of contemporary popular forms."[48]

One effective means of exposing the ideological dimensions of specific kinds of knowledges is to give students, as I discussed in the previous chapter, ideologically distinct texts about the same or similar events. For example, have students collect news articles from ideologically different sources. Note that it is important, especially for new "readers," to pick exaggerated texts. As Theodor Adorno famously said in the context of psychotherapy, in the exaggerations there are truths, and by using texts that are obviously ideological, students can begin to name and locate the perspective accordingly. They can do this by discussing whose interests are being privileged in the texts, as well as the social and political implications of this privileging, and, through comparison, they can note the absences in the texts themselves. In the final analysis, students must learn how to read the absences in texts in order for a text's ideological force to become manifest.

This type of activity—the juxtaposition of ideologically distinct texts—encourages an understanding of ideology in a way that makes it real for students. No longer does it occupy the realm of the philosophical alone. Nor does ideology stay anonymous, hiding behind the veil of common sense. Rather, it comes to be understood as that which structures our lived experiences and often distances our understanding of those experiences through the use of dominant discursive and material practices. From this perspective, ideology comes to be defined not only through its implications, but through its relationship to dominant power as well. The underbelly of ideology is hegemony, and it is equally important that students begin to get a sense of this concept as a social process of commonsense construction, or a process by which a consensus of common sense is formed.

Hegemony is a concept that is fundamental to cultural studies of critical pedagogy because it implicates the sphere of culture as a site of teaching and learning. Culture, in this context, represents the primary field of social experiences, learning, and most importantly, the space and place in which common sense is manufactured. *This process of psychosocial coordination is the mechanism by which ideology and its effects are made transparent.* This is not to say that hegemony is the pedagogical process of establishing false consciousness, if by false consciousness we mean that workers, for example, are ignorant of all the dimensions of capitalism. On the other hand, hegemony does describe a process in which discursive absences are generated, and those parts to the narrative that are left in place are represented as the whole.[49] In this context, a concerted effort to mystify social, cultural, and economic processes generates falsities. What constitutes our unconsciousness are those things that are "invisible, given the concepts and categories that we are using."[50]

Teaching students about hegemony is one of the most difficult and important concepts in cultural studies of critical pedagogy. It is difficult because students are often quite resistant to the notion that their common sense has been constructed from some force outside of themselves. Students who have been raised in the era of neoliberalism with its vulgar individualism find it daunting in some cases to accept that systemic and institutional power affects the choices they make, the questions they ask, and the future they imagine.

I break the concept of hegemony down through an extremely, and admittedly, oversimplified and somewhat banal illustration. I ask the students in the class why men generally choose to wear pants to class instead of dresses. This seemingly innocent question has never failed to disrupt their commonsense assumptions about what is appropriate to wear if you are a male college student in the northeast of the United States. This is not to say that they all came to the next class wearing dresses. The question is asked in an effort to make them aware of the pedagogical processes that made them unconsciously put on pants everyday instead of a dress. In this way, students begin to develop an awareness of how their individual thought processes are part of a larger social process, in which decisions about clothes are only one small part. Once this reflective activity is underway, the task is no longer to persuade a student as to the validity of the hegemonic process. Rather, it is to delve more deeply into other circuits of production and representation in an effort first to reveal the wholes as parts, and then to name and connect the parts to form, if not a whole, a more comprehensive understanding of social, political, and cultural processes. In direct terms, this strategy asks students to question why that which is considered common is common and how it got that way.

Obviously related is the concept of identity, or more accurately, social and personal identifications. The concepts of social and personal identifications are important because they provide a framework for taking up how and why we position ourselves, or are positioned, the way we are in the social and political milieu. Getting at these questions often means taking a detour through our experiences as racialized, class-organized, and gendered individuals. But again, in the age of neoliberal hegemony, the task is to have students begin to register these identifications socially and politically. Many students still understand themselves within the logic of Descartes: "I think therefore I am." This construction of subjectivity at worst denies the social aspects of our individuality. At best, it relegates the social to the periphery of ontological studies.

The feminist position (generally) situates the self in relation to other selves. Instead of "I think therefore I am," "We think therefore I am" creates the conceptual framework in which to examine the relationship between social and personal identifications and the power/knowledge nexus that organizes those identifications, hence, privileges certain positionalities over others. Granted, the complexity of identifications, given their interlocking relationships to each other, presents a pedagogical challenge. Nevertheless, it is important for students to begin to examine how certain identifications carry with them the capacity to legitimate or delegitimate others.

For "white" students, for example, it is imperative that they begin to recognize the political processes that not only situate "black" and "brown" students in derogatory and exclusionary ways, but how the identification of "white" as a historically positive position works to subjugate those who are not "white." Having students take an accounting of white privilege can do this. I have used the example of racial profiling to begin to peel away the hegemony of white supremacy. It is enough, initially at least, to have students understand just one example of white privilege in order to get them to question other realities in which white privilege might be at work. As long as one concrete example can be understood, then the task again, like that of hegemony, is not to persuade students as to the validity of the concept, but to get them to delve more deeply into the mechanisms of domination as they manifest themselves in the process of identity construction. The question is no longer, Are there institutional forces at work in society? Rather, the question becomes, Where are they and what are their social and political implications for our ability to live in a free and just society? Other questions that beg to be asked in this context are, What knowledges are working to legitimate these mechanisms of domination? How do the media and other cultural formations help to transform perspective into truth? How does power work to validate the knowledges that legitimate domination and/or specific economic and social formations? How are the identifications we make constrained by the power/knowledge nexus?

The move into a dialog about the relationship between power and knowledge is informed, in large part, by Foucault's work.[51] But it is not necessary to subject students, especially undergraduates, to the complexities of his work in order to teach them the general principles of power/knowledge. I begin by asking students how they understand the relationship between knowledge and power. Most reply that a person who acquires knowledge will have power. I then ask my students to reflect on historical narratives. Columbus "discovering" America is an easy example. But teachers should not ignore the obvious simply because it is obvious or has already been revised in a more radical way. In my experience, many students have come to understand the revised Columbus "discovery" story as more accurate than what they were taught in elementary school, but nevertheless they often see it as an imposition of "politically correct" thinking, rather than an example of power writing history on one hand, or insurgency rewriting history on the other.

Having students reflect on who writes the historical narratives (the winners of historical struggle) and how those narratives shape our understanding of the past, present, and future begins to rearticulate the relationship between knowledge and power to one in which power defines, creates, and legitimates knowledge. No longer seeing learning as a question of simply acquiring knowledge (in the singular), but rather as one of making distinctions between different knowledges and the powers that struggle over their legitimacy, students begin to "read" power through a critique of knowledge. "Critique," as Foucault explains, "is not a matter of saying that things are not right as they are. It is a matter of pointing out on what kinds of assumptions, what kinds of familiar, unchallenged, unconsidered modes of thought the practices that we accept rest."[52]

In the cultural sphere—one of the primary sites for the construction of "truths"—representations play a fundamental role in how we see each other and view society. As such, there is no longer a clear line delineating where representations end and where "reality" begins. Not a digression into a vulgar postmodernism, rather this position acknowledges that what appears outside the circuit of representation is, in part, understood by how it is represented.[53] In other words, our capacity to imagine and think otherwise and to transform reality is directly linked to our ability to construct and deconstruct representations.

Conceptually, the notion of representations seems straightforward. But, in my experience, students sometimes have trouble making the leap between representations and their ability to "teach" what is normal and what is strange. Students should be encouraged to interrogate representations in an effort to demystify the notion that they simply reflect reality. Some of the questions I encourage them to ask are, Who has created the representation? Whose "gaze" are we seeing? Are the representations "one dimensional?" That is, do the representations present a narrow perspective of our human capacities? What are the political implications of the representations? For example, if African American men are often portrayed as criminals in the media, do policing policies directed at them make sense? In this context, the criminalization of poverty and "blackness" in judicial and policing practices is *consistent* with dominant representations. When representations are understood as simply reflective, then the critical process gets short-circuited because the material reaction to representations is defended as an appropriate response to a "truth," as opposed to a condition of force.

As a brief example, profiling black males is justified by some law enforcement agencies because, it is argued, black men are more apt to be involved in illegal activity. The argument fails to consider that if black males are profiled and picked up and/or pulled over to a greater degree than whites, it goes to reason that a higher incident of criminal behavior will be discovered. The fact that matters here is not that more black males are involved in criminal behavior than whites, a dubious assertion at best, but that more are under surveillance and, as a consequence, are caught in illegal activities. In short, it is the consistency between representations and political and social policy that suggests a seamless articulation of reality. The questions I encourage my students to ask using the evaluative principles as theoretical reference points attempt to disrupt that consistency by revealing the process by which it has been created.

These five evaluative markers provide students with a critical vocabulary. With this new vocabulary they can begin to put some distance between themselves and the realities in which they live. As such, the questions that they ask of objective realities change. The poster project that I give my students asks them to exercise this new critical vocabulary through a critique of media and other cultural artifacts. The project gives students an opportunity to do a "cultural study of critical pedagogy," creating articulations in an effort to reveal the anonymity of established power and some of its effects. More specifically, I ask students to link (articulate) representations to larger formations of power, critically reflect on the "absences" within texts, and discuss the political implications of these articulations on people's ability to act in and upon the world.

🍎 Poster Project

As Giroux, Kellner, Kincheloe, Steinberg, hooks,[54] Bordo, Grossberg, Hall, and Horkeimer and Adorno,[55] to name only a few, have shown that how we understand "reality" and what we understand about reality are significantly influenced by how that reality is represented. As such, my course entitled "Media and Intercultural

Communications" is developed around the notion of representations. The poster project is an activity for my undergraduates, although I believe that it is an appropriate project for many different levels of students. My students are asked to create a map that explicitly draws connections between representations and larger formations of power. This activity encourages students to ask questions like, Who creates the representation? To what effect? In whose interest? What kinds of attitudes, behaviors, and identities are denigrated? Which ones are celebrated? What is it to be "normal?" Who and/or what is abnormal? Why? How do we come to our commonsense assumptions about the world? How is gender/race/class/sexuality represented? "Who" (i.e., ideologically, culturally, economically, racially) is behind the camera?

This project also engages students in the creative and imaginative process. Breaking into and out of dominant representations, the articulatory process is part of reconstituting the sociological imagination. As you will see, there are many different ways to do this project. The main thing here is that students are actively learning how to do cultural studies. They are learning what it means, and what is at stake, in creating linkages between representations and larger formations of power; they are engaging the relationship between power/knowledge and truth; and they are beginning to complicate their own relationship to media and the world that media helps to construct.

One important aspect to this project is the presentation of it. Students are given ten to fifteen minutes to present their projects to the class. This allows them an opportunity to "write" the accompanying narrative. It also gives the other students an opportunity to ask questions and critically engage the presenter. I turn briefly to a few of the actual projects to demonstrate the efficacy, as well as some of the challenges, of teaching/learning cultural studies of critical pedagogy.

One student, a freshman, chose the dollar bill as an object for critique. But she did not just photocopy a dollar bill; she drew it by hand in pencil. Her rendition of the dollar was presented to the class on a large poster board. In and around the "dollar," she wrote small narratives about the relationship she found between the white man on the bill and the economic iniquities that she saw in society. She problematized the normality of the image by bringing attention to its whiteness and gender. She also highlighted the "In God We Trust" idiom, forming more than a casual relationship between religion and capitalism. Finally, she discussed the notions of greed and power and how the dollar has come to mean more than currency alone, but rather how it symbolizes a way of life defined by the pursuit of material values.

Many students took up representations of women in the media. These students cut out representations of women and pasted them on their poster boards in various patterns. No words accompanied the images, but during the presentation these students created articulatory narratives that pointed out the logic of their thinking.

Most of these presentations interrogated the hypersexualized images of women, but this by no means suggests uniformity in these presentations or perspectives. What was fascinating, and eventually the point, was that students engaged in the critical process of questioning not only the images, but each other. Some of the students believed that these hypersexualized images were damaging to a women's ability to feel good about herself physically, but resisted the notion that they constrained a women's ability to participate in the job market or democratic life. They were encouraged to create linkages between "beauty" and power. Others felt that it was the responsibility of the models in the ads to resist the seduction of fame and money in the service of self-respect, while others critically located the images within the larger formations of capitalism and patriarchy. During these presentations, students were encouraged to evaluate the images using the five evaluative markers. This gave them an opportunity to reflect upon their own work, just as it gave them the critical tools to evaluate their peers' work.

An exchange student from Poland, who chose to explore anti-Semitic representations, completed the last project I will discuss. Coming from a country historically antagonistic toward Jews, this project was both an effort to inform others, as well as an opportunity for this woman to understand her own culture's bigotry, something that she had discussed openly in class. She unrolled a huge poster board approximately seven feet tall and three feet wide, by far the largest used in the class. She divided the board in half, one side portraying anti-Semitic representations and narratives (jokes, fables, myths), while the other half showed more complex representations of Jews. It was a sophisticated project, creating articulations between religious dogma and political repression; anti-Semitism and cultural hegemony; and power and knowledge. Interestingly, it also showed how deeply ingrained the hegemony of anti-Semitism is in certain cultures. Despite her efforts to break into this cultural and political hegemony, on occasion she legitimated it. In one instance, she chose a photo of a Hasidic Jew as an example of an anti-Semitic representation, in effect creating an articulation that justifies domination on account of difference. In this instance, she failed to evaluate the representation in terms of power/knowledge and was left with an analysis that left untroubled the process of normalization. Nevertheless, the project illustrates one student's struggle to "see" and "read" social reality in articulatory terms, that is, as a process of relations with specific cultural, political, and pedagogical implications.

❧ Conclusion

Teaching people how to do cultural studies is a political strategy that helps create distance between people and their immediate surroundings. It is a counterhegemonic strategy in that it disrupts the continuity of common sense, which by default reifies what is *because* it is. Cultural studies of critical pedagogy is, in short, a theory/method that builds a bridge between what is and what could be. In this neoliberal era of corporate media domination and a politico-moral conservatism that reeks of McCarthyism, I would argue that it is imperative for people to evaluate the social, economic, and political spheres using more than Christian morality as a compass. With these evaluative markers—hegemony, identity, ideology, representations, and power/knowledge—we can begin to take a more complex accounting of the politics of everyday life, the politics that are both everywhere and, consequently nowhere, all at the same time.

I think these examples provide an interesting account of what it means to merge cultural studies, critical pedagogy, and critical literacy, without reducing them to a method of interpretation or teaching recipe on one hand or restricting them at the level of the theoretical on the other. I hope this work provokes educators and other political workers to actively create new conditions of hope through the institution of oppositional social and cultural forms, the interrogation of popular cultural forms, and the production of cultural forms that reflect new political relationships, based in democratic ideals and insurgent political lessons. From music and film to poetry and dance, the innovation of cultural forms and the resurrection of "dissident understandings of past and present political realities"[56] help revitalize our social and political imaginary. Through new cultural formations, I believe we can reclaim histories, memories, and knowledges, while upsetting exclusionary traditions.

In order to challenge and transform what for many is an oppressive social condition, performance artist/intellectual Guillermo Gomez-Pena suggests that we could begin by imagining more "enlightened cartographies: a map of the Americas with no borders; a map turned upside down; or one in which the countries have borders that are organically drawn by geography, culture, and immigration, and not by the capricious hands of economic domination and political bravado."[57] Strategically utopian, political practices of the imagination force cynicism to the margins of political discourse. By redrawing the borders of possibility, we can move closer to what Gomez-Pena calls a "Fourth World,"

> a conceptual place where the indigenous peoples meet with the diasporic communities. In the Fourth World, there is very little place for static identities, fixed nationalities, 'pure' languages, or sacred cultural traditions. The members of the Fourth World live between and across various cultures, communities, and countries. And our identities are constantly being reshaped by this kaleidoscopic experience.[58]

The aspiration of collective freedom is a democratic hope rooted in the belief that through the political organization of public space, we can create the kind of social environment that is conducive to unlearning neoliberal lessons of exclusion and elitism, while disrupting the geopolitical landscape so that we are encouraged to explore linguistic, cultural, and sexual freedoms. This kind of freedom works within the parameters of democratic authority, striving to balance liberty, equality and justice with individual desire, social autonomy, and collective responsibility. It is a freedom that must struggle to institute social formations that support the democratization of power. And it is a freedom that, in the end, must no longer be approached as a noun, but, instead, must be considered a *verb*! In this potent form, freedom signifies, not a thing, but the manner by which we become something other than what we are.

Conclusion

Democratic Education for a Neoliberal Age

Education must be guided by the *principles*, not the practices, of a regime.[1]

The principles of a deliberative *democratic* regime are mutual respect, justice, self-governance, hope, and equity.[2] These principles should shape the direction and formation of the systems and institutions that help organize the social and political spaces of a society. They also connote a significant knowledge base as well as skills and dispositions (see chapter 5) that people should have to participate in the reproduction and/or transformation of the many different social structures that help organize the political landscape. As such, they should significantly influence the manner by which education and schooling is theorized and practiced. Unfortunately, deliberative democracy is overwhelmed by the demands of neoliberalism.

The principles of a neoliberal regime, by contrast, are economic efficiency, limited government, "financial essentialism," and "polyarchic" rule.[3] These principles, as I outlined in chapter 1, have given rise globally to organizations like the IMF and the World Bank. The recent practices of neoliberal regimes like the United States are direct articulations of these principles. Joseph Stiglitz notes that during his tenure as chairman of President Clinton's Council of Economic Advisers and as senior vice president and chief economist of the World Bank from 1997 to 2000, an "irrational exuberance" about the market overwhelmed the democratic sensibilities of many people who were charged with making decisions about the direction of the "new" economy specifically and the social welfare of public and private life generally.[4] He writes, "the [Clinton] administration seemed to accept the notion that the bond market, or financial markets more generally, knew the best way forward. The financial markets, it seemed, represented America's best interests as well as their own. This seemed like nonsense to me."[5] Stiglitz insightfully acknowledges that although finance is an important dimension of twenty-first century life, it is "a special interest group like many others."[6] Throughout this book, I have discussed many different spheres that are influenced by neoliberal rule. From local school reform to global literacy initiatives, neoliberal rule has effectively altered the way "free" societies think about and practice democracy and capitalism.

In this closing chapter, I argue in defense of democratic education. Amy Gutmann argues that "conscious social reproduction is the primary ideal of democratic education."[7] In this model, society is reproduced within the principled constraints of nonrepression and nondiscrimination, two principles that "preserve the intellectual and social foundations of democratic deliberations. A society that empowers citizens to make educational policy, moderated by these two principled constraints, realizes the democratic ideal of education."[8] Gutmann's argument is not a critique of existing educational models as much as it is a philosophical defense of deliberative democratic education. She argues that democratic education should work to empower citizens to participate in educational and political decision making because it is the most equitable means of achieving just ends.

She defends the need for a principled theory of education by arguing that without it we are unable to evaluate the practices and policies that go along with the management of education. How are we to know what a "better" education means outside of a principled theory of education, she asks? Stated another way, a principled theory of education answers the vital questions, Why teach? Why learn? How should we teach? What should we learn? It offers a means to judge the policies and practices of teachers, administrators, and anyone else involved in the educational enterprise.

More specifically, Guttman defends a democratic theory of education on the grounds that it can best answer the question, Who will make decisions about what, how, and why we should teach.[9] A democratic theory of education, unlike functional, liberal, and conservative theories, Gutmann argues, answers the question of "how citizens should resolve their disagreements over educational policy."[10] In a *deliberative* democracy, all people, not simply experts, should be part of a deliberative debate about educational issues. This should increase not only our understanding of educational needs, but also our understanding of each other as part of a community with shared concerns. This does not mean that people will agree. "The most distinctive feature of a democratic theory of education is that it makes a democratic virtue out of our inevitable disagreement over educational problems."[11]

But for democratic education to be meaningful in our neoliberal age, it has to come to terms with the savage inequalities in our schools that Jonathan Kozol brought to our attention more than ten years ago, as well as the savage inequities that inform neoliberal globalization.[12] As I have noted in previous chapters, the gap under neoliberal rule between those who possess and control economic and political power and those who do not has grown since Kozol's striking account of educational inequality. Stiglitz notes that globalization, "as it was actually practiced" by the United States, "tended to make poor societies more rather than less unequal."[13] These inequities help reproduce society by rationalizing themselves within a discourse of freedom and choice on one hand and containment, enforcement, and deception on the other. The former are problematic when theorized outside of power and resources, and the latter are directly incompatible with the principles of deliberative democracy. They are not, however, incompatible with the principles of U.S. democracy or what Noam Chomsky more directly describes as a polyarchy. Chomsky points out, from the perspective of elite opinion regarding the democratic fiasco of the 2000 presidential elections, that "the elections did not reveal a flaw of U.S. democracy, but rather its triumph."[14] Likewise, the inequality that perverts our local schools and the global landscape is a triumph of neoliberalism, not its failure.

In light of these brutal delineations of power and authority, the only authentic democratic education is one that must struggle both to improve and equalize the educational system by teaching students how to organize across cultural interests, struggle against institutional and ideological power, and imagine social life through and beyond the acceptable parameters of dominant knowledge. The playing field is not flat and any form of democratic education that assumes it is does so at the expense of its own relevancy. To be more than a philosophical defense, Gutmann's theory of deliberative democracy should be contextualized more specifically within the reality of political and economic repression and inequality.

This is the point at which issues of social justice coincide with the ideals of democratic education. As R. W. Connell writes, referring to a more Platonic notion of justice, "Individual equality is the condition, not the goal, of a just *social order*."[15] Balancing power, in this context, is a condition of democratic education, not simply its goal. What does it mean to include the condition of "balance" as a principled constraint in a theory of democratic education? It could mean that we must redistribute that which is already in place, albeit placed inequitably. This formulation might create balance in one sense (i.e., empirically), but it does not follow that that which has been distributed is transformed in any meaningful way. Left out of this formulation of justice is the fact that what is being redistributed is not necessarily in the best interests of those who are now being included. For the principle of balance to mean more than the redistribution of a questionable good, it would have to include a notion of content as well as form.[16] Stated another way, *what* is being distributed should be subjected to the same kind of deliberations as the distribution itself. The latter minus the former might bring about a degree of equality, but fail to improve upon the status quo. Without both dimensions considered we would achieve a disruption in practice, but we would fail to provoke a change in principle.

Transforming the principles of education as they exist under neoliberal rule is the ideal goal of a *critical* deliberative democratic education (not unlike what Freire attempted in São Paulo, as I discuss in chapter 4). Transformation at this level suggests a pedagogical strategy that links the spheres of schooling and education. Like I discussed in chapter 6, this requires both a critical vocabulary as well as a radical curriculum. A critical vocabulary works at the level of consciousness, "language" being the medium by which we make sense of the world. Learning a new language shifts our sociological gaze from one that recognizes only those things that have been designated as different, to one that views normalcy as a constructed referent within and across knowledge domains.

Learning new languages implies developing new literacies. Literacy, as I discussed in chapters 2 and 5, entails more than the basic skills of decoding, phonics, and comprehension. Literacies of critical deliberative democracy refer to the fluencies with which one participates in a vast array of "social" discourses. This necessitates a pedagogy that is responsive to new technologies, the arts, media (corporate and public), political ideologies, power and propaganda, oppression, and the function of authority. Extending Connell's ideal of justice, mass-based critical literacies are the condition, not the goal, of deliberative democracy.

Likewise, a radical curriculum that is built up around critical literacies should reflect both a political and social commitment to the principles of deliberative democracy. Politically, a radicalized curriculum should be cosmopolitan in nature, meaning that knowledges, histories, and art from around the world should be taught *in conjunction with,* and not at the expense of, more localized texts. In an age of globalization, it is the articulation between and among different glocal texts that makes them meaningful. Articulations should be created that bring attention to the relationship between texts and power. This does not mean that all studies are reduced to an examination of power per se; it means that because power circulates and affects all knowledges, it should never be too far out of view. From historical research and the truths it uncovers, to the aesthetics of literature, power is always circulating, always *creating,* forever active.

Power, understood in these terms, should be something that citizens of a critical deliberative democracy should not only analyze, but possess in the form of authority. As I discussed in chapters 3 and 4, authority is a necessary dimension of democratic communities because people should have a significant level of control, guided by principled constraints, over how their institutions function. Authority also refers to the power certain discourses have to create identities, legitimate certain realities, and validate conceptions of difference that are conducive to the deliberation of resources. Authority, in this context, should be measured and critiqued for how it enlivens democratic relations or for how it closes them down.

Critical deliberative democracy is, finally, a creative endeavor. It demands a creative mind, an imagination that can trouble existing conceptualizations of what is practical and possible. The creative process bridges the political at the levels of the personal and the social. It engages the imagination and shakes it out of inertia. The imagination, as I am using the word here, refers to the imaginative powers of the social mind to conceptualize the world—from its microcenters to its global frontiers—beyond the parameters of the sensible, normal, and acceptable. Getting beyond the practical is not to ignore it or to reduce it to the theoretical; it means recognizing the limitations of the practical in terms of setting the imagination free to explore ideas, attitudes, and behaviors that are strange and unfamiliar. In this context, the imagination should be engaged for its creative potential, for its capacity to disrupt the kind of common sense manufactured by powerful social and political forces. The practice of using one's imagination is not to be left to artists alone. Teachers and other political workers should be the stewards of their own imagination and the dreams that come forth.

Through the creation of poetry, film, sculpture, and other artistic initiatives—initiatives that do not necessarily take up political concerns directly—teachers and others concerned with the principles and practices of critical deliberative democracy will be helping to develop the skills and dispositions needed to be reflective civic agents. This will occur because creative arts, as places where theory and practice converge, are places of becoming: Identities are resisted and reproduced, geopolitical borders are redrawn, languages are invented, sounds are given voice, voices are given volume, streets become stages, and what is becomes what might be.

The creative process, understood this way, introduces hope as a principle of conscious political participation. Without hope, critical deliberation—struggle—is a nonsensical practice. Hope is a precondition of deliberation; it is the foundation of transformation. Neoliberalism is hostile to hope, as it exists as part of the democratic project of deliberation and decision making. Neoliberalism assumes that its formulation of economic and political life should be beyond the reach of democratic change. Hope is reduced to a mode of dreaming that includes, above all else, material wealth. Absent from this formulation is the hope for equity, cultural plurality, respect across difference, and the possibility of critical deliberations about the most important social agencies, like education, finance, health care, media, and trade. In this context, hope is a radical concept because it demands no less than the transformation of all local and global institutions that are hostile to critical deliberative democracy and the principles that support it.

Notes

Introduction

1. Sehr, David T. (1997). *Education for Public Democracy* (p. 5). Albany: State University of New York Press.

2. Ibid., p. 4.

3. Comaroff, Jean, and Comaroff, John L. (2001). "Millennial Capitalism: First Thoughts on a Second Coming." In *Millennial Capitalism and the Culture of Neoliberalism* (p. 14). Durham, NC: Duke University Press.

4. Ibid., p. 15.

5. Coronil, Fernando. (2001). "Toward a Critique of Globalcentrism: Speculations on Capitalism's Nature." In *Millennial Capitalism and the Culture of Neoliberalism* (p. 70). Durham, NC: Duke University Press.

6. Ibid., pp. 70–71.

7. Ibid., p. 77.

8. Ibid.

9. Giroux, Henry A. (2001). *Theory and Resistance in Education*, 2nd Edition. New York: Bergin and Garvey Press.

10. Giroux, Henry A. (1991). *Border Crossings* (p. 2). New York: Routledge.

11. Ibid.

12. Ibid., pp. 3–4.

13. See Allington, Richard L., Ed. (2002). *Big Brother and the National Reading Curriculum*. Portsmouth, NH: Heinemann Press.

14. See Freire, Paulo, and Macedo, Donaldo. (1987). *Literacy: Reading the Word and the World*. New York: Bergin and Garvey; Macedo, Donaldo. (1994). *Literacies of Power: What Americans Are Not Allowed to Know* Boulder, CO: Westview Press; Purcell-Gates, Victoria, and Waterman, Robin. (2000). *Now We Read, We See, We Speak: Portrait of Literacy Development in an Adult Freirean-based Class*. New York: Lawrence Erlbaum Associates.

15. Gee, James Paul. (2001). "What Is Literacy." In Ed. Patrick Shannon, *Becoming Political, Too* (p. 6). Portsmouth, NH: Heinemann Press.

16. Ibid., p. 1.

🎵 Chapter One

1. Marcuse, H. (1969). *An Essay on Liberation*. Boston: Beacon Press.

2. McChesney, R. W. (1999). "Introduction." In N. Chomsky, *Profit over People: Neoliberalism and Global Order* (p. 7). New York: Seven Stories Press.

3. Bourdieu, P. (1998, December). *Utopia of Endless Exploitation*. Retrieved July 8, 2003, from *Le Monde Diplomatique*: http://mondediplo.com/1998/12/08bourdieu.

4. Jessop, B. (2002). "Globalization and the National State." In Eds. S. Aronowitz and P. Bratsis, *Paradigm Lost* (p. 208). Minneapolis: University of Minnesota Press.

5. McChesney, Ibid., p. 9.

6. Hursh, D. "Neoliberalism and the Control of Teachers, Students, and Learning." Retrieved July 8, 2003: http://eserver.org/clogic/4-1/hursh.html.

7. Palast, G. (2003). *The Best Democracy Money Can Buy* (pp. 153–158). London: Plume.

8. Ibid., p. 154.

9. Ibid.

10. Ibid.

11. Ibid.

12. Ibid., p. 155.

13. Stiglitz in Palast, Ibid., p. 155.

14. Ibid.

15. Ibid., p. 156.

16. Bourdieu, Ibid.

17. Ibid., pp. 1–2.

18. Palast, G. (2000); Harvey, D. (2000). *Spaces of Hope*. Berkley: University of California Press.

19. Bourdieu, Ibid., p. 1.

20. John and Jean Camaroff quoted in Giroux, H. (2002, Winter). "Neoliberalism, Corporate Culture, and the Promise of Higher Education." *Harvard Educational Review*, 72(4): pp. 439–464.

21. Bourdieu, Ibid.

22. Ibid., p. 2.

23. Ibid., p. 2.

24. Giroux, Ibid., pp. 439–464.

25. Ibid.

26. Castoriadas, C. (1999). In Bauman, Z. (1999), *In Search of Politics* (p. 84). Stanford, CA: Stanford University Press.

27. John and Jean Camaroff quoted in Giroux, Ibid., pp. 439–464.

28. McChesney, Ibid., p. 11.

29. Bauman, Z. (1999). *In Search of Politics* (p. 84). Stanford, CA: Stanford University Press.

30. Giroux, Ibid., pp. 439–464.

31. Ibid.

32. Bauman, Ibid., p. 88.

33. Giroux, Ibid., pp. 439–464.

34. Bauman quoted in Giroux, Ibid., 439–464.

35. Giroux, Ibid., pp. 439–464.

36. Ibid.

37. Ibid.

38. See www.mtv.com/onair/cribs/.

39. Chomsky, N. (1999). *Profit over People* (pp. 59–60). New York: Seven Stories Press.

40. Althusser, L. (1971). "Ideology and the Ideological State Apparatuses (Notes toward an Investigation)." In Trans. B. Brewster, *Lenin and Philosophy and Other Essays* (p. 22). New York: Monthly Review Press.

41. Ibid., p. 24.

42. Ibid.

43. Aronowitz, S., and Bratsis, P. (2002). "State Power Global Power." In *Paradigm Lost* (p. xxiii).

44. Bauman, Z. (1998). *Globalization* (p. 60). New York: Columbia University Press.

45. Held, D. (1995). *Democracy and the Global Order* (p. 92). Stanford, CA: Stanford University Press.

46. Bauman, Ibid., p. 64.

47. Held, Ibid., p. 92.

48. Bauman, Ibid., pp. 66–67.

49. Ibid., p. 69.

50. Held, Ibid., p. 91.

51. Bauman, Ibid., p. 69.

52. Macedo, D. "The Colonialism of the English Only Movement." Retrieved from *ER Online* on July 30, 2003: www.aera.net/pubs/er/arts/29–03/macedo01.htm. As Macedo insightfully points out, "The position of U.S. English Only proponents is not very different from the Portuguese colonialism that tried to eradicate the use of African languages in institutional life by inculcating Africans through the educational system in Portuguese only with myths and beliefs concerning the savage nature of their cultures" (p. 2).

53. Held, Ibid., pp. 123–124.

54. Bauman, Ibid., p. 69.

55. Ibid., p. xx.

56. Ibid.

57. Nico Poulantzas quoted in Aronowitz and Bratsis, Ibid., p. xix.

58. Ibid., p. 68.

59. Ibid., p. 70.

60. Ibid., pp. 70–71.

61. Held, Ibid., pp. 99–140.

62. For complete discussion, see Bauman, Z. (1998). "After the Nation-State—What?" In *Globalization* (pp. 55–76).

63. Althusser, Ibid., pp. 6–7.

64. Althusser, Ibid., p. 18.

65. Subcomandante Marcos quoted in Bauman, Ibid., p. 66.

66. Chomsky, N. (2000). *Chomsky on MisEducation* (p. 17). Ed. Donaldo Macedo. New York: Roman & Littlefield.

67. Willis, P. (1981). *Learning to Labor*. New York: Columbia University Press.

68. Althusser, Ibid., p. 30.

69. Giroux, H. (2001). "Private Satisfactions and Public Disorders." *Journal of Advanced Composition*, 21(1): p. 6.

70. Ibid.

71. Michael Parenti quoted in Weiner, Eric J. (2003). Beyond Doing Cultural Studies: Toward a Cultural Studies of Critical Pedagogy." *The Review of Education, Pedagogy, and Cultural Studies*, 25(1): pp. 55–73.

72. Raymond William quoted in Weiner, Ibid.

73. Weiner, Ibid.

74. Giroux, Ibid., p. 23.

75. McChesney, R. (2000). *Rich Media, Poor Democracy*. Champaign: University of Illinois Press.

76. Giroux, Ibid., p. 24.

77. Held, Ibid., p. 15.

78. Aronowitz, S. (1996). *The Death and Rebirth of American Radicalism* (pp. 181–182). New York: Routledge.

79. Gee, J. P. (2001). "What Is Literacy?" In Ed. P. Shannon, *Becoming Political, Too* (p. 2). Portsmouth, NH: Heinnemann Press.

80. Marcuse, H. (1964). *One Dimensional Man* (p. 5). Boston: Beacon Press.

81. Ibid., p. 9.

82. Ibid., p. 9.

83. See Stevenson, R. (June 27, 2003). "Bush Calls for Changes in Africa and to Promote Trade." *New York Times*. Section A, p. 1, col., 5. For an explicit account of neoliberalism's brutality see, Chomsky, *Profit over People*; Palast, *The Best Democracy Money Can Buy*; Harvey, *Spaces of Hope*.

84. Hursh, D. "Neoliberalism and the Control of Teachers Students, and Learning." Retrieved July 8, 2003, from http://eserver.org/clogic/4–1/hursh.html.

85. Marcuse, Ibid., p. 5.

86. Ibid., p. 6.

87. Lemert, C. (1997). *Social Things*. New York: Rowman & Littlefield.

88. Giroux, H. (1997). *Pedagogy and the Politics of Hope* (p. 9). New York: Westview Press.

89. Ibid., pp. 9, 12.

90. Blackmore quoted in Hursh, "Neoliberalism and the Control of Teachers Students, and Learning." Retrieved on the Internet on July 8, 2003, from http://eserver.org/clogic/4–1/hursh.html.

91. Giroux, Ibid., p. 123.

92. Stanley Aronowitz, conversation.

93. Spring, J. (1998). *Education and the Rise of the Global Economy* (pp. 152–153). New York: Lawrence Erlbaum Inc.

94. Ibid., 151.

95. State Board President's Address. (2002). *Public Education in New Jersey.* Produced under the direction of the Office of Public Communications.

96. Aronowitz, S. (2000). *The Knowledge Factory* (p. 50). Boston: Beacon Press.

97. Aronowitz, Stanley, and Defazio, William. (1994). *The Jobless Future* (p. xxi). Minneapolis: University of Minnesota Press.

98. Ibid., p. 85.

99. Retrieved August 4, 2003, from New Jersey Core Curriculum Standards: www.state.nj.us/njded/cccs/02.

100. Retrieved August 4, 2003, from New Jersey Core Curriculum Standards: www.state.nj.us/njded/abbotts/resources/models_by_cohort_s.shtml; For a list of reform models and their foci see: www.nwrel.org/scpd/catalog/modellist.asp; For New Jersey's "Reading First" initiatives see www.state.nj.us/njded/readfirst/Five/Fluency.shtml. Note that in the "Reading First" online literature, the National Reading Panel Report is referenced as a guide "based on research." For a serious challenge to the legitimacy of that research, see Allington, Richard. (2002). *Big Brother and the National Reading Curriculum.* Portsmouth, NH: Heinnemann Press.

101. Apple, M. (1982). "Curricular Form and the Logic of Technical Control." In Ed. Michael Apple, *Cultural and Economic Reproduction in Education* (p. 249). London: Routledge and Kegan Paul.

102. Retrieved August 7, 2002, from New Jersey Core Curriculum Standards: www.state.nj.us/njded/cccs/drafts/career.pdf.

103. Aronowitz and Defazio, Ibid., p. 85.

104. Ibid., p. 85.

105. See www.nwrel.org/scpd/catalog/SampleSites.asp?ModelID=10.

106. Retrieved August 25, 2003, from www.nwrel.org/scpd/catalog/ModelDetails.asp?ModelID=10.

107. See www.bbn.com/arpanet/index.html.

108. Aronowitz and Defazio, Ibid., p. 14.

109. Ibid., p. 95.

110. Retrieved August 7, 2002, from New Jersey Core Curriculum Standards: www.state.nj.us/njded/cccs/drafts/career.pdf.

111. Spring, Ibid., p. 142.

112. Retrieved August 7, 2002, from New Jersey Core Curriculum Standards: www.state.nj.us/njded/cccs/drafts/career.pdf.

113. Horkheimer, M. and Adorno, T. (2002). *Dialectic of Enlightenment.* Stanford, CA: Stanford University Press; Lipman, M. (1991). *Thinking in Education.* New York: Cambridge University Press.

114. Retrieved September 8, 2003, from www.state.nj.us/njded/cccs/08langintro.html.

115. Ibid.

116. Ibid.

117. Ibid.

118. Retrieved September 8, 2003, from www.state.nj.us/njded/abbotts/resources/models_by_cohort.shtml.

119. Retrieved September 8, 2003, from www.successforall.net/curriculum/readroot.htm.

120. See Arlington, *Big Brother and the National Reading Panel.*

121. Jessop, Ibid., p. 208.

122. Ibid.

123. Ibid.

124. Giroux, H. (1999). *The Mouse that Roared: Disney and the End of Innocence.* Lanham, MD: Rowman & Littlefield.

125. Cutler, A. D. (2002). *Deans Message,* from www.montclair.edu/pages/cehs/MessagefromDean.htm.

🎵 Chapter Two

1. Social structures, however invisible to the "untrained" eye, are organizing and enduring entities that condition how individuals experience everyday life. As C. Lemert states, "Still, structures appear to people in the course of daily life as through a mysterious fog. As I've said, it is very hard to say with precision exactly what a social structure is. Yet we must, if only because the practical sociologies by which people live and move are constantly drawn toward attempts to explain how and why structures so inexorably determine what individuals can and cannot do, even who they are." Lemert, Charles. (1997). *Social Things* (p. 128). New York: Rowman & Littlefield.

2. See http://home.howstuffworks.com/question47.htm.

3. Jenkins, Linda B. and Kirsch, Irwin S. (1994). *Executive Summary from Adult Literacy in New Jersey* (p. 8). Princeton, NJ: ETS.

4. Kaestle, Carl F., Campbell, Anne, Finn, Jeremy D., Johnson, Sylvia T., and Mikulecky, Larry J. (2001). *Adult Literacy and Education in America.* Washington, DC: U.S. Department of Education.

5. They can be saved from what is left conspicuously ambiguous in this highly politico-religious discourse. But the notion that they need to be saved from oppressive operations of power, manifested in a reduced social welfare commitment, is never discussed. This "silence," of course, leaves us with the implicit understanding that they need to be saved from themselves, their families, and their communities.

6. For example, see Goodstein, Lori. (February 23, 2003). "Anti Drug Program Lauded by Bush Is More Ministry than Treatment Center." *New York Times:* p. 18, Sect. 1; Lictblau, Eric. (January 23, 2003). "Bush Plans to Let Religious Groups Get Building Aid." *New York Times:* p. 1, Sect. A.

7. Explaining the fetish that the prison-industrial complex represents, Eric Schlosser writes, "Three decades after the war on crime began, the United States has developed a prison-industrial complex—a set of bureaucratic, political, and economic interests that encourage increased spending on imprisonment, regardless of the actual need. The prison-industrial complex is not a conspir-

acy, guiding the nation's criminal-justice policy behind closed doors. It is a confluence of special interests that has given prison construction in the United States a seemingly unstoppable momentum. It is composed of politicians, both liberal and conservative, who have used the fear of crime to gain votes; impoverished rural areas where prisons have become a cornerstone of economic development; private companies that regard the roughly $35 billion spent each year on corrections not as a burden on American taxpayers but as a lucrative market; and government officials whose fiefdoms have expanded along with the inmate population. Since 1991 the rate of violent crime in the United States has fallen by about 20 percent, while the number of people in prison or jail has risen by 50 percent. The prison boom has its own inexorable logic. Steven R. Donziger, a young attorney who headed the National Criminal Justice Commission in 1996, explains the thinking: "If crime is going up, then we need to build more prisons; and if crime is going down, it's because we built more prisons—and building even more prisons will therefore drive crime down even lower." Schlosser, Eric. (December 1998). "The Prison Industrial Complex," *The Atlantic Online*, at www.theatlantic.com/issues/98dec/prisons.htm.

8. Harrison, Paige M. and Karberg, Jennifer C. (2003). www.ojp.usdoj.gov/bjs/pub/pdf/ pjim02.pdf.

9. White paper for the 1999 National Literacy Forum entitled "Adult and Family Literacy in the United States: Key Issues for the 21st Century," at www.nifl.gov/nifl/policy/whpap.html.

10. Regarding state prison population growth from 1990 through 2000, the U.S. Department of Justice reports, "Overall, the increasing number of drug offenses accounted for 27% of the total growth among black inmates, 7% of the total growth among Hispanic inmates, and 15% of the growth among white inmates (table 19)." Harrison, Paige M. and Beck, Allen J. (July 2002). *U.S. Department of Justice, Bureau of Justice Statistics, Prisoners in 2001* (p. 13). Washington, DC: U.S. Deptment of Justice.

11. As Carl Boggs points out, using data from the Sentencing Project, "while blacks constitute only 13 percent of regular drug users, they account for 35 percent of those arrested for possession, 55 percent of those convicted, and 74 percent of those jailed. . . . As Diane Gordon argues, U.S. drug policy is an attack on poor, urban minorities." Boggs, Carl. (2000). *The End of Politics* (pp. 55–56). New York: Guilford Press.

12. Wagner, Daniel. "EFA Thematic Study on Literacy and Adult Education," (p. 2) http://literacyonline.org/products/ili/pdf/OP0001.pdf.

13. Ibid., p. 4.

14. Ibid., pp. 4–5.

15. Ibid., p. 5.

16. For Literacy and Poverty scale see Kirsch, Irwin S. (1998). "Literacy in America: A Brief Overview of the NALS." In Ed. M. Cecil Smith, *Literacy for the 21st Century* (p. 15). Westport, CT: Praeger. Note that the 2003 poverty level, for a family of four, is $18,400 or $353.84 per week! http://aspe.hhs.gov/poverty/03poverty.htm

17. See www.fool.com/foolu/askfoolu/2002/askfoolu020404.htm.

18. See Hull, Gylinda, Ed. (1997). *Changing Work, Changing Workers*. New York: State University of New York Press; Lemert, *Social Things*; Shannon, Patrick. (1998). *Reading Poverty*. Portsmouth, NH: Heinemann Press; Aronowitz, Stanley and Defazio, William. (1997). *Jobless Future*. Minneapolis: University of Minnesota Press.

19. Lemert, Ibid., p. 124.

20. Lewis, Justin. (1997). "Myth of the Liberal Media." *Media Education Foundation*. Northhampton, MA.

21. Venezky, Richard L. and Kaplan, David. "Literacy Habits and Political Participation." In Smith, Ibid., pp. 109–122.

22. Ibid., p. 122.

23. Palast, Greg. (2003). *The Best Democracy Money Can Buy* (pp. 11–12). London: Plume.

24. Ibid., pp. 28–29.

25. Edward Herman and Noam Chomsky point out in detail how this process works in Herman, Edward and Chomsky, Noam. (1998). *Manufacturing Consent*. New York: Pantheon Books.

26. Palast, Ibid., p. 14.

27. Ibid., pp. 14–15.

28. See Lewis, Ibid.; McChesney, Robert. (1999). *Rich Media, Poor Democracy*. Chicago: University of Illinois Press.

29. Bloom, Harold. (2001). *How to Read and Why* (p. 32). New York: Touchstone Books.

30. Smith, M. Cecil and Reder, Stephen. "Introduction: Adult Literacy Research and the National Adult Literacy Survey." In Smith, Ibid., p. 4.

31. Gee, James Paul. (1994). *The Social Mind*. Westport, CT: Greenwood Publishing.

32. Hall, Stuart. (1997). "The Work of Representation." In Ed. Stuart Hall, *Representation* (p. 19). London: Sage.

33. Connell, R. W. (1993). *Social Justice and Education* (p. 16). Philadelphia: Temple University Press.

34. See Ibid.; Bowles, Samuel and Gintis, Herbert. (1977). *Schooling in Capitalist America*. New York: Dimension; Willis, Paul E. (1981). *Learning to Labor*. New York: Columbia University Press; Anyon, Jean and Williams, William Julius. (1997). *Ghetto Schooling*. New York: Teachers College Press; Giroux, Henry A. (1998). *Schooling and the Struggle for Public Life*. Minneapolis: University of Minnesota Press; Aronowitz, Stanley and Giroux, Henry. (1993). *Education Still under Siege*. New York: Bergin and Garvey; Freire, Paulo. (1993). *Pedagogy of the Oppressed*. New York: Continuum Publication Group; Apple, Michael. (1982). *Cultural and Economic Reproduction in Education*. New York: Routledge, Kegan and Paul; Giroux, Henry. (2001). *Theory and Resistance in Education*. New York: Bergin and Garvey.

35. Connell, Ibid., p. 19.

36. Ibid., p. 16.

37. See Edwards, E., Hanson, A., and Raggett, P. (1996). *Boundaries of Adult Learning*. London: Routledge; Thorpe, M., Edwards, R., and Hanson, A. Eds. (1993). *Culture and Process of Adult Learning*. London: Routledge.

38. Adams, F. and Horton, M. (1986). *Unearthing Seeds of Fire: The Idea of the Highlander*. Winston-Salem, NC: John F. Blair.

39. Ibid., p. 113.

40. Ibid., p. 115.

41. Ibid.

42. Ibid.

43. Ibid., p. 117.

🎵 Chapter Three

1. Fromm, Erich. (1941). *Escape from Freedom* (pp. 240–241). New York: Rinehart and Co.

2. Giroux, Henry. (1997). *Pedagogy and the Politics of Hope*. Boulder, CO: Westview Press.

3. Jay, Martin. (1973). *The Dialectical Imagination* (p. 92). Boston: Little Brown.

4. Ibid., p. 89.

5. Ibid., p. 89.

6. Ibid., p. 91.

7. Ibid., p. 92.

8. Ibid., p. 93.

9. Ibid., p. 103.

10. Ibid., p. 103.

11. Ibid., p. 105.

12. Weiler, Kathleen. (1992). "Introduction." In Eds. K. Weiler and C. Mitchell, *What Schools Can Do: Critical Pedagogy and Practice* (pp. 1–12). New York: State University of New York Press.

13. Britzman, Deborah. (1992). "Decentering Discourses in Teacher Education." In Weiler and Mitchell, Ibid., p. 153.

14. Best, Steven and Kellner, Douglas. (1991). *Postmodern Theory* (p. 256). New York: Guilford.

15. Rorty, Richard. (1998). *Achieving Our Country*. Cambridge, MA: Harvard University Press.

16. Bordo, Susan. (1997). *Twilight Zones*. Los Angeles: University of California Press.

17. Aronowitz, Stanley. (1998). "Introduction." In *Pedagogy of Freedom* (p. 10). New York: Rowman & Littlefield.

18. Fromm, Erich. (1995). *The Fear of Freedom*. New York: Routledge.

19. Ibid., p. 220.

20. Ibid., p. 221.

21. Aronowitz, Ibid., p. 4.

22. Ibid., p. 3.

23. Arendt, Hannah. (1968). *Between Past and Future* (pp. 149, 151). New York: Viking Press.

24. Ibid., p. 96.

25. Fromm (1995), Ibid., p. 144.

26. Ibid.

27. Ibid.

28. Ibid.

29. Ibid.

30. Ibid.

31. Foucault, Michel. (1980). *Power/Knowledge*. New York: Pantheon.

32. Macedo, Donaldo. (1994). *Literacies of Power*. Boulder, CO: Westview.

33. Giroux, Henry A. and McLaren, Peter. (1991). "Leon Golub's Radical Pessimism: Toward a Pedagogy of Representation" *Exposure*, 28(12): pp. 18–33.

34. Fromm (1941), Ibid., p. 251.

35. Ibid., p. 253.

36. McChesney, Robert W. (1997). *Corporate Media and the Threat to Democracy*. New York: Seven Stories Press.

37. Fromm (1941), Ibid., p. 251.

38. Ibid., p. 250.

39. Connell, R. W. (1993). *Schools and Social Justice*. Philadelphia: Temple University Press.

40. Castoriadis, Cornelius. (1991). "The Nature and Value of Equity." In *Philosophy, Politics, Autonomy: Essays in Political Philosophy* (p. 137). New York: Oxford University Press.

41. Ibid.

42. Aronowitz, Stanley. (1991). "The Unknown Herbert Marcuse." *Social Text*, 58: p. 50.

43. Ibid., p. 49.

🍎 Chapter Four

1. See for a broad range of perspectives on critical education and its relationship to leadership, power, authority, domination, and resistance: Apple, Michael W. (1990). *Ideology and Curriculum*, 2nd ed. New York: Routledge; Apple. (2000). *Official Knowledge*, 2nd ed. New York: Routledge; Aronowitz, Stanley and Giroux, Henry A. (1993). *Education Still under Siege*. New York: Bergin and Garvey; Britzman, Deborah P. (1992). "Decentering Discourses in Teacher Education." In Eds. Kathleen Weiler and Candace Mitchell, *What Schools Can Do: Critical Pedagogy and Practice*. New York: State University of New York Press; Ellsworth, Elizabeth. (1997). *Teaching Positions*. New York: Teachers College Press; Ellsworth, Elizabeth. (August 1989). "Why Doesn't This Feel Empowering?" *Harvard Educational Review*, 59: pp. 297–325; Freire, Paulo. (1998). *Pedagogy of Freedom*. New York: Rowman & Littlefield; Freire, Paulo and Macedo, Donaldo. (1987). *Literacy: Reading the Word and the World*. Boston: Bergin and Garvey; Giroux, Henry A. (1983). *Theory and Resistance in Education*. New York: Bergin and Garvey; Giroux. (1984). "Marxism and Schooling: The Limits of a Radical Discourse." *Educational Theory*, 34(2); Giroux. (1988). *Teachers as Intellectuals*. New York: Bergin and Garvey; Giroux. (1988). *Schooling and the Struggle for Public Life*. Minneapolis: University of Minneapolis; Giroux. (1992). *Border Crossings*. New York: Routledge; (1992) "Critical Literacy and Student Experience: Donald Grave's Approach to Literacy." In Ed. Patrick Shannon, *Becoming Political*. Portsmouth, NH: Heinemann; Giroux. (1997). *Pedagogy and the Politics of Hope*. Boulder, CO: Westview Press; Giroux. (2000). *Impure Acts*. New York: Routledge; Giroux, Henry A. and Simon, Roger I. "Schooling, Popular Culture, and a Pedagogy of Possibility." In Weiler and Mitchell, Ibid.; Greene, Maxine. (1973). *The Teacher as Stranger*. Belmont, CA: Wadsworth Publishing; Gur-Ze'ev, Ilan. (1998). "Toward a Nonrepressive Critical Pedagogy." *Educational Theory*, 48(4): pp. 463–486; hooks, bell. (1989). *Talking Back*. Boston: South End Press; hooks. (1995). *Teaching to Transgress*. New York: Routledge; Hunter, Ian. (1994). *Rethinking the School*. New York: St. Martin's Press; Lather, Patti. (1991). *Getting Smart*. New York: Routledge; Lather. (Fall 1998). "Critical Pedagogy and Its Complicities." *Educational Theory*, 48(4); Luke, Carmen. (Summer 1996). "Feminist Pedagogy Theory: Reflections on Power and Authority." *Educational Theory*, 46; Macedo, Donaldo. (1994). *Literacies of Power*. Boulder, CO: Westview Press; McLaren, Peter. (Fall 1998). "Revolutionary Pedagogy in Post-Revolutionary Times: Rethinking the Political Economy of Critical Education." *Educational Theory*, 48(4): pp. 431–462; McLaren. (1997). *Revolutionary Multiculturalism*. Boulder,

CO: Westview Press; Simon, Roger. (1992). *Teaching against the Grain*. Toronto: OISE Press; Simon. (1992). "Empowerment as a Pedagogy of Possibility." In Shannon, Ibid; Weiler, Kathleen. "Introduction." In Ibid., pp. 1–12.

2. See Gramsci, Antonio. (1971). *Selections from the Prison Notebooks of Antonio Gramsci*. Eds. and Trans. Quintin Hoare and Geoffrey Nowell Smith. New York: International Publishers.

3. Mouffe, Chantel. (1979). "Hegemony and Ideology in Gramsci." In Ed. Chantel Mouffe, *Gramsci and Marxist Theory* (pp. 224–225). New York: Routledge.

4. See Giroux, *Border Crossings, Pedagogy and the Politics of Hope*, and *Schooling and the Struggle for Public Life*.

5. Aronowitz, Stanley. "Introduction." In Freire (1998), Ibid., p. 13.

6. Freire, Ibid., p. 53.

7. For an overview of these positions and the devastating effects that they have on public life see Unger, Roberto Mangabeira and West, Cornel. (1998). *The Future of American Progressivism*. Boston: Beacon Press; McChesney, Robert W. (1997). *Corporate Media and the Threat to Democracy*. New York: Seven Stories Press; Chomsky, Noam. (1999). *Profit over People*. New York: Seven Stories Press; Castoriadis, Cornelius. (1991). *Philosophy, Politics, Autonomy: Essays in Political Philosophy*. New York: Oxford University Press; Aronowitz, Stanley. (Spring 1999). "The Unknown Herbert Marcuse." *Social Text* 58(17): p. 1.

8. Aronowitz, "Introduction," Ibid., p. 10.

9. del Pilar, Maria. (1998). "Cadiz, Pia Lindquist Wong, Carlos Alberto Torres" *Education and Democracy* (p. 45). New York: Westview Press.

10. Arendt, Hannah. (1968). *Between Past and Future* (p. 106). New York: Viking Press.

11. Said, Edward. (1996). *Representations of the Intellectual* (p. 60). New York: Vintage Books.

12. See del Pilar, Ibid.

13. Freire, Paulo. (1993). *Pedagogy of the City*. Trans. Donaldo Macedo (p. 19). New York: Continuum.

14. Ibid., 22.

15. del Pilar, Ibid., pp. 47–48.

16. Ibid., 75.

17. Ibid., 213.

18. Ibid., 249.

19. Ibid., 250.

20. See Hunter, Ibid.; Ellsworth, Ibid.

21. Giroux, Henry. (2000). "Pedagogy of the Depressed: Beyond the New Politics of Cynicism" (unpublished manuscript).

22. Featherstone, Liza. (Fall 2000). "A Common Enemy: Students Fight Private Prisons." *Dissent:* p. 78.

23. Brenkman, John. (1995). "Raymond Williams and Marxism." In Ed. Christopher Prendingast, *Cultural Materialism: On Raymond Williams* (p. 244). Minneapolis: University of Minnesota Press.

24. The notion of popular power, as it used here, refers to revolutionary actions brought about by a "popular" minority in defense of certain ideological concerns that conflict with those that occupy positions of dominant power. Contrast this use with Freire's concern with popular schooling, and things can get confused. Freire's concern with popular schooling certainly reflects a concern

with popular power, but not in a revolutionary context. Rather, his notion of popular schools and the "popular power" that they can organize is in the context of democratic power. Here, the "popular" signifies a plurality organized in democratic terms and around democratic struggle. In the first instance, the "popular" represents a faction that is in direct, and often violent, opposition to the dominant power structure. Understand, I am not making a claim that violence and revolution are not sometimes the only remaining option, but historically, violent revolution has reproduced structures of violence, even with the best intentions driving the violent actions. But it is hard to imagine apartheid in South Africa falling without violence, just as it is difficult to imagine the American Revolution without violence. On the other hand, Havel's "velvet revolution" moved totalitarianism without a full-scale war. It is hard to know when the last resort to violence is, in fact, the last resort. It is also difficult, if not impossible, to anticipate the social consequences of violence as it is taking place.

25. Maria del Pilar discusses the role of the democratic state in terms of methods and practices. As a method, democracy is seen as a system of political *representation*. As a practice, democracy is associated with political *participation*. del Pilar, Ibid., pp. 40–41.

26. Steven Lukes argues that there are three main perspectives on power. The first he describes as one dimensional. One-dimensional power "involves a focus on behavior in the making of decisions on issues over which there is an observable conflict of (subjective) interests, seen as express policy preferences, revealed by political participation." The position connoted by a claim to "governmentality" adheres to this one-dimensional view of power. See Lukes, Steven. (1979). *Power* (p. 15). London: The Macmillan Press; see also Marcuse, Herbert. (1991). *One-Dimensional Man*, 2nd ed. Boston: Beacon Press, for his now famous discussion of how the dominant forms of rationality repress people into thinking and acting "one-dimensionally" in regard to "values, aspirations, and ideas."

27. Keane, John. (2000). *Vaclav Havel: A Political Tragedy in Six Acts* (p. 345). New York: Basic Books.

28. Ibid., p. 424.

29. Radical democracy has been understood differently by different theorists, but despite differing interpretations, it does possess a few unifying principles. They could be understood as a dedication to liberty and equality, an investment in the practice of political struggle, a dedication to expanding political agency, and the need to interrogate modern democracy's uncomfortable relationship with the workings of capital. As David Trend sees it, "For many on the left, the concept of radical democracy provides . . . an alternative framework. Radical democrats argue that traditional democracy has failed to deliver on its promises of equality and civic participation. They accuse liberal democracy in particular of being too willing to sacrifice the interests of diverse groups in the name of a broad consensus. Most importantly, radical democrats claim that democratic principles underlie critiques of capitalism, and the creation of an egalitarian society will entail extending these democratic principle into ever expanding areas of daily life: work, education, leisure, and home." Trend, David. (1996). "Introduction." In Ed. David Trend, *Radical Democracy* (pp. 2–3). New York: Routledge. For the diversity of positions within this "paradigm" see the other provocative essays in *Radical Democracy*.

30. Giroux (1997), Ibid., p. 82.

31. Keane, Ibid., p. 244.

32. Ibid., p. 246.

33. See, for example, van der Bogert, Rebecca and Williams, Vivian. (1998) *Conceptual and Practical Issues in School Leadership*. San Francisco: Jossey- Bass; Begley, Paul T. and Leonard, Pauline E.

(1999). *The Values of Educational Administration.* London: Falmer; Taylor, Robert L. and Rosenbach, William E. (1996). *Military Leadership: In Pursuit of Excellence,* 3rd ed. Boulder, CO: Westview Press.

34. Mouffe, Chantel. (1992). "Citizenship and Political Identity." *October:* pp. 30–31.

35. Ibid., 31.

36. Arendt, Ibid., p. 146.

37. Ibid., p. 148.

38. Bauman, Z. (1999). *In Search of Politics* (p. 129). Stanford, CA: Stanford University Press.

39. Ibid., p. 3.

40. So I am not misunderstood, let me explain that this is not a return to the argument of "clarity" versus abstraction. The argument for clarity, I agree, was primarily and often just a way to hide a conservative ideology behind the veil of linguistic critique. Common to that argument was a call to do away with words like "praxis" and "oppression," but as Macedo and Freire have argued, as has Giroux, who has often been the target of these assaults, these calls for clarity simply helped to obfuscate the material injustices that they wanted to describe. When confronted with the cogent response that the Los Angeles "riots," as they were described in the dominant press, would have been more clearly described as an uprising, the "conservative" critiques advocating clarity had very little to say, falling back on the highly contentious claim of journalistic objectivity, which has been obliterated by intellectuals from Camus to Chomsky. Another more recent example can be found in the dominant press when the terminology "underprivileged" is used to describe those groups that are clearly under a state of economic and cultural siege by dominant powers. By using the term *underprivileged,* not only is the emphasis taken off those who are privileged, but it totally obfuscates the relationship between the two. In other words, the terminology implies no systemic connection between the privileged and underprivileged. The suggestion, unspoken of course, is that those who are privileged are magically taking advantage of a system that is already just, equal, and free. Rather than critique and challenge the humaneness of the system, the task is to look to the underprivileged for the cause of their situation. In this example, not unlike the L.A. example, emphasis and responsibility, with the help of terminology, get placed upon the victims of injustice as opposed to the larger systems at work that help to create an environment that is inherently unjust. Clarity is certainly an important issue, but needs to be understood as part of the discussion around ideology, power, and identity. A call for clarity that makes a claim to being outside of these theoretical referents obfuscates its own political position. See Freire, Paulo and Macedo, Donaldo. *Literacy: Reading the Word and the World;* Giroux. *Border Crossings.*

41. See Giroux, Henry A. and Simon, Roger I. (1989). *Popular Schooling and Everyday Life.* New York: Bergen and Garvey.

42. Giroux, Henry. (1999). *The Mouse that Roared* (p. 6). New York: Rowman & Littlefield; See also Bloch, Ernst. (1988). *The Utopian Function of Art and Literature,* Trans. Jack Zipes and Frank Mecklenburg. Cambridge, MA: MIT Press; Bloch. (1986). *The Principle of Hope.* Trans. Neville Plaice, Stephen Plaice, and Paul, Knight. Vol. 1. Cambridge, MA: MIT Press; Rabinach, Anson. (Spring 1977). "Unclaimed Heritage: Ernst Bloch's *Heritage of Our Times and the Theory of Fascism.*" *New German Critique:* p. 8.

43. Mouffe, Chantel. (1988) "Hegemony and New Political Subjects: Toward a New Concept of Democracy." In Eds. Cary Nelson and Larry Grossberg, *Marxism and the Interpretation of Culture* (pp. 100–101). Urbana: University of Illinois Press; (March–April 1989) "Towards a Radical Democratic Citizenship," *Democratic Left,* XVII(2): p. 7; (1992) "Citizenship and Political

Identity," *October:* pp. 30–31; (1992) "Feminism, Citizenship and Radical Democratic Politics." In Eds. Judith Butler and Joan Scott, *Feminist Theorize the Political* (pp. 378–379). New York: Routledge; Mouffe. (1993). *The Return of the Political.* London: Verso; Mouffe. (2000). "Which Ethics for Democracy?" In Eds. Majorie Garber, Beatrice Hanssen, and Rebecca Walkowitz, *The Turn to Ethics.* New York: Routledge.

44. For racism as a politics of exclusion see Goldberg, David Theo. (1993). *Racist Culture.* Oxford: Blackwell. For a discussion of raciology and how colonialization functioned as a paradigmatic element within modernity, see Gilroy, Paul. (2000). *Against Race.* Cambridge, MA: Harvard University Press.

45. See Giroux. *Border Crossings.*

46. See for example, Sanchez, Victor. (1995). *The Teachings of Don Carlos.* Santa Fe, NM: Bear and Company. In this book, Carlos Castaneda and Don Carlos's ideas about power, practice, responsibility, and human energy (agency) are put into a methodological context. For more philosophical texts dealing with these issues, see Castaneda, Carlos. (1968). *The Teaching of Don Juan: A Yaqui Way of Knowledge.* Berkeley: University of California Press; Castaneda. (1974). *Journey to Ixtlan: The Lessons of Don Juan.* New York: Washington Square Press; (1981) *The Eagle's Gift.* New York: Simon and Schuster; Castaneda. (1992). *Tales of Power.* New York: Washington Square Press; and O'Sullivan, Edmund. (1999). *Transformative Learning.* New York: Zed Books.

47. Freire (1998), Ibid., pp. 23, 25.

48. Historian Robin D. G. Kelley triggered my thoughts concerning the relationship between imagination, dreaming, culture, and politics. During a lecture he gave at Penn State University on March 23, 2000, he spoke powerfully about the need to think politics beyond the traditional registers of "action," "organization," and "participation." Never suggesting that these were not vital in the face of the New Right's repression, oppression, antidemocratic ideology, and reprehensible social policies, he nonetheless advocated for "culture as a space of dreaming." By this he meant that in cultural invention, such as music, art, and literature, we find an imagined future very different from what we have now. This imaginative process, he argued, was vital if society was to be transformed. It is not enough simply to "put out fires." Rather, we must also recognize the art of dreaming through cultural activity as a political moment, not simply as an aesthetic or empty utopian sign.

49. Mouffe (1988), Ibid., pp. 100–101.

🕮 Chapter Five

1. Reed, Charles B. (February 23, 2001). *The San Diego Union-Tribune,* p. B-9.

2. Gee, James Paul. (1999). "Reading and the New Literacy Studies: Reframing the National Academy of Sciences Report on Reading" *Journal of Literacy Research:* p. 342.

3. Aronowitz, Stanley and Giroux, Henry. (1993). *Education Still Under Seige* (p. 62). Westport, CT: Bergin and Garvey.

4. *Star Tribune* Metro Edition (Minneapolis, May 12, 2001), p. 22A.

5. Taylor, Curtis. (April 26, 2001). *Newsday,* Queens Edition, pp. A06, 386.

6. Ibid., B9.

7. Miner, Barbara. (2000). "Making the Grade." *The Progressive* (August): p. 40.

8. See Kozol, Jonathan. (1991). *Savage Inequalities*. New York: Crown; Aronowitz and Giroux, Ibid; and Glenn-Paul, Dierdre. (2000). "Rap and Orality" *Journal of Adolescent and Adult Literacy*, 44(3): pp. 246–252.

9. See Willis, Paul. (1977). *Learning to Labor*. New York: Columbia University Press; and Marable, Manning. (1996). *Speaking Truth to Power: Essays on Race, Resistance, and Radicalism*. Boulder, CO: Westview.

10. Kohn, Alfie. "The Real Threat to American Schools." *Tikkun*, (March–April): p. 60.

11. Ibid.

12. See Gee, Ibid., p. 358; Edmundson, J., and Shannon, P. (1998). "Reading Education and Poverty," *Peabody Journal of Education*, 73(3–4): pp. 104–126; and Daniels, H., Zemelman, S., and Bizar, M. (1999). "Whole Language Works." *Educational Leadership*, (October): pp. 32–37.

13. Gee, James Paul. (1992). "What Is Literacy?" In Ed. P. Shannon, *Becoming Political* (pp. 21–28). Portsmouth, NH: Heinemann.

14. Kozol, Ibid.

15. Simon, Roger. (1992). "Empowerment as a Pedagogy of Possibility." In Shannon, Ibid., pp. 142–155.

16. Gee (1999), Ibid., p. 342.

17. Freire, Paulo. (1998). *Pedagogy of Freedom*. New York: Rowman & Littlefield.

18. Macedo, Donaldo. (1994). *Literacies of Power*. Boulder, CO: Westview.

19. Macedo, Donaldo. (2000). "Introduction." In Ed. D. Macedo, *Chomsky on Miseducation* (p. 10). New York: Rowman & Littlefield.

20. Worsham, L. and Olson, Gary A. (1998). "Staging the Politics of Difference: Homi Bhaba's Critical Literacy" *Journal of Advanced Composition*, 18(3): p. 11.

21. Sehr, David T. (1997). *Education for Public Democracy*. New York: State University of New York Press.

22. Ibid.

23. Gee (1992), Ibid., p. 21.

24. Gunster, Shane. (2000). "Gramsci, Organic Intellectuals, and Cultural Studies." In Eds. John A. Grank and John Tam Bornino, *Vocations of Political Theory* (pp. 245–246). Minneapolis: University of Minneapolis Press.

25. Boggs, Carl. (2000). *The End of Politics* (pp. 55–56). New York: Guilford.

26. Stuart Hall quoted in Giroux, Henry A. (1999). "Doing Cultural Studies: Youth and the Challenge of Pedagogy" *Harvard Educational Review*, 6(3) (Fall): pp. 298–299.

27. Noam Chomsky in Macedo, Donaldo, Ed. (2000). *Chomsky on Miseducation* (p. 21). New York: Rowman & Littlefield.

28. Freire, Ibid.

29. Ibid., p. 68.

30. Bauman, Z. (1999). *In Search of Politics* (pp. 2–3). Stanford, CA: Stanford University Press.

31. Worsham, L. and Olson, Gary A. (1999). "Hegemony and the Future of Democracy: Ernesto Laclau's Political Philosophy." *Journal of Advanced Composition*, 19:(1): p. 10.

32. Stanley Aronowitz cited in Giroux, Henry A. (1997). *Pedagogy and the Politics of Hope* (p. 52).

Boulder, CO: Westview.

33. Gee (1992), Ibid., p. 23.

34. Ibid.

35. Willis, Paul. (1977). *Learning to Labor.* New York: Columbia University Press.

36. Drew, Julie. (1998). "Cultural Composition: Stuart Hall on Ethnicity and the Discursive Turn." *Journal of Composition Theory,* 18(2): p. 198.

37. Gee (1992), Ibid., p. 24.

38. Derrida, Jacques. (2000). "Intellectual Courage: An Interview." In Trans. Peter Knapp, *Culture Machine,* at http://culturemachine.tees.ac.uk/journal.htm.

39. Chomsky, Noam. (1999). *Profit over People.* New York: Seven Stories Press.

40. Arendt, Hannah. (1968). "Introduction." In Walter Benjamin, *Illuminations,* Ed. H. Arendt, Trans. Harry Zohn (p. 3). New York: Schocken.

41. Campo-Flores, Arian. (September 18, 2000). "The New Face of Race." *Newsweek:* pp. 38–41.

42. Geiger, H. Jack. (December 1, 1997). "The Real World of Race." *The Nation:* pp. 27–29.

43. Campo-Flores, Ibid., p. 40.

44. Ibid.

45. Geiger, Ibid., p. 27.

46. Ibid.

47. Lee Mun Wah. (1994). *The Color of Fear* [video recording]. Berkeley, CA: Stir-Fry Productions.

48. McLaren, Peter. (1997). *Revolutionary Multiculturalism* (p. 282). Boulder, CO: Westview.

49. Geiger, Ibid., p. 29.

50. Bernstein, Richard. (October 6, 2001). "Counterpoint to Unity: Dissent." *New York Times:* A13, A15.

51. Foucault, Michel. (1977). *Power/Knowledge.* Trans. C. Gordon et al. (p. 114). New York: Pantheon.

52. Ibid., p. 59.

53. Ibid., p. 131.

54. Ibid.

See Shannon, Patrick. (1997) *The Struggle to Continue.* Portsmouth, NH: Heinemann.

🏵 Chapter Six

1. Freeman, Cynthia A. and Wartenberg, Thomas E. (1995). "Introduction." In Eds. C. Freelander and T. Wartenberg, *Philosophy and Film* (p. 3). New York: Routledge.

2. Parenti, Michael. (1992). *Make Believe Media.* New York: St. Martin's Press.

3. See Worsham, Lynn. (2001). "Going Postal: Pedagogic Violence and the Schooling of Emotion." In Eds. H. Giroux and K. Myrisides, *Beyond the Corporate University* (pp. 230–251). New York: Rowman & Littlefield.

4. See Gee, James Paul. (1992). "What Is Literacy." In Ed. Patrick Shannon, *Becoming Political* (pp. 21–28). Portsmouth, NH: Heinemann.

5. See Hall, Stuart. (1997). "Interview with Stuart Hall: Culture and Power." *Radical Philosophy,* 86

(Nov/Dec): pp. 24–41; Aronowitz, Stanley. (1993). *Roll over Beethoven*. Hanover, NH: Wesleyan University Press.

6. See Giroux, Henry A. (1994). "Doing Cultural Studies: Youth and the Challenge of Pedagogy." *Harvard Educational Review*, 64: pp. 278–299; Bordo, S. (1997). *Twilight Zones*. Los Angeles: University of California Press; Kinchloe, J. (2002). *The Sign of the Burger*. Philadelphia: Temple University Press.

7. Hall, Stuart. (1996). "Cultural Studies and Its Theoretical Legacies." In Eds. D. Morley and K. H. Chen, *Critical Dialogues in Cultural Studies* (p. 268). New York: Routledge.

8. Giroux, Henry A. (2000). *Impure Acts* (pp. 128–129). New York, Routledge.

9. Ibid.

10. See Grossberg, Lawrence. (1998). "'The Cultural Studies' Crossroads Blues," *European Journal of Cultural Studies* 1(1): pp. 65–82; and Wright, Handel Kashope. (2000). "Pressing Promising, and Paradoxical: Larry Grossberg on Education and Cultural Studies." *The Review of Education/Pedagogy/Cultural Studies* 22(1): pp. 3–22.

11. See Giroux, Henry A. (1998). *Channel Surfing*. New York: St. Martin's Press; Giroux. (1999). *The Mouse that Roared*. New York: Rowman & Littlefield; Giroux. *Impure Acts*; Giroux. (2002) *Breaking into the Movies*. New York: Blackwell.

12. Giroux (2002), Ibid.

13. Miner, Barbara. (2000). "Making the Grade." *The Progressive* (August): pp. 40–43.

14. Downing, John D. H. (1997). "Cultural Studies, Communication and Change: Eastern Europe to the Urals." In Eds. Marjorie Ferguson and Peter Golding, *Cultural Studies in Question* (p. 191). London: Sage.

15. Best, Steven and Kellner, Douglas. (1991). *Postmodern Theory* (p. 259). New York: Guilford.

16. Ibid.

17. Sholle, David. (1995). "Buy Our News: The Melding of News, Entertainment in the Totalized Selling Environment of the Postmodern Market." In Eds. P. McLaren, R. Hammer, D. Sholle, and S. Reilly, *Rethinking Media Literacy* (p. 151). New York: Peter Lang.

18. Giroux (2001), Ibid., p. 1.

19. Ibid.

20. Ibid., pp. 5–6.

21. Ibid., p. 21.

22. Ibid., p. 24.

23. Grossberg, Ibid., p. 68.

24. Giroux, Henry A. (Fall 1999). "Doing Cultural Studies: Youth and the Challenge of Pedagogy." *Harvard Educational Review*, 6(3): p. 295.

25. Giroux (2001), Ibid., p. 24.

26. Giroux (1999), Ibid., "Doing Cultural," pp. 295–296.

27. Ibid., p. 296.

28. Ibid.

29. Ibid.

30. Ibid.

31. Macedo, Donaldo. (1994). *Literacies of Power* (p. 21). Boulder, CO: Westview.

32. The phrase "doing theory" came from Paul Youngquist at Penn State, who taught a graduate class entitled "Doing Theory."

33. See Kellner, Doug. (1990). *Television and the Crisis of Democracy*. Boulder, CO: Westview; Kellner. (1995). *Media Culture*. New York: Routledge.

34. Kellner (1995), Ibid., p. 116.

35. Ibid., p. 100.

36. Ibid., p. 93.

37. Kincheloe, Ibid.

38. Ibid., p. 5.

39. Ibid., p. 11.

40. Slack, J. D. (1996). "The Theory and Method of Articulation in Cultural Studies." In Eds. D. Morley and K. H. Chen, *Critical Dialogues in Cultural Studies* (p. 113). New York: Routledge.

41. Ibid.

42. Ibid., p. 114.

43. Ibid.

44. Giroux (1988), Ibid., *Teachers*.

45. Hall, Stuart. (1996). "The Problem of Ideology." In Eds. D. Morley and K. H. Chen, *Critical Dialogues in Cultural Studies* (pp. 25–46). New York: Routledge.

46. Volosinov, V. N. (1973). *Marxism and the Philosophy of Language*. Trans. L. M. and I. R. Titunik (pp. 35–36). New York: Seminar Press.

47. Hall, Stuart. (1996). "On Postmodernism and Articulation." In Eds. D. Morley and K. H. Chen, *Critical Dialogues in Cultural Studies* (p. 137). New York: Routledge.

48. Aronowitz, Stanley and Giroux, Henry A. (1993). *Education Still under Siege*. New York: Bergin and Garvey.

49. Hall (1996), Ibid "The Problem . . . ," p. 26.

50. Ibid., p. 37.

51. Foucault, Michel. (1980). *Power/Knowledge*. Trans. C. Gordon. New York: Pantheon.

52. Foucault, Michel. (1990). "Practicing Criticism." In Ed. L. D. Kritzman, *Politics, Philosophy, Culture* (pp. 152–158). New York: Pantheon Books.

53. Stuart Hall cited in Giroux (1994).

54. See bell hooks. (1995). *Teaching to Transgress*. New York: Routledge; hooks. (1989). *Talking Back*. Boston: South End Press.

55. Adorno, T. and Horkheimer, M. (1972). *Dialectic of Enlightenment*. Trans. John Cumming. New York: Seabury Press.

56. Long, Elizabeth. (1997). "Engaging Sociology and Cultural Studies." In Ed. E. Long, *From Sociology to Cultural Studies* (p. 19). Malden, MA: Basil Blackwell.

57. Gomez-Pena, Guillermo. (1996). *The New World Border* (p. 6). San Francisco: City Lights.

58. Ibid., p. 7.

◉ Conclusion

1. Gutmann, A. (1999) *Democratic Education,* 2nd ed. (p. 19). New Jersey: Princeton Press.

2. Gutmann's study of deliberative democracy is extensive and complex. By taking up her model of deliberative democracy, I only hope to give the reader a basic sense of some of her arguments, but make no claim to be dealing comprehensively with her total theory of democratic education.

3. Chomsky, N. (2003) *Hegemony or Survival* (p. 5). New York: Metropolitan Books. Chomsky explains polyarchy as a system of political decision making where the elite are responsible for decisions vis-à-vis public ratification.

4. Stiglitz, J. (2003) *The Roaring Nineties* (p. 10). New York: W. W. Norton and Company.

5. Ibid., pp. xiv–xv.

6. Ibid., p. xv.

7. Gutmann, Ibid., p. 45.

8. Ibid., 14.

9. Ibid., 7–8.

10. Ibid., p. 11.

11. Ibid.

12. Kozol, J. (1991) *Savage Inequalities.* New York: Harper Collins; Stiglitz, Ibid.

13. Stiglitz, Ibid., p. 23.

14. Chomsky, Ibid., p. 139.

15. Connell, R. W. (1993) *Schools and Social Justice* (p. 16). Philadelphia: Temple University Press.

16. Ibid.

Index

TEACHING

❧CONTEMPORARY❧

SCHOLARS

Joe L. Kincheloe & Shirley R. Steinberg
General Editors

This innovative series addresses the pedagogies and thoughts of influential contemporary scholars in diverse fields. Focusing on scholars who have challenged the "normal science," the dominant frameworks of particular disciplines, *Teaching Contemporary Scholars* highlights the work of those who have profoundly influenced the direction of academic work. In a era of great change, this series focuses on the bold thinkers who provide not only insight into the nature of the change but where we should be going in light of the new conditions. Not a festschrift, not a re-interpretation of past work, these books allow the reader a deeper, yet accessible conceptual framework in which to negotiate and expand the work of important thinkers.

For additional information about this series or for the submission of manuscripts, please contact:

Joe L. Kincheloe & Shirley R. Steinberg
c/o Peter Lang Publishing, Inc.
275 Seventh Avenue, 28th floor
New York, New York 10001

To order other books in this series, please contact our Customer Service Department:

(800) 770-LANG (within the U.S.)
(212) 647-7706 (outside the U.S.)
(212) 647-7707 FAX

Or browse online by series:

WWW.PETERLANGUSA.COM